JACK OF
ALL TRADES

The Stackpole Military History Series

THE AMERICAN CIVIL WAR
Cavalry Raids of the Civil War
In the Lion's Mouth
Witness to Gettysburg

WORLD WAR I
Doughboy War

WORLD WAR II
After D-Day
Airborne Combat
Armor Battles of the Waffen-SS,
    1943–45
Armoured Guardsmen
Arnhem 1944
The B-24 in China
The Battalion
The Battle of France
The Battle of Sicily
Battle of the Bulge, Vol. 1
Battle of the Bulge, Vol. 2
Battle of the Bulge, Vol. 3
Beyond the Beachhead
Beyond Stalingrad
The Black Bull
Blitzkrieg Unleashed
Blossoming Silk Against the Rising Sun
Bodenplatte
The Breaking Point
The Brigade
The Canadian Army and the Normandy
    Campaign
Clay Pigeons of St Lô, The
Critical Convoy Battles of WWII
A Dangerous Assignment
D-Day Bombers
D-Day Deception
D-Day to Berlin
Decision in the Ukraine
The Defense of Moscow 1941
Deliverance at Diepholz
Destination Normandy
Dive Bomber!
Eager Eagles
Eagles of the Third Reich
The Early Battles of Eighth Army
Eastern Front Combat
Europe in Flames
Exit Rommel
The Face of Courage
Fatal Decisions
Fist from the Sky
Flame On
Flying American Combat Aircraft of
    World War II, Vol. 1
For Europe
Forging the Thunderbolt
For the Homeland
Fortress France
The German Defeat in the East,
    1944–45
German Order of Battle, Vol. 1
German Order of Battle, Vol. 2
German Order of Battle, Vol. 3

The Germans in Normandy
Germany's Panzer Arm in World War II
GI Ingenuity
Goodbye, Transylvania
The Great Ships
Grenadiers
Guns Against the Reich
Hitler's Final Fortress
Hitler's Nemesis
Hitler's Spanish Legion
Hold the Westwall
Infantry Aces
In the Fire of the Eastern Front
Iron Arm
Iron Knights
Japanese Army Fighter Aces
Japanese Naval Fighter Aces
JG 26 Luftwaffe Fighter Wing War Diary,
    Vol. 1
JG 26 Luftwaffe Fighter Wing War Diary,
    Vol. 2
Kampfgruppe Peiper at the Battle of
    the Bulge
The Key to the Bulge
Kursk
Luftwaffe Aces
Luftwaffe Fighter Ace
Luftwaffe Fighter-Bombers over Britain
Luftwaffe Fighters & Bombers
Luftwaffe KG 200
Marshal of Victory, Vol. 1
Marshal of Victory, Vol. 2
Massacre at Tobruk
Mechanized Juggernaut or Military
    Anachronism?
Messerschmitts over Sicily
Michael Wittmann, Vol. 1
Michael Wittmann, Vol. 2
Mission 85
Mission 376
The Nazi Rocketeers
Night Flyer / Mosquito Pathfinder
No Holding Back
Operation Mercury
Panzer Aces
Panzer Aces II
Panzer Commanders of the
    Western Front
Panzergrenadier Aces
Panzer Gunner
The Panzer Legions
Panzers in Normandy
Panzers in Winter
Panzer Wedge, Vol. 1
Panzer Wedge, Vol. 2
The Path to Blitzkrieg
Penalty Strike
Poland Betrayed
Red Road from Stalingrad
Red Star Under the Baltic
Retreat to the Reich
Rommel Reconsidered
Rommel's Desert Commanders
Rommel's Desert War

Rommel's Lieutenants
The Savage Sky
The Seeds of Disaster
Ship-Busters
The Siege of Brest 1941
The Siege of Küstrin
The Siegfried Line
A Soldier in the Cockpit
Soviet Blitzkrieg
Spitfires & Yellow Tail Mustangs
Stalin's Keys to Victory
Surviving Bataan and Beyond
T-34 in Action
Tank Tactics
Tigers in the Mud
Triumphant Fox
The 12th SS, Vol. 1
The 12th SS, Vol. 2
Twilight of the Gods
Typhoon Attack
The War Against Rommel's Supply Lines
War in the Aegean
War of the White Death
Warsaw 1944
Winter Storm
The Winter War
Wolfpack Warriors
Zhukov at the Oder

THE COLD WAR / VIETNAM
Cyclops in the Jungle
Expendable Warriors
Fighting in Vietnam
Flying American Combat Aircraft:
    The Cold War
Here There Are Tigers
Jack of All Trades
Land with No Sun
Phantom Reflections
Street without Joy
Through the Valley
Tours of Duty
Two One Pony

WARS OF AFRICA AND THE MIDDLE EAST
The Rhodesian War

GENERAL MILITARY HISTORY
Battle of Paoli
Cavalry from Hoof to Track
Desert Battles
Guerrilla Warfare
The Philadelphia Campaign, Vol. 1
Ranger Dawn
Sieges
The Spartan Army

JACK OF ALL TRADES

An American Advisor's War in Vietnam, 1969–70

Ronald L. Beckett

STACKPOLE
BOOKS

Published by
STACKPOLE BOOKS
5067 Ritter Road
Mechanicsburg, PA 17055
www.stackpolebooks.com

Printed in the United States of America

10 9 8 7 6 5 4 3 2 1

FIRST EDITION

Cover design by Wendy A. Reynolds
Photos from author's collection

Library of Congress Cataloging-in-Publication Data

Names: Beckett, Ronald L., author.
Title: Jack of all trades : an American advisor's war in Vietnam, 1969-70 / Ronald L. Beckett.
Description: First edition. | Mechanicsburg, PA : Stackpole Books, [2016] | Series: Stackpole military history series | Includes bibliographical references.
Identifiers: LCCN 2015034725 | ISBN 9780811717540
Subjects: LCSH: Vietnam War, 1961-1975—Personal narratives, American. | United States. Army—Officers—Biography. | United States. Army—Military life. | Community development—Vietnam. | Vietnam War, 1961-1975—???ong Nai.
Classification: LCC DS559.5 .B394 2016 | DDC 959.704/34—dc23 LC record available at http://lccn.loc.gov/201503472

This book is dedicated to the memory of
Maj. Tran Thanh Xuan, Army of the Republic of Vietnam,
district chief of Dinh Quan District, Long Khanh Province—
friend, soldier, and esteemed professional, who, better than
us all, knew what the end would be.

Contents

Preface ix

PART ONE—GOING BACK 1
   1. The Beginning 3
   2. Duty Calls 7
   3. Cinnamon 10
   4. Getting the Job 14
   5. Headin' Upcountry 21

PART TWO—FIRST IMPRESSIONS 27
   6. Dinh Quan District 29
   7. Home Sweet Home 33
   8. The Team 36
   9. Counterparts 44

PART THREE—THE CULTURE 51
  10. The Clash of Cultures 53
  11. The Magic Red Seal 62
  12. "Dawk" and Other Delights 66
  13. Spirited Adventures 73

PART FOUR—TEAM LIFE 77
  14. The Dinh Quan Surf and Raquette Club 79
  15. The Sauna 86
  16. Outhouse #2 89
  17. The Inferno 95
  18. The Shower and Bath House 98

19. Hollywood Goes to War 101
20. The Dinh Quan Power and Light Company 106
21. Snakes Alive 110
22. Going to Saigon 117

PART FIVE—THE BATTLE FOR HEARTS AND MINDS ... 125
23. Pacification 127
24. USAID 135
25. Chicken Man 139
26. Miracle Rice 144
27. This Little Piggy Went to Market 147
28. TV Comes to Dinh Quan 151
29. Security Operations 154
30. Chopper Day 168
31. Phung Hoang: The Phoenix Program 173
32. The Hamlet Evaluation System 183

PART SIX—MEMORABLE EVENTS 187
33. The Great Ambush 189
34. The Crash 193
35. R&R 197
36. The Thai Traveling Show 203
37. My Lai 208

PART SEVEN—CLOSING SCENES 211
38. Vietnamization: The Beginning of the End 213
39. The Painting 217
40. Final Thoughts 222

Postscript: Worst Practices 227
Glossary 233
Bibliography 235
Acknowledgments 239

Preface

This is a book about events and moments worth preserving, a book about the American war in Vietnam. It is not, however, a book about war in the traditional sense. Neither is it a book about heroism, though it has heroes, nor a book of protest, though it is sometimes critical. This is simply a book about people and places and events that marked my third tour of duty in Vietnam. It is a book bound loosely by the thread of human experience—a book the writing of which has moved me to laughter and resurrected emotions long thought forgotten.

American screenwriter Steven Shagan once remarked to a disappointed colleague, "Be glad you had the moment." War, like life, is made up of moments, some singular and some strung together into seemingly endless hours and days. Those who have experienced war know all too well those moments—moments of sorrow, camaraderie, exhilaration, fear, violence, compassion, sacrifice, and brutality. We know them because they come unexpectedly, punctuating the stifling monotony and boredom that characterize the primary war experience. Vietnam was no exception. Most of the books about the Vietnam War published in recent years have dealt with such moments, and most have consequently focused on the combat experience.

This book is different. It is a book about the advisory experience, an experience unique unto itself. In it you will find no recounting of battles or firefights, and no in-depth analysis of strategy or tactics. There are very few political messages or moral judgments. Rather, this is a collection of true vignettes, reminiscences, and often humorous anecdotes, not necessarily in chronological order, arising from one advisory team's experiences. More specifically, it is the story of a seven-man American District Advisory Team in Dinh Quan District, Long Khanh Province, in the Republic of Vietnam from April 1969 to June 1970.

I have tried to frame these stories within the context of the advisory experience, the war itself, and the political events that engulfed us all at that time. In retrospect, I recognize that the events of this book were shaped as much by decision makers in Washington as they were by the participants in that remote Vietnamese district.

The characters I write about were real people doing the best they could, often in unreal situations. Where most of them are now, I do not know. I only remember them from those moments when our paths crossed and the shutter of life's camera caught us. This book attempts to capture those moments, preserving them like so many dog-eared photos collecting dust in boxes across this nation.

After years of observing our nation's denial and its conscious effort to "put Vietnam behind us," I am pleasantly surprised to note that talking about the Vietnam experience is now fashionable, as witnessed with Robert McNamara's recent *mea culpa*. In addition, the recent commemoration of the twentieth anniversary of the fall of Saigon and the official end of the war have prompted renewed discussion. I believe all of this is healthy as well as historically appropriate.

More than a quarter of a century having elapsed since I lived these events, the details may be fuzzy or some facts may seem to have been embellished over time. I regret that I did not more faithfully record the details of my experiences as they occurred, yet I am grateful still for having "had the moments."

I have tried wherever possible to introduce humor into this account. Although war is a brutalizing experience, it also has a lighter side. Humor is where you find it, often in the most unexpected places—you just have to recognize it. Over my career—and Vietnam was no exception—I experienced many amusing incidents and misadventures, which I have shared with friends and acquaintances. They generally are entertained, and invariably at the end of the evening, someone will say, "You ought to write a book!" Well, now I have, and I am counting on each of them to buy a copy!

Ronald L. Beckett, 1999

PART ONE

Going Back

CHAPTER 1

The Beginning

Alarms sounded silently in my head as we snaked our way along the nearly deserted, narrow two-lane road, our pace frequently slowed by the erosion and potholes that marked the crumbling asphalt strip. Heavy jungle, shadowy and foreboding in its quest to reclaim its natural dominance, encroached upon the cleared right-of-way, often within feet of the road. This was madness: four lightly armed Americans in a lone vehicle traveling along the southern edge of War Zone D, an area of dense jungle notorious as a stronghold and major base of operations for the Viet Cong (VC). All my training and previous Vietnam experience came rushing back, warning me of our vulnerability.

It was 0930 on 30 April 1969, and I was riding shotgun in Maj. Roger V. Havercroft's jeep, moving northeast on Highway 20 in Long Khanh Province. I was en route to assume command of the Dinh Quan District Advisory Team in the northern part of the province. Havercroft was driving, and two NCOs from his Kiem Tam District Advisory Team were riding in the back of the jeep. They were looking forward to visiting their American counterparts on the Dinh Quan team, but had come along primarily to provide security on the trip. Somehow, I wasn't comforted. The VC could practically reach out and touch you almost anywhere along this part of the route. My body involuntarily tensed as we approached particularly hazardous stretches of the road—I could envision the explosive violence of the ambush that I believed was sure to come.

During the first 10 kilometers of the journey, we had traveled through generally populated areas, encountering cleared farmland, banana and rubber plantations, small villages and hamlets, and an

3

occasional Vietnamese military outpost. There was a noticeable presence of Regional Force (RF) and Popular Force (PF) soldiers, but
equally noticeable was their apparent lack of concern for security.
Most were lounging about or walking casually beside the road, often
unarmed. As we traveled northward, the population and military
presence continued to diminish until eventually we found ourselves
alone, with only the jungle surrounding us. My anxiety had increased
proportionately to our growing isolation.

I couldn't help contrasting this trip with those I had taken four
years earlier in Vietnam while serving as a company commander in
the 1st Infantry Division. By division policy, we had traveled in heavily armed convoys. Vehicles were sandbagged or had armor plating,
and air cover often flew overhead. Radio communications ensured
that division artillery fire support was instantaneously on call. On
occasion, armored personnel carriers led the way. We had taken
every precaution. In stark contrast, this trip ignored all the rules that
I had learned.

Reluctant to reveal my growing apprehension, I cautiously mentioned my concerns to Havercroft, who simply smiled. I had learned
my first lesson as an advisor: risk-taking, normally a currency to be
spent carefully, was an inherent part of an advisor's job. It was a high-
stakes game, and advisors often found themselves wagering great
sums at a time.

Traffic on the road was sporadic, mostly logging trucks or vehicles
laden with a variety of produce headed for Saigon. The city of Dalat,
some two hundred kilometers away on the Cao Nguyen plateau at the
northern terminus of Highway 20, was noted for its small farms,
which produced tons of fresh fruits and vegetables, coffee, and tea
that were trucked daily along this route. These farms increased dra-
matically in number during the war, becoming a major source of
fresh fruits and vegetables for the U.S. Armed Forces.

Approximately twenty-five kilometers into the trip, we came to
the La Nga River, which marked the border between Kiem Tam District and Dinh Quan District. I noticed immediately that the steel
girder bridge spanning the river had been blown, its center span
sprawled awkwardly in the riverbed below—yet another reminder of
the enemy's invisible presence. Engineers had replaced the missing
span with a standard World War II "Bailey bridge," whose narrow

width restricted traffic to a single lane. Except for occasional confrontations between harried Vietnamese truck drivers, it seemed to work reasonably well.

About a hundred meters from the western bank of the river was a U.S. compound housing Company D, 169th Engineer Battalion, whose mission was to straighten and improve a 40-mile stretch of the road. Sharing the compound was one section (two guns) of a 155mm howitzer battery that provided fire support to both Kiem Tam and Dinh Quan Districts. In a separate compound at the western end of the bridge was a Vietnamese RF Company charged with securing what remained of the bridge. A U.S. mobile advisory team (MAT), consisting of five men, was also assigned there to advise and assist the RF Company.

On the eastern side of the bridge (Dinh Quan District) about a hundred yards from the river was the small hamlet of La Nga. As we drove past, I noted the hamlet's single distinguishing mark—a small Roman Catholic church. The routine of daily activities was well underway in the hamlet by this hour, and the presence of four Americans didn't appear to raise an eyebrow.

As we drove from the bridge to the district capital in Dinh Quan Village, I tried to take in every detail. That 10-kilometer stretch was completely unpopulated and even more thickly forested, with trees and underbrush growing within feet of the highway on both sides. Occasionally there were logging trails or what appeared to be heavily traveled footpaths leading off into the jungle. I later learned that these paths served as major north–south arteries for Viet Cong and North Vietnamese Army (NVA) units moving into and out of War Zone D. (My uneasiness was vindicated less than three weeks later, when the Vietnamese 18th Division fought a major engagement with a North Vietnamese Division attempting to move south across precisely this stretch of road.) On this day, however, except for the infrequent traffic, all was quiet, and there was no sign of life.

A glance at the 1:50,000 scale map resting on my lap told the story: the entire sheet was a solid sea of green. This green mass, indicating jungle, was broken only by a single line representing Highway 20. In the center, astride the highway, was a small white elliptical hole—the village of Dinh Quan. Never has isolation been more graphically depicted.

I felt a tremendous sense of relief when we rounded a bend and the jungle melted away. Before me lay a large cleared plain checkered with small farm plots and rice paddies. The sun reflecting off the flooded paddies outlined the signature rock outcroppings of the remote village that was to be my home for the next fourteen months. I had arrived.

We know little about where things really begin or where they will end, but a series of singular events over the previous five months had culminated in my being in this place at this moment. It was a strange feeling, and while I didn't understand it, I somehow sensed that I was destined to be here.

CHAPTER 2

Duty Calls

Destiny, it seemed, and the call to duty had first come in the guise of a disturbing early morning phone call from the Department of the Army. "Good God! This can't be happening," I thought, as I hung up the phone. I had just been ordered back to Vietnam for my third tour of duty. It seemed unfair; while most of my career-officer peers had served one tour by this time, I still knew many who had not been to Vietnam at all.

It was the fall of 1968, and I was a brand new army major attending graduate school at the University of Alabama. The Vietnam War was far away, and not many wild-eyed antiwar radicals were in residence in Tuscaloosa, Alabama. Sure, there was a little protest movement on campus, but the local chapter of the Students for a Democratic Society was small, poorly organized, and not taken very seriously. Most of the student body were either amused by their efforts or ignored them altogether. I had been sent to 'Bama at the army's expense to get a master's degree in political science and was anticipating a follow-on assignment at my alma mater, the United States Military Academy, as an instructor in the Social Sciences Department. Having completed two tours in Vietnam, I did not expect to return for a third. I was enjoying university life and looking forward to the more relaxed pace associated with instructor duty at the academy.

Things were going well at Alabama. I was with my family, I was successfully meeting the challenges of academia, Bear Bryant was coaching, "Snake" Stabler was quarterbacking, and life on campus was fun and carefree. Much to my surprise, when I completed my master's degree in August, the Department of the Army granted permission for me to remain and enter the doctoral program. Life was good.

It was November, and I was three months into my doctorate course work, when the call came from the Officers' Assignment Branch in Washington telling me my Ph.D. program was being curtailed, and I would soon receive orders, not to West Point, but back to Vietnam—this time on the advisory side of the war. I tried to convince the assignments officer that this wasn't fair and that there must be some mistake. Failing that, I tried to convince him to defer my orders to Vietnam for a few months, reminding him of the army's investment in my Ph.D. program and that I would only need until May to complete my doctoral course work. I knew the university would allow me to complete my doctoral dissertation in absentia once I returned from Vietnam.

I might as well have been talking to the wall. The only thing that bureaucratic son-of-a-bitch cared about was filling his quota. He tried to convince me that I had been requested by name, implying that my assignment was somehow critical to the war effort. I wasn't buying, but it didn't matter—he didn't have to sell. Fair or not, reasonable or not, like it or not, I was going back.

I completed the semester in January 1969, made my farewells, and moved my family to Fayetteville, North Carolina. I was temporarily assigned to the John F. Kennedy Special Warfare Center at Fort Bragg, where for the next six weeks I was enrolled in the Military Assistance Training Advisors (MATA) course. We found a house in a quiet neighborhood off-post where my wife, Nan, and my five-year-old daughter, Natasha, would live for the year I was to be in Vietnam. All the post facilities were nearby, and there were lots of other waiting wives and children to keep them company.

The MATA course consisted of training in a variety of subjects including communications, explosives, survival, counterinsurgency warfare, psychological operations, and weapons. The training, which was supposed to prepare officers and NCOs for advisory assignments in Vietnam, was for the most part superficial, lacking both substance and depth. There was also a crash course in the most rudimentary elements of the Vietnamese language. My assessment at the end of the course was that I was ill-prepared to be an advisor and even less prepared to speak the language. About the best I could muster was a *Chao Ong*, which translated as "Hello, Mister." A few members of the class had orders for follow-on language training at the Department of

Defense Language Schools in Monterey, California, or Fort Bliss, Texas, or at the Foreign Service Language School in Washington, DC. Unfortunately, I was not among them. Despite my apprehension about my lack of preparation, April found me saying goodbye to my family and for the third time boarding a plane bound for the Republic of Vietnam.

I was truly distressed about being assigned to the Military Assistance Command Vietnam (MACV) and about the prospect of being an advisor. The conventional wisdom was that an advisory assignment was strictly second-class. For a career officer, service in a U.S. unit was what counted for selection to service schools, choice future assignments, and early promotions. I had served in the 1st Infantry Division in 1965–66, and I knew the general disdain with which advisory jobs were viewed. The combination of second-class status, poor preparation and training, and the perceived negative career impact had a predictable effect on those chosen. Career officers made every effort to avoid advisory assignments, and once selected, they made every effort to transfer into U.S. units once they got to Vietnam. Accordingly, most of the officers in my MATA class considered themselves only "temporary help" and stated openly that they planned to be advisors only until they could land a job in a U.S. unit. I confess that my own reaction to being assigned to MACV was no different from that of my MATA classmates or any of the other thousands of U.S. officers fingered for advisory assignments—I was not happy. I would go to Vietnam, but once there, I would do everything in my power to get reassigned to an American unit. I was a major, I had been to Vietnam twice, and I knew my way around. There was no way I was going to spend a year as an advisor!

As I boarded the flight to San Francisco for the first leg of my journey back to Vietnam, little did I know that not only would events prove me wrong, but that I would end up voluntarily extending my advisory tour to fourteen months. My assignment as district senior advisor of Dinh Quan District in Long Khanh Province proved to be one of the most rewarding personal and professional experiences of my life.

CHAPTER 3

Cinnamon

In everyone's life there are those moments and events, seemingly insignificant, the details of which are inexplicably and indelibly etched in our memories. We only know that as the years come and go, the memory of those events remains as clear and fresh as if they had occurred the evening before. Such is my memory of Cinnamon.

As the Braniff flight from Travis Air Force Base, California, to Vietnam roared down the runway and lifted off into the darkness, most everyone aboard sat quietly, absorbed in their own thoughts. I tried to think about what lay ahead, but my thoughts kept drifting back to the evening before. I had arrived at Travis by way of San Francisco early in the afternoon, only to learn that my flight to Vietnam had been delayed and now wasn't scheduled until the following evening. After checking in and confirming flight information, I caught the bus back to San Francisco for the evening. I found a cheap hotel with a small sign in the front window proclaiming "Servicemen Welcome." The hotel was showing its age but was clean, and the elderly man serving as desk clerk and bellhop was friendly. I checked in, dropped my bags in my small room, and spent the remainder of the afternoon riding the cable cars and sightseeing in the Fisherman's Wharf area. Realizing that this would be my last chance for a while to enjoy a really fine meal, I found a suitable restaurant and proceeded to stuff myself, then took a walk to settle my meal before returning to the hotel. As I approached the tarnished brass revolving door that guarded the entrance to the hotel lobby, the glare of neon caught my eye. Across the street and halfway down the block was a small bar. The flashing neon sign above the door proudly proclaimed "Best Topless Dancers in SF!" With still a few hours to kill before bedtime, this seemed like an interesting diversion—and since they claimed to be the *best* in San Francisco, I felt some obligation to see for myself. I never imagined that more than twenty-five years later I would be writing about that night's events and recalling them in every detail.

It took a few minutes for my eyes to adjust to the near darkness inside, and when they did, I found myself in a long, narrow room with a bar running about halfway down the right side. Tables occupied the center and left half of the room, and I noted perhaps a dozen people in the place, all seemingly engaged in their own conversations. I climbed onto a worn leather stool at the end of the bar, giving me an unobstructed view of the entire room. Farther down the right wall, beyond the bar, was a platform perhaps four feet above the floor. It was surrounded by a small brass railing, and a shiny brass pole extended up from the center of the floor to the ceiling. Loud, pulsating music was blaring, and overhead lights bathed the platform in an array of constantly changing colors. On the platform was a somewhat attractive full-figured redhead, adorned only in a glittering G-string, mechanically going through her routine and seemingly oblivious to the audience half-watching her from the darkness. If this was San Francisco's best, I was glad I hadn't wandered into one of the city's lesser-ranked joints. (I recall making some comment to that effect to the bartender—a humorless dried-up character who didn't even crack a smile.)

Sipping my Jack Daniels and water, I followed the ever-changing parade of dancers, some good, most fair, some downright awful, but nearly all with identical expressions of indifference. After several hours and several more drinks, I half-noticed a figure slipping onto the stool next to mine. I casually turned to acknowledge this new presence and was pleasantly surprised to find myself face-to-face with a beautiful blond, about twenty-five, with the deepest blue eyes I had ever seen. She was wearing a silk wrap that was loosely tied in front, providing a tantalizing glimpse of cleavage. I recognized her as one of the few performers who was not only a good dancer, but also gorgeous. When she had danced earlier, conversations had stopped, and she had the rapt attention of everyone in the room. Fully clothed, she would have stopped a parade; clad only in a G-string, she took your breath away. She smiled warmly and said, "Hi, I'm Cinnamon." I

smiled back, as much in response to her name as to her presence. I
assumed Cinnamon was her stage name, borrowed no doubt from
Mission Impossible, a popular TV series at the time featuring an attractive blonde female character named Cinnamon.

After a few minutes of small talk, she asked, noting my haircut
and black low-quarter shoes, "Are you army or Marines?"

"Army," I replied, adding that I was en route to Vietnam for the
third time and flying out the following day. She talked for a few minutes about Vietnam and friends she had who were serving there,
adding that she hated the war for what it was doing to our country
and to our young people. She grew quiet for a minute, then leaned
over next to me and, speaking softly into my ear, said, "For a hundred
dollars, I could make this the most memorable night of your life." I
could feel her breath in my ear and the warmth of her body as she
leaned against my arm. Every nerve ending in my body sprang to
attention! She paused for a moment, as if to let her words sink in,
and then said, "Do you understand?" Unable to speak, I only nodded.
My mind was racing: $100—shit, it might as well have been $100,000!
I was boarding a plane for Vietnam in a few hours, and you didn't go
to a war zone with a lot of money. A hasty mental inventory told me I
had $35 or $40 tops on me at the time. I managed to mumble something to the effect that her offer was certainly inviting, but I didn't
think I would be able to take her up on it. She smiled, feigning disappointment, although at the time I was convinced her expression was
genuine. In a moment she leaned over again, kissed me on the
cheek, and whispered, "Take care of yourself in 'Nam and come back
safely." I weakly thanked her as she slid off the stool. As she started to
walk away, she paused and, looking back, said softly, "If you change
your mind, I get off at one." With that, she walked the length of the
bar and disappeared behind a curtained door at the far end. Her
scent hung heavy in the air for the next several minutes. It was a
scene right out of a Mickey Spillane novel.

I downed the remains of my drink, got up casually, and strolled to
the men's room, where I spent the next three minutes doing a frantic
search and inventory of my fiscal assets. My hotel bill was paid and my
bus ride back to Travis taken care of. I had paid for my drinks, and
my only anticipated expenses would be meals the next day—I could
skip a couple of those. My search, however, had turned up a grand

total of $38.77, and I knew with that meager sum negotiations were out of the question. Forlornly, I returned to my post at the bar.

Ten minutes later, Cinnamon was back on the stage. It seemed to me that her every gesture and look were directed at me. It was more than I could stand, so I quickly downed my final drink, gave an appreciative nod, and returned alone to my hotel room. By the time I showered and settled in, it was well past midnight. Cinnamon would be getting off in a few minutes. The "most memorable night of my life," she had said—a tall promise, but for that single moment on an April night in San Francisco, I believed her.

As my flight winged its way westward the following evening, I found it hard to forget the events of the previous night. More than twenty-five years later, the memory lingers, vividly intact.

CHAPTER 4

Getting the Job

The screech of the Boeing 707's oversized tires biting into the runway startled me awake. We had landed at Hickam Air Force Base in Honolulu, Hawaii. It was 0230 as we disembarked so that the plane could be refueled. Despite the hour, I phoned Ben McPherson, an old friend from my days with the 25th Division in Hawaii. We had a brief telephone reunion, and he brought me up to date on several mutual friends who had likewise recently passed through Hawaii either heading to or returning from Vietnam. It was good talking with him, although at that hour I'm not sure how happy he was to hear from anyone.

The remainder of the flight included refueling stops at Wake Island, Guam, and Clarke Air Force Base in the Philippines. At each stop, we disembarked, were fed, and had several hours to kill; I managed to dash off a postcard to my family from every layover, chronicling my trip across the Pacific.

The three-hour stop at Wake Island was memorable for several reasons. First, I was amazed at how small the island was. The airstrip literally ran from one end of the island to the other. Someone had fashioned a hand-painted sign and stuck it atop a sand dune, proclaiming it to be fifteen feet above sea level and the highest point on the island. Rusting hulks of ships lay offshore, visible reminders of the fierce fighting that had taken place there in the early days of World War II. I could envision that small detachment of American sailors and Marines and imagine the helplessness they must have felt as they waited for the Japanese invasion that would ultimately overwhelm them.

What was most unforgettable, however, was the greeting we received as we disembarked the plane for breakfast. We stumbled along in the early morning darkness to the nearby mess hall. There, silhouetted in the doorway, was the biggest, meanest-looking mess sergeant I had ever seen. In a sleeveless T-shirt, with his hairy arms crossed and sweat running off his body, he looked like a caricature that the fertile mind of Bill Mauldin might have created. As we approached, he growled, "Gentlemen, welcome to Wake Island. I prepared a hot breakfast for you—eggs, pancakes, bacon, sausage, home fries, biscuits, and gravy. I have just one rule in my mess hall: you are welcome to take all you want, but you'd better eat all you take!" I noted that every one of my traveling companions, from private to colonel, took careful measure of the food they put on their trays as they moved down the serving line.

The last leg of the trip from the Philippines to Saigon was a little livelier, as apprehension was growing, especially for those heading to Vietnam for the first time. Tension mounted as we got closer, culminating in an audible gasp as the plane made its sudden diving descent to reduce exposure to possible ground fire. "Welcome to Vietnam," I thought.

We touched down at Tan Son Nhut Airport in Saigon at 1330 the afternoon of 24 April. Stepping off the air-conditioned plane onto the tarmac and into the stifling 100+ degree heat reminded me of yet another reason I was unhappy to be back in Vietnam. As we made our way into the airport, we passed an assembled group of soldiers, airmen, and marines waiting to board our plane for their trip home. Cries of "FNGs" (fucking new guys), "cherries," and "fresh meat" greeted us as they hooted and cheered our arrival. Each had some tidbit of advice to shout to the arriving replacements. Among the mass I spotted Maj. Carlos "Matt" Matthews, a friend from my 1st Division days. His wife, Donna, was also waiting in Fayetteville, North Carolina. Matthews had just completed a tour as an advisor to an Army of the Republic of Vietnam (ARVN) regiment. We spoke briefly, and he wished me well before I was prodded to move on with my group. There were more than 530,000 Americans in Vietnam at that time, and as I rode the bus to the reception center at Camp Alpha, I mentally tried to calculate the odds not only of our meeting in that airport, but also of his leaving on the very plane I had arrived on. I quickly gave up, however, as the sights, sounds, and smells of Vietnam rushed through the screen mesh covering the open windows of the bus, bringing back vivid memories of my two previous tours.

After a brief welcome, orientation, and initial processing at the reception center, we were free for the rest of the day. I quickly separated myself from my traveling companions and set about my business—I was looking for a job! If I was going to be an advisor (at least until I could wrangle myself into a U.S. unit), then I wanted to get one of the better positions. My first effort was to contact Maj. Fred Hillyard at the Vietnamese Airborne Division. The Vietnamese Airborne was the elite division in the Vietnamese Army, and as such it was a good place for advisory duty. Hillyard arranged for me to meet with the division senior advisor the next morning.

My interview at the Airborne Division, however, was disappointing. A battalion advisor's position was available, and because of my experience as an infantry company commander in Vietnam, the position was mine for the asking. Fate seemed to be working against me, however, as there was one small glitch. The army had just announced an initiative that would decrease the size and scope of advisory teams assigned to combat divisions, reducing them from full-blown advisory teams to smaller "combat assistance teams"—in today's parlance, "downsizing." The concept was that the advisor's role would transition from advising to combat support. I was told that when the reduction came in the very near future, many of the Airborne Advisory Team personnel would be reassigned elsewhere in the country. The senior advisor had already announced that longevity would determine who remained with the division, so within a few months I'd likely be reassigned (with no voice in the matter) or back on the street looking for a job—and there wasn't much demand for officers with only a few months remaining on their tours. As tempting as the airborne assignment was, I didn't want to take that risk. But while destiny was closing that door, it was opening another.

For the rest of that day, I continued to in-process and receive "in country" briefings. Between briefings, I attempted to fight my way through four or five switchboards—frequently getting disconnected—as I tried to reach Lt. Col. Max Lake, who I had been told was the Regional Force/Popular Force (RF/PF) Advisor in III Corps, one of the four Corps Tactical Zones (CTZ) into which the Republic of

Vietnam had been divided for command and control. Each area was the responsibility of a Vietnamese Amy corps commanded by a Vietnamese lieutenant general. American command and control paralleled the Vietnamese, with an American three-star not only commanding all U.S. forces within the corps, but also serving as the U.S. senior military advisor for that region. Each of the four corps had an American Deputy for Civil Operations and Revolutionary Development Support (DEPCORDS), normally a civilian. The DEPCORDS was responsible for all aspects, military and civil, of the pacification program. Within each corps were a number of provinces (Vietnamese political subdivisions equivalent to a state), each of which had a U.S. advisory team, generally commanded by an army colonel, lieutenant colonel, or equivalently ranked civilian foreign service officer. The province senior advisors reported directly to the DEPCORDS.

Max Lake had been the battalion executive officer when, as a new captain, I had served in the 2nd Battalion of the 18th Infantry, 1st Infantry Division, at Fort Riley, Kansas, in 1964. My hope was that Max could personally help me find a job or at least put me in contact with someone who could. When I finally succeeded in getting through to his office that evening, I was informed that he had just been reassigned as the province senior advisor (Advisory Team 49) in Long Khanh Province, about seventy kilometers from Saigon. After several more frustrating hours with the phone system, I finally reached him in Xuan Loc, the province capital, around 2200 hours. When I explained my dilemma, Max replied that I must be living right, because it just so happened that he had a vacant district senior advisor (DSA) position, and that the job was mine if I could get myself assigned to his team. He advised me to contact Col. Elmer R. Ochs, senior military advisor and deputy to the DEPCORDS in III Corps, to see if he would pull some strings. I knew Colonel Ochs from my cadet days at West Point, when he was assigned there as a company tactical officer. Max also promised to work from his end on my behalf. I slept better that night.

Despite repeated attempts throughout the following day, I was unable to contact Colonel Ochs. Meanwhile, the bureaucratic process ground on, and in midafternoon I received my official assignment: a joint operations staff (J-3) slot at MACV headquarters. I could not have imagined a worse assignment! As a major in the rank-heavy J-3 shop (the J-3 was a major general), I pictured my primary responsibilities as either the coffee pots or the wastebaskets. Disappointment doesn't begin to describe my state of mind. I had been yanked out of graduate school four months short of completing my doctoral coursework and rushed back to Vietnam for a third time for this? Dejected, I drew my meager bag of "Saigon equipment," received my room assignment at the Idaho Bachelor Officers' Quarters (BOQ), and finished out the day in more briefings. I was to report for duty at MACV headquarters at 0800 the following morning.

The more I thought about it, the angrier I got. I made up my mind not to go quietly. I would not spend a year of my life stuck in a meaningless staff job in Saigon. If I raised a ruckus, what's the worst that could happen? They couldn't send me to Vietnam—I was already there! Some people thought (and still think) I was crazy to want to give up the "good life" in Saigon. After all, it offered all the conveniences and creature comforts of big city living—good food, air-conditioned quarters, night life, clean working conditions, hot and cold running whores (if you were into that), and relative safety. But the truth is, Saigon would have driven me crazy.

When Captain Gardner, the personnel officer responsible for assignment of incoming officers, arrived for work at 0700 the next morning, I was waiting. I reminded him that during the early stages of the in-processing, he had promised to work with all officers back for their second tour to get them assignments of their choice. I told him that since I was back for my third tour in five-and-a-half years, I should definitely receive some special consideration regarding my ultimate assignment. He was sympathetic, but didn't think there was much he could do. I told him about the DSA vacancy in Long Khanh Province and that all I needed was to be released from my J-3 assignment. He agreed to help and telephoned the appropriate folks in the personnel office at MACV headquarters. They reluctantly agreed to release me, but only if I was acceptable to Colonel Ochs and if Captain Gardner could find a replacement with similar qualifications within three days. I looked apprehensively at the eight-inch stack of files sitting on Gardner's desk—these were the incoming majors. What were the odds that someone with the necessary qualifications could be in that small pile? I was hopeful, but not optimistic.

At that moment, fate again intervened. Gardner's phone rang. He answered and suddenly became very deferential to the person on the other end. "Yes, Sir! Yes, Sir! He is sitting right here in my office now, Sir. No, Sir, he is not going to MACV headquarters. Yes, Sir, I understand! III Corps is fine, Sir. I'll personally take care of it, Sir!" With that, Captain Gardner hung up, looked over at me with renewed respect, and said, "How do you know John Vann?" When I replied that I knew of Mr. Vann but had never met the man personally, Gardner said, "Well, he sure as hell knows you! He just directed me to send you to III Corps to be a district senior advisor. He said he'd personally call Colonel Ochs. He also said if for some reason III Corps didn't work out that I should send you to him in IV Corps!"

John Paul Vann was legendary in army circles. As a lieutenant colonel, he had served in Vietnam in the early sixties as a division senior advisor. He fell into disfavor with the senior American military leadership in Vietnam for strongly and publicly disagreeing with the optimistic reports being sent back to Washington about conditions in Vietnam. His military career dead-ended, and he subsequently retired from the army and returned to Vietnam as a U.S. Agency for International Development (USAID) official. He rose rapidly on the civilian side, becoming the DEPCORDS in III Corps Tactical Zone (CTZ) in 1967 and taking the position of DEPCords in IV CTZ in 1969. In 1971, in an unprecedented move, Vann, a civilian, was placed in command of all forces, civilian and military, in II Corps Tactical Zone. He was killed in a plane crash in Vietnam during the latter part of the war, and later became the subject of Neil Sheehan's best-selling biography, *A Bright Shining Lie.*

For a moment I sat there stunned. Then it hit me: I had a job—a real, meaningful job! I had escaped the drudgery of a menial staff assignment in Saigon. Things were finally looking up! Now all I needed was a replacement for the J-3 job.

Energized by Vann's call, Captain Gardner launched a diligent search into the pile of majors' records. Near the bottom of the pile he found what he was looking for: an infantry major with company-level combat command time and experience as an S-3 (Operations) Air staff officer—the same magical qualifications that had originally earmarked me for the J-3 job. I thought back to the bullshit line that the Infantry Branch Majors' assignment officer had fed me when I was at Alabama: "You were requested by name." Right!

In any event, some unnamed major, at that very moment en route to Vietnam, had just been redirected to the J-3 staff at MACV. I asked Gardner not to tell me the guy's name—I would sleep better not knowing. Over the years, I have managed to rationalize my actions by believing that Major "X" really was pleased to get a Saigon assignment.

I later learned that John Vann's interest in me stemmed from his association with Maj. Paul T. DeVries, my West Point roommate. DeVries had worked for John Vann in 1968 when Vann was the DEPCORDS for III CTZ. DeVries was the Deputy RF/PF Advisor for III Corps during that period and, as such, had frequent contact with Vann. DeVries had impressed him with his candor, thoroughness, and insight in assessing the RF/PF units in III Corps. When DeVries left Vietnam in December 1968, he told Vann that I had orders for MACV, was due in country in late April, and that I was a pretty good guy. Fortunately for me, John Vann was listening.

Over the intervening years, I have often reflected upon the incredible coincidence of Vann calling the reception center on the very day and at the precise moment that I was sitting beside the assignment officer's desk. It exceeds the bounds of reasonable probability, and I can only attribute it to fate.

CHAPTER 5

Headin' Upcountry

It boggled my mind. I could not believe what I was seeing as I stared from the bus window. It was 0900 on 28 April, and I was on the shuttle bus to the Civil Operations and Revolutionary Support (CORDS) compound in Bien Hoa, traveling through the heart of the Long Binh complex on the Saigon–Bien Hoa Highway. What had been jungle in 1965 when (as S-4 of the 2nd Battalion, 18th Infantry, 1st Infantry Division) I had been plunked down there was now a glistening sea of asphalt—acre upon acre populated by hundreds of administrative and logistical support units and supply depots of every type. Home of the II Field Force headquarters, U.S. Army Vietnam headquarters, and countless other commands, there were now clubs, swimming pools, a Chinese restaurant, bowling alleys, tennis courts, miniature golf courses, theaters, and libraries—all the amenities that a small city might afford. This was the lair of the REMFs (GI slang for rear echelon motherfuckers), so despised—or perhaps secretly envied—by the grunts in the boonies. Only four years earlier it had been a fetid mud hole that my battalion had wrestled the local Viet Cong to control. We were sniped at and mortared nightly. Local operations made frequent contact, and on at least two occasions our base camp was attacked. We had prevailed, but at considerable cost.

Our former battleground was now a giant parking lot. The jungle was gone, and the terrain had been bulldozed, reshaped, and paved over; except for the railroad, not a recognizable feature remained. I tried to explain to a lieutenant sitting across the aisle from me how disconcerting the striking visual contrast was. He looked skeptical, and I understood—had I not experienced it, I doubt I would have believed it either. I turned back to the window, determined to keep my thoughts to myself for the remainder of the trip.

As mentioned previously, III Corps was one of the four geographic CTZs into which the Republic of Vietnam had been divided for command and control. I Corps was the northernmost corps tactical zone, with IV Corps (Mekong Delta region) in the far south. III Corps constituted the heart of South Vietnam; located in the south central part of the country, it included Saigon and the eleven surrounding provinces. Also within the III Corps borders were War Zones C and D, the Iron Triangle, and the Rung Sat Special Zone—all major Viet Cong strongholds.

John Vann, so instrumental in my fate, had left the DEPCORDS position in III Corps in February 1969 and was assigned to take over those same duties in the IV Corps area in the hope that he could work the same miracle in building the CORDS team in IV Corps that he had in Bien Hoa.

The shuttle bus finally made its way through the heavy traffic and swung through the gates into the CORDS compound. I got off the bus with the other passengers and was looking around at the unimpressive array of small buildings when a sergeant appeared and directed our small group into the largest of the buildings, where we had the pleasure of yet more in-processing and a briefing on the CORDS organization and mission. The CORDS concept was unique. It brought together under one command all the major players necessary for the pacification program: the State Department, the U.S. Agency for International Development, the Central Intelligence Agency, the U.S. Information Agency, and the U.S. military. CORDS advisors, both civilian and military, were assigned to each of Vietnam's forty-four provinces and all of its 250 districts. I would be the district senior advisor (DSA) in the Xuan Loc District of Long Khanh Province.

A series of short briefings about Xuan Loc District followed: the intelligence situation, USAID programs, the Regional and Popular Forces in the district, the Revolutionary Development Program, the security of the villages and hamlets, and an assessment of the Vietnamese district chief and his staff. As the parade of briefing officers marched by, the information, numbers, and details they poured out was overwhelming. I felt like a man trying to drink from a firehose.

Next I met with Charles Whitehouse, the DEPCORDS, and Colonel Ochs, his military deputy. They formally welcomed me, and we talked briefly about the many pacification initiatives underway in Long Khanh Province and the challenges I faced in the months ahead. Whitehouse, Vann's replacement, had only been aboard a few days himself.

Late in the afternoon, Lieutenant Colonel Lake arrived to pick me up and escort me back to Long Khanh Province headquarters in Xuan Loc. I still had no weapon—my Saigon-issue pistol had been reclaimed when my orders were changed to Advisory Team 49, and my new weapon was conveniently waiting for me at province head-quarters in Xuan Loc. Thus, Max and I, armed with a single M16 rifle between us, drove the 45-kilometer trip up Highway One in a goose-drowning rainstorm, not uncommon during the monsoon season, which was just beginning. Visibility ranged from bad to awful; at times we could barely see 20 feet in front of the jeep. Adding to my anxiety was the rapidly fading daylight and Max's apparent belief that if you drove fast enough, the bad guys couldn't get you. I wasn't sure which I feared more, being killed in an ambush along the deserted road or dying in a mud hole pinned under an overturned jeep. My newfound lucky streak held, however, and we arrived safe and sound shortly before dark.

During the ride, Max told me that he had changed his mind about my assignment and instead of becoming the DSA of Xuan Loc District, I would be the DSA of Dinh Quan District, the northernmost of the province's three districts. Unfortunately for me, all the briefings I had just received had been about programs and activities in the Xuan Loc District!

Upon our arrival at the Province Advisory Team headquarters compound in Xuan Loc, Max introduced me around. I was greeted warmly and told by nearly everyone how fortunate I was to get assigned to Advisory Team 49 and especially to be taking over the Dinh Quan District team. After a delicious dinner, I spent the evening chatting with various members of the province team and noting with pleasant surprise the living conditions at the compound. It all seemed very comfortable: television, movies, electric appliances of every sort, hot and cold running water, toilets that flushed, a thoroughly provi-sioned bar, tables set with linen and china, and dinner prepared and

served by white-coated Vietnamese servants. Many of the senior officers and civilians on the team had their own air-conditioned trailers—
true luxury in an unexpected locale.

My accommodations for the night were in the comfortable trailer
of one of the senior staffers who happened to be on R&R (Rest &
Recuperation) leave at the time. I couldn't help but smile as Gen.
William Tecumseh Sherman's famous quote flicked through my
mind: "War is Hell!" General Sherman notwithstanding, I spent a
restful night in air-conditioned splendor, disturbed only by periodic
firing of harassment and interdiction (H&I) rounds from an ARVN
105mm howitzer battery positioned nearby. Only the outgoing
artillery fire reminded me that I was back in a combat zone. It was a
strange and somewhat unsettling feeling.

The following day, I processed in, was briefed on Dinh Quan District by various elements of the province staff, and paid a courtesy call
on Lt. Col. Bui Duc Diem, the Vietnamese province chief, and Vu
Van Khuong, his civilian deputy for administration. In the afternoon,
Maj. Roger Havercroft, district senior advisor at Kiem Tam District,
picked me up, and we drove north on Route 20 to his district headquarters. Kiem Tam was the third district in the province and was
located along Highway 20 between Xuan Loc and Dinh Quan. Rog
and I had been friends since our days in the same cadet company at
West Point. I enjoyed the evening spent with him in Kiem Tam
recalling old times, catching up on mutual acquaintances, and trying
to learn from him just what a DSA was supposed to do. He gave me a
brief orientation, some good advice, and confirmed what I already
knew: my job was a demanding one, requiring much more than just
military skills. He also emphasized that it was a dangerous assignment. The DSA commanded a small team (three to ten men,
depending upon the team composition) and lived with the Vietnamese, often in very remote locations. Coordination of the pacification program was the team's principal focus. Duties were broad and
included military operations and combat support activities, liaison
with U.S. military units and civilian agencies, advice and training for
regional and local forces, and assistance to district officials on a wide
range of governmental activities and programs—everything from sanitation, education, and economic development to intelligence operations and security.

John Vann, while serving as the DEPCORDS for III Corps, had established the standards and expectations against which advisors were to be measured. These were later formally codified in a Policy Guidance and Information memorandum.

Expectations for Advisors

I expect each advisor, within 30 days after his assignment, to be the world's leading expert on the functional and geographic area of his assignment. As an example, for a District Senior Advisor, this involves a knowledge of the size, ethnic makeup, religious adherence and political breakout of the population of the district; the authorized, assigned and the present-for-duty strengths of the RF/PF, National Police, RD Cadre, and the People's Self-Defense Force; the family name, age, education, place of birth, religion, political connections, past assignments, strengths and weaknesses of the District Chief, and to only a slightly lesser degree, the major personalities of the district, both GVN and VC; the price of rice, fish sauce, beef, fish, pork, beer, soft drinks, labor, sampan motors, transport, etc., and their trend over the past 12 months; a history of the district, its physical characteristics and its potential for development; the number of identified and estimated VCI and their *de facto* organizational structure; the number of primary and secondary classrooms, the shortage (if any) of school teachers and the percentage of children eligible who are enrolled at both primary and secondary levels; the number, types and productivity and potential of major private industries within the district; the enemy order of battle and how it has changed in the past two years; an intimate knowledge of the name and location of all contested hamlets and the actions necessary to improve them to an acceptable level; the number and type of medical facilities either in the district or accessible from the district and an evaluation of their adequacy; the most decorated or otherwise outstanding RF soldier and PF soldier within the district; the average daily numbers of rounds fired by each tube of sector artillery and a knowledge of whether or not the fire was

observed and to the extent that it was harassment and inter-
dictory fires (H&I); the status of major items of equipment
authorized within the district, to include radios (PRC-25s,
PRC-10s, and HT-1s), mortars, machine guns, starlight scopes,
M-79s, Claymore mines and vehicles; effectiveness and organization of the District Intelligence Operations Coordination
Center (DIOCC); and the performance of the principal personalities within the DIOCC; knowledge of the ten "most
wanted" VCI on the black list; status of RF and PF housing
and plans for improvement; knowledge of the existence or
non-existence of an RF/PF recruiting plan, steps underway to
improve it, monthly attrition rate of RF/PF and number of
individual fillers currently at the training center.*

This expertise was to encompass the social, religious, political,
economic, and military aspects of his district. The advisor was not
only expected to have this knowledge, but also to put it to use effectively in pursuit of the numerous pacification objectives. It was a hell
of a challenge, but with the experience of two previous tours, and
buoyed by my recent successful escape from Saigon, I was brash
enough to believe I was up to it.

Up to it or not, I was eager to get started; I had been in Vietnam
for six days and had still not arrived at my assigned post. Havercroft
was to deliver me to my team the following morning. I slept reasonably well that night, but at one point was haunted by a recurring
dream of a young Major "X" in Saigon who had just been told he was
being assigned to J-3 MACV.

---

* Vann, John P., Memorandum, 2d Regional Assistance Group, RVN, Subject: Policy
  Guidance and Information Memorandum 1, dated 5 June 1971 (National Archives,
  Washington, DC).

PART TWO

First Impressions

CHAPTER 6

Dinh Quan District

The jeep's gears growled in protest as Havercroft tried to downshift in order to negotiate a particularly bad section of the decaying highway. Ahead in the distance lay Dinh Quan and my new assignment. I tried to remember what I had been told during my several briefings, but there had been so much and it came so fast, it all now seemed hazy. I did manage to recall that the district was about forty kilometers wide (west to east) and sixty-five kilometers long (north to south), and that despite its relatively large size there were only about 16,400 inhabitants—legal ones at least. Since the northern 40 percent of the district was located in War Zone D, a notorious Viet Cong stronghold, there were always numerous other inhabitants who were not counted among our official population. I also recalled that the district was relatively new, having been established only thirteen years earlier. Most of the inhabitants had been resettled from contested areas in other parts of the country by the government or were refugees fleeing the war. In 1967 the portion of the district west of the La Nga River (about one-third of the original district) had been broken away to form Kiem Tam District.

The official population was predominately Vietnamese, but there were sizable groups of Chinese and Montagnards as well. The Montagnards (mountain people) were primitive aborigines who lived in the central highlands. They were fierce fighters who trusted neither the South Vietnamese government nor the Viet Cong. Considered inferior, they were looked down upon by the Vietnamese. (Discrimination, it seems, knows no ethnic, religious, nor geographic boundaries.) The U.S. Special Forces had great success in earning their trust and in training, equipping, and organizing them into Civilian

Irregular Defense Groups (CIDG). Operating from fortified camps in the mountains, they were effective in disrupting North Vietnamese Army (NVA) supply routes.

The Montagnards in Dinh Quan had fled their mountain homes to escape the war. They had their own hamlets and to the extent possible, elected to be alone. In addition, the district population was sprinkled with a few Cambodians and several other smaller minorities, including the twenty-two Americans assigned to the district: seven in the advisory team at Dinh Quan and fifteen others assigned to three (later four) mobile advisory teams co-located with the Regional Force Companies stationed within the district. There was an equally diverse religious representation: Catholic, Protestant, Buddhist, Animist, Confucist, and a particularly unusual sect the Vietnamese called the "Coconut People." (The name was obviously derived from their appearance—they dressed totally in brown Buddhist-type garb with a brown turban wound atop their heads. As far as I was able to determine, their religious beliefs combined elements of numerous eastern religions.)

Dinh Quan was a rural district in every sense of the word—its location, its economy, its infrastructure, its lack of sophistication, and its values. The economy was dependent upon three basic sources of income: farming (both rice and vegetables), logging (the surrounding jungle and forests were rich in valuable hardwoods), and serving as a stopover for truckers running the long stretch of highway between Saigon and Dalat.

The dominant terrain feature of the area was a Hershey Kiss–shaped hill that towered above the western edge of the village. On top were a Vietnamese artillery position and a company of Regional Force soldiers. Nui Dang Cai, better known as "Artillery Hill," rose 300 feet above the surrounding plain, providing a vantage point from which the artillery pieces could fire in all directions and give maximum coverage to the central part of the district.

Just beyond the hill was Tin Nghia, a Montagnard community, the first of five hamlets that made up the village of Dinh Quan. Farther along, the hamlets Trung Hieu, Hoa Thuan, and Truong van Phuc ran together, making it impossible to distinguish where one ended and another began. Doan Ket, the final hamlet of the village stood separate several hundred yards up the highway. Houses and small businesses lined both sides of the highway, most of them small wooden buildings with tin roofs. The village was full of activity of every kind.

Because it was a rural village, the traditional peasant garb of black pajamas and conical straw hats was predominate, but western-style slacks and shirts were also in evidence among many men in the village. A few younger girls and women were dressed in the traditional *Ao Dai*, a long, flowing tunic split all the way up the sides to the waist and worn over silk trousers. Not unexpectedly, soldiers were everywhere.

The hamlets extended outward 75 to 100 meters on the south side of the highway, but only 25 meters on the north side, as giant rock outcroppings prevented further expansion in that direction. These strange outcroppings rising out of the plain were Dinh Quan's major, and perhaps only, claim to fame and the source of the village's nickname, "Rock City." The granite formations, apparently creations of the ice age, were composed of huge boulders (as big as 150 feet in diameter), many mysteriously stacked two and three high and towering more than 100 feet into the air. They were an impressive sight, and Americans came from all over to see them and to visit the Buddhist shrine and gardens that were intricately carved into one area. The rocks' origins were the subject of much speculation. (In an attempt to resolve the mystery, SFC Michels, the team medic and medical advisor, sent a sample of the rocks for analysis to an acquaintance at Penn State University. The geology department there responded that without question it was Rocky Mountain granite from the western United States!)

A number of local legends had sprung up as to the rocks' origin. One legend, shared with me by our Vietnamese housekeeper, was that long ago, as the Vietnamese from the north had begun their move south, they were resisted by inhabitants of the Kingdom of Champa, currently central South Vietnam. A great battle took place at Dinh Quan, and according to legend, afterward the Vietnamese soldiers camped on the site of the village to regroup and to celebrate their victory over the Chams. When they broke camp to move farther south, the stones they were using for chess pieces were stacked or scattered about the battlefield. According to local lore, over hundreds of years these pieces of stone had grown into the existing giant boulders.

A series of rather rickety ladders allowed soldiers to climb up and down to man the sentry posts and fighting positions perched atop the highest formations. I later learned that a bunker atop one of the rocks was the final rallying position for members of the advisory team should our compound be overrun. I recall only too well the trepidation with which I hauled my 200-pound body up those ladders to inspect the positions. I couldn't imagine what it would be like trying to get up there under fire carrying all my gear! Later in my tour, *The Hurricane*, a monthly magazine published by II Field Force in Vietnam, ran a feature story about the rocks and their origins.

Beyond the village to the south were approximately four square kilometers of open fields and paddies, and beyond the fields lay the jungle. Near the eastern end of the village, there was a thriving marketplace offering a variety of fruits, bread, vegetables, meats, fish, and fowl of all sorts. In addition, there were several small restaurants, a barber shop, vehicle repair shop, and other small facilities that had sprung up to accommodate the needs of the highway travelers.

Truckers caught in Dinh Quan for the night would sleep in their trucks or sling a hammock on the undercarriage. In all the months I spent there, I never failed to be amazed when I saw a truck pulled over to the side of the highway undergoing what in army parlance would have been called "depot-level" maintenance: major engine and transmission repair! The Vietnamese were geniuses at keeping these old trucks running. (Having once served as a battalion motor officer, I can say with confidence that the army's Ordnance branch could have learned a lot about field maintenance from these truck drivers.)

Beyond the marketplace were the military compounds, which housed the district government, local military units, the National Police, and the Dinh Quan District Advisory Team, my new command. As we approached the gate that hot and humid April morning, I took a deep breath and murmured, half aloud, the standard warning from my childhood games: "Ready or not, here I come!"

CHAPTER 7

Home Sweet Home

The road ahead was blocked temporarily by an ancient bus bulging with people, live chickens and ducks, produce, and baskets and bags of all sorts. It groaned in protest as it inched its way through the congested village street. As it moved on, we turned left into the district headquarters on the eastern edge of the village. My first reaction was utter disappointment. I don't know what I was expecting, but this sure as hell wasn't it! The compound was small, rundown, and dirty, with only a tangled web of rusting barbed wire separating it from the highway. A determined troop of Girl Scouts could have overrun the place! The compound ran parallel to the road for about a hundred meters and extended roughly eighty meters rearward, with rock formations making up the western and northern boundaries. To the east was the National Police compound. Beyond that, except for a Buddhist temple and the village high school, both of which stood alone, it was open.

On the south side of the road, opposite the district headquarters, was another military compound housing the 621 Regional Force Company, one of the district's five RF companies. Adjacent to that compound was a very crude military hospital—"infirmary" might have been more descriptive, although in retrospect I believe even that term may have been generous.

The district compound itself contained a dozen or so buildings, the most impressive being the district headquarters, a yellowish stucco building directly opposite the gate about fifty meters from the road. To the left of the headquarters building were several others, mostly wooden and tin structures. However, sitting prominently in their midst was another stucco building, the District Intelligence Operations Coordination Center (DIOCC), from which the infamous

Phoenix Program operated. To the right of the headquarters was a smaller stucco building that served as the district chief's house, and behind it were several more wooden structures that housed the officers and men assigned to the headquarters.

To the far right were the compound's well and the American advisory team house, a low rectangular building approximately forty-five feet wide and eighteen feet deep with an asphalt shingle roof. It was built on a concrete slab and had wooden clapboard walls up to about four feet and screen wire from there to the ceiling. An extension on one end provided a small radio room and an extra bedroom. A 4-foot-high stone wall had been erected across the entire front of the structure, ostensibly to protect the team from rocket-propelled grenades (RPGs) or other fire from the highway. I often thought it would be a pretty poor RPG gunner who couldn't put a round above the wall and through the flimsy screen right into the team house.

In front of the house were a graveled parking area, a smaller wooden building that served as an overflow bunkhouse for engineers working the highway or for other American visitors, and a wholly inadequate team bunker constructed of rock.

First impressions? Perhaps—with a stretch of the imagination—a nice place to visit, but I wouldn't want to live there!

Not surprisingly, the inside of the team house did little to change my opinion. Entering the screen door directly into the 16-foot by 18-foot combination living room, dining room, and kitchen, I noted two sofas and two cushioned chairs along the walls; dominating the left side of the room were several smaller tables pushed together to form a larger dining room table, which was surrounded by eight folding chairs. I soon learned that this was an all-purpose table—a place for dining, game playing, planning, preparing reports, letter writing, and other assorted activities. A white sheet, which served as the movie screen, hung casually on the wall behind the table.

On the right side, a counter extended out from the wall, separating the kitchen area from the rest of the room. Pots, pans, small appliances, and limited foodstuffs were stored on shelves beneath the countertop, and a variety of canned goods were stored on shelves along the rear wall. A simple electric refrigerator was on the rear wall.

From the back door I could see a lean-to–style metal roof extending rearward from the right side of the exterior wall and under it several wooden work surfaces that served as washstands. To the left were an 8-foot by 12-foot storage shed that housed a large freezer and the bulk of the team's food supplies, and a small makeshift tower topped by an aircraft wing tank from which water flowed for the open-air shower. In the center of the "backyard" was a small wooden outhouse, a "one holer," with a "piss tube" protruding from the ground nearby. Finally, about thirty meters to the rear was a shed housing the generators that supplied power to the entire compound.

The rest of the house consisted of a tiny 6-foot by 10-foot radio room and small individual rooms for each team member. There were seven bedrooms inside and one—accessible only from the outside—in the small addition that had apparently been tacked on after the house was built. The rooms were small (roughly seven by eight feet), with only enough space for a bunk, a footlocker, a small table, and a chair. There were no doors, so strips of beads or colored plastic hung bordello-style in the doorways to provide some semblance of privacy. Small as the rooms were, they nonetheless afforded each team member his own coveted private space.

The district senior advisor's room, which was in the right rear corner of the building, was slightly larger—a luxurious 8 by 10 feet. It had a built-in bed consisting of a table-like platform topped with a mattress and enveloped in a mosquito net. Two storage drawers were built under the bed, a small table and chair stood sentry in one corner, and a round chair woven of colored plastic strips—which looked to me like one of the conical straw hats worn by the Vietnamese turned upside down and mounted on legs—sat in the other. A goose-neck lamp sat on the table, and an oscillating fan mounted on the wall struggled futilely against the oppressive heat. A *Playboy* centerfold, apparently the parting gift of a previous senior advisor, was thumb-tacked to one wall. Miss February's "come hither" welcoming smile seemed appropriate for the occasion. The only thing missing was a framed needlepoint piece proclaiming "Home Sweet Home." I chuckled to myself, reminded of Victor McLaglen's great line from the classic western movie *She Wore a Yellow Ribbon*. As the burly veteran cavalry sergeant, he greeted the returning John Wayne with, "Welcome home, colonel darling!" Though I was just a major, it seemed to fit. Be it ever so humble, for the next fourteen months, this was to be my home.

CHAPTER 8

The Team

Members of the Dinh Quan team, alerted by the Kiem Tam radio operator that we would be arriving in late morning, were all present to greet me, although looking somewhat apprehensive.

My briefings at Province HQ in Xuan Loc had included some information about the individual team members, so I knew that my predecessor, Maj. Ronald Finnerty, had departed several weeks before and that Capt. Charles "Chuck" Backlin was acting senior advisor. Backlin welcomed me and introduced me to the other team members. Officially there were seven members on the team (including me); however, I quickly discovered that there were several unofficial team members, including two Vietnamese interpreters; a Vietnamese housekeeper/cook and her two nieces who did the laundry and cleaning; several enlisted men from D Company, 169th Engineer Battalion, who were temporarily residing with us while they operated a local rock crusher; and two dogs adopted by the team. In addition, three U.S. mobile advisory teams—consisting of five Americans each who lived and worked with the Vietnamese Regional Force companies located in various parts of the district—also came under my purview. The composition of the team's seven official positions were as follows:

Title	Rank
District Senior Advisor (DSA)	Major
Intelligence Officer/Deputy DSA	Captain
Weapons/Training Advisor	Sergeant First Class
Village/Hamlet Security Advisor	Sergeant First Class

Title	Rank
Operations/Intelligence Advisor	Sergeant First Class
Team Medic/Medical Advisor	Staff Sergeant
Radio/Telephone Operator (RTO)	Specialist 4th Class

Each team member had specific advisory duties and responsibilities, and allegedly the specific background, skills, and training to meet those requirements and responsibilities. Each of us had a principal Vietnamese counterpart with whom he worked, but our duties brought us into daily contact with scores of Vietnamese and took us to all parts of the district. Individual initiative and the ability to work without supervision were essential to success. As might be expected, some were better than others in such an environment.

Close living and complete interdependence required a sense of teamwork and trust. While we were a military organization with a specific chain of command, we were also a team of distinct individuals dependent on an intricate web of interpersonal relationships. Our successful operation hung on that web. In short, we were much like a family, complete with all the rewards and frustrations of any family unit. Personal friction in such an environment can be damaging beyond description.

I was fortunate to inherit a team that, by and large, got along well, had a sense of humor, and, thankfully, was professionally competent. None were terribly thrilled about being in Vietnam, and all would have preferred to be in an American unit, but to their credit they accepted their fates and did their jobs. Some were better than others in working with the Vietnamese, but all were effective.

It was an interesting cast of characters that greeted me on that steamy morning in April 1969; of course, that cast would change over the next fourteen months. When I departed in June 1970, none of the original American team members remained.

During my tour I was fortunate to have two topnotch deputies. Capt. Charles "Chuck" Backlin, Infantry officer, was West Point Class of 1966, twenty-nine years old, and unmarried. Prior to Vietnam, Chuck had served two years with the 3rd Armored Division in Germany. He was friendly and a little shy, but extremely popular with the

Vietnamese. A reliable team player, Chuck was a good officer and an able advisor, respected by all with whom he served. His duties included intelligence operations and responsibility for the Phoenix Program in the district. He had been with the district for about five months when I arrived, but remained with me for only three months before being transferred to the Xuan Loc district team to serve as the deputy and help resolve problems that team was experiencing.

First Lt. (later captain) Robert Hughes was a Military Intelligence officer, married, from Panama City, Florida, and had been a practicing attorney. Bob arrived in June 1969 as a brand-new lieutenant, fresh out of Intelligence School at Fort Holabird, Maryland. The army had just reassessed its policy of having Infantry officers run the intelligence operations of the Phoenix Program at province and district levels, and had decided to staff those positions with Intelligence officers instead. This was a long overdue move, in my opinion. I have nothing against Infantry officers, being one myself, but this job was clearly more suited for Intelligence officers, who have the requisite training and background. Bob was in the second Holabird class shipped directly to Vietnam to serve in these roles. He was bright, outgoing, highly effective, fun-loving, and well liked by the Vietnamese.

The third officer on the team for most of my tour was 1st. Lt. Ray Wingo, Military Intelligence, actually a member of the U.S. 199th Infantry Brigade assigned as liaison to Dinh Quan district. Since serving as liaison to a seven-man team was in itself not a full-time job, Ray doubled as a team officer, participating fully in all activities and carrying his load of the responsibilities. Ray's military intelligence training made him a valuable asset, and his contacts with the 199th provided us with valuable material resources not available through normal channels. (As Mr. Rogers might have said, "Can you say the word 'scrounger,' boys and girls?") An avid photographer, Ray captured many moments of the "advisory war" with his ever-present camera.

SFC Robert Kirkbride, Infantry, was the team's senior noncommissioned officer (NCO) during most of my tour. Assigned officially as the weapons/training advisor, he was also the team "First Sergeant." A professional soldier and a great guy, Kirkbride was a doer, a problem solver, and a leader. He had great instincts, sound judgment, a good sense of humor, and a "thing" for Diana Ross and the Supremes.

Other team members during my tour included:

SFC Robert Kraft, Infantry, operations/intelligence advisor
SFC Gradie Sanders, Infantry, operations/intelligence advisor
SFC James King, Infantry, village/hamlet security advisor
S/Sgt. Joseph M. *"Bac-si"* Michels, Medical Corps, medical advisor/
    medic
S/Sgt. Francis Parker, Medical Service Corps, medical advisor/
    medic
Spc. 4 John Houston, radio/telephone operator

Except for Houston, the RTO, all the enlisted team members were professional career soldiers ("lifers" in GI vernacular). Backlin and I, both West Pointers, likewise were professional soldiers.

Houston was a reluctant draftee from Chicago who was brought into the army under "Project 100,000." The word on the street in Chicago was that if you tested very poorly on the Armed Forces Qualification Tests, you would not be inducted, so Houston deliberately did so, anticipating that his "low IQ" would disqualify him from having to serve. His timing was bad, however, as Secretary of Defense Robert McNamara—in a political move to avoid having to touch existing deferments, which he feared would evoke greater protest—announced a program under which the Armed Services were going to admit 100,000 individuals who had scored poorly, and through remedial programs transform them miraculously into effective soldiers. Predictably, those drafted under Project 100,000 were predominately minorities and poor, received little or no remedial training, and ended up in disproportionate numbers in the infantry. I heard years later that the casualty rate among that group was more than twice the army's average. Houston got caught in the trap! Ironically, he actually was a bright young man, and had he taken the test properly, his higher scores would likely have resulted in his avoiding the stigma and drudgery of the program and might well have landed him in a better job elsewhere in the army. He was a good soldier and a valued team member. Because he was young, *Ba*, our Vietnamese housekeeper, treated him like her own son and could barely be consoled when he left, crying nonstop throughout the day.

We had a number of interpreters, both civilian and military, who served with the team during my fourteen months. Provided by the Vietnamese government, their ability to speak, read, and write English varied widely; many had only the most basic command of English, but because the demand for interpreters was so great nationwide, they were pressed into service. Since none of the team members spoke Vietnamese, and very few of the Vietnamese officials with whom we worked spoke any English, we were uncomfortably dependent on Vietnamese interpreters with generally marginal abilities. This lack of basic communication skills, regrettably common on advisory teams, resulted from the army's lack of selectivity in assigning advisors and failure to provide requisite language training; it was to plague us throughout my tour.

During my fourteen months, except for one brief period, we always had at least two (sometimes three) interpreters assigned to the team, one of whom was a civilian, the others military. In late January 1970, we found ourselves with only one interpreter. It was an impossible situation, since normal team operations took team members all over the district each day and an interpreter was essential. In addition, translating documents that were brought for my signature or had been acquired through intelligence operations was nearly a full-time job for one interpreter. The lack of interpreters was having a serious negative impact on our ability to get the job done, but my repeated requests to the province team had shown no results. My frustration finally got the better of my judgment, and in a fit of emotion I sent a personal message to Lieutenant Colonel Scott, who had replaced Lieutenant Colonel Lake as the province senior advisor, accusing him of either not knowing what was going on or of callously ignoring our needs. I knew that province headquarters had a number of interpreters and they could certainly afford to lend us one until the Vietnamese provided a suitable replacement. Scott's reaction was swift and predictable: he jumped on the first available chopper, flew to Dinh Quan, and royally chewed my ass. I had it coming and accepted it accordingly. The next morning, however, a chopper from Xuan Loc arrived with two interpreters aboard. The incident was never mentioned again.

Of all the interpreters who worked for us, by far the most proficient, and the mainstay for the team, was Sergeant Cuong. Cuong, a schoolteacher by trade, was drafted, promoted to sergeant, and made an interpreter on the basis of his ability to speak English. He was a good man who understood Americans and did his best to keep us from screwing up our interpersonal relationships with the Vietnamese. Bright, knowledgeable, and well-educated, he nonetheless succumbed to a number of Vietnamese superstitions. From time to time he would subject himself to "treatment" by a local medicine man we referred to as the "witch doctor." The treatment, which Cuong swore made him feel better, consisted of placing the open mouths of large drinking glasses against his skin on his chest and back. The glasses had been preheated and were very hot; as they subsequently cooled, the air contracted, creating a strong sucking action that allegedly sucked out evil spirits and other bodily ailments. The net result was large, perfectly round purple welts all over his body. We ragged Cuong pretty hard about this practice, but while acknowledging that there was no scientific basis for the treatment, he was convinced it worked.

Without question, the two most popular members of the team were our mascots—two mongrel dogs named Baron and AWOL. Baron was black as charcoal and although a mixed breed, resembled a small Doberman. He was the brighter of the two dogs. AWOL was bigger, clumsier, and dumber, but he was the more lovable of the two; tan and dirty black, he somewhat resembled a German shepherd. Both were there when I arrived, and both were there when I left. No one on the team really knew when or how the team had acquired the dogs, but they were healthy and well fed, and living with a team of Americans, they received a lot of attention. In a society that regards dogs as potential foodstuff, it was rather surprising that the dogs survived as long as they did. They wandered freely throughout the village without incident; since they frequently accompanied us in the jeep, they were probably recognized by the villagers as the team's dogs and spared the stew pot.

Finally there was *Ba* (Mrs.) Huynh Ngoc Mai and her three nieces: *Co* (Miss) Lien, *Co* Huong, and *Co* Tuyet. They were addressed simply as *Ba* and *Co*. Generally only one or two of the nieces would accompany *Ba* each day. When the team had originally come to Dinh Quan and sought local help with the cleaning, laundry, marketplace shopping, and cooking, the district chief had brought over *Ba* and her teenage nieces. Because *Ba* was the wife of the Dinh Quan village chief, there were no other candidates for the job. They would arrive by 9:00 A.M. and depart in late afternoon every day except Sunday.

The pay was very good by Vietnamese standards, and at *Ba*'s insistence all the pay went to her, and then she paid the younger girls. How much they actually received was something we were never able to find out. Whenever we inquired, she would respond in her singsong tone, "*Beaucoup Ps,*" which translated as "many piasters." She'd then cackle and go about her work.

Even today, across the span of thirty years, *Ba* remains in my memory as a character in her own right. She was small, I believe about forty-five years old, although the rigors of village life had aged her physically beyond her years, and her teeth were black as a result of years of chewing on betel nut, an opiate common in rural Vietnam. She was a good person and treated us like her own family. She was intelligent and had a good sense of humor. When we jokingly accused her of being a VC spy (and she may well have been), she would react with a wide grin and animated head-shaking and arm-waving gestures. "No VC! No VC!" she would cry, then she would laugh wildly. Like AWOL and Baron, *Ba* and the *Co*s preceded me and were there to see me off, providing my tour with a small thread of constancy uncharacteristic of the setting and circumstances.

I discovered early in my tour that an incredible amount of the team's time and energy was by necessity spent on self-support. A major shortcoming of the advisory organization was the absence of any support structure. Teams did it all themselves—they built, repaired, and maintained their houses; scrounged materials and repair parts; repaired vehicles, generators, and appliances; acquired and prepared their own food; generated their own electricity; and provided their own water. Among the Americans, duties were shared; some, such as radio watch, were on a roster basis, while others, such as tending the generator, running the movie projector, or the always pleasant chore of burning the shit from the outhouse, were handled on a less formal basis. We all did our part. Individual skills and experience often dictated who performed what chores. It was SFC Kirkbride's role as team first sergeant to ensure that these necessities were taken care of while minimizing the impact these requirements had on our duties and responsibilities as advisors. It was often a difficult trade-off.

Amazingly, the chemistry among the team members worked well. The team house was a pleasant place to be, and everyone was comfortable. As a result, we were able to focus our attention and energy on the job at hand. I believe we were an effective advisory team; we cared about the Vietnamese, and, despite our limitations, we did our best to improve the quality of life of the people of Dinh Quan District.

CHAPTER 9

Counterparts

Capt. Tran Thanh Xuan stood up as I entered his office. He greeted me fluently in English: "I am pleased to meet you, Major Beckett. Welcome to Dinh Quan." He offered me a seat and asked if I would join him in a cognac. My briefings at province headquarters had all indicated that Captain Xuan was the cream of the crop—intelligent, professional, and pro-American. I couldn't help but smile; somehow Lady Luck had continued to follow me, even to this remote Vietnamese district 9,000 miles from home.

Captain Xuan was an interesting figure with a life story itself worthy of a book. Bright and articulate, he was a man of integrity and a leader possessing good instincts and common sense. He was the consummate professional soldier. Physically, he was a handsome man—trim and fit, perhaps 5 feet 4 inches tall, in his mid-thirties. I thought he bore a remarkable resemblance to the Vietnamese vice president, Air Marshal Nguyen Cao Ky. Captain Xuan was the district chief, and as such was my counterpart. Over time, he also became my friend.

To a great extent, the nature of an advisor's relationship with his counterpart determined his ultimate success or failure in the job. Establishing trust and rapport was critical; however, such relationships require time and careful cultivation. The Vietnamese were well aware that the Americans would come for a year and then be replaced. By and large, with each new advisor, the Vietnamese took a "wait and see" posture, with the burden for developing the relationship falling primarily on the U.S. advisor. Fortunately, the advisor held the key to the material resources and the combat support that the Vietnamese wanted and needed, so there was leverage to be applied. I sensed, however, that the Vietnamese understandably resented the use of this less-than-subtle leverage. Additionally, an advisor could always go over the head of his counterpart by having the American chain of command put pressure on his counterpart's superior. As might be expected, these efforts were offensive to the Vietnamese, and while they sometimes worked, in the long run they destroyed rapport and proved to be counterproductive.

Another irritant to the Vietnamese was the fact that, while many of them had years of combat experience, knew the terrain and the enemy, and had considerable experience in fighting a guerrilla-style war, most U.S. advisors came to the job with no combat experience and little knowledge of the enemy or guerrilla warfare. In addition, the advisors were frequently younger and junior in rank to the Vietnamese they were there to advise, had no Vietnamese language skills, lacked the necessary cultural sensitivity and understanding, and had received little training for the position. But perhaps most frustrating of all was the fact that when all the obstacles had been overcome, a relationship established, and a degree of effectiveness developed, it was then time for the advisor to rotate, and the cycle began again with the arrival of a new advisor. It must have been a painfully difficult process for the Vietnamese.

In my observation, the successful advisor was one who established a partnership with his counterpart—a relationship of mutual respect in which issues could be discussed and solutions found, and in which no one won or lost. The successful advisor could never lose sight of the fact that his role was to advise and assist, and that the ultimate responsibility for accomplishing the mission rested with his Vietnamese counterpart—a difficult concept for many Americans to accept.

Unlike many advisors, I assumed this role with several things in my favor. First, I had two previous tours in Vietnam. My tour with the 1st Infantry Division had provided me considerable combat experience and with that came credibility. Second, I was very lucky to have Tran Thanh Xuan as a counterpart.

Captain Xuan and I shared a number of common experiences in our backgrounds. He was a graduate of the Vietnamese Military Academy at Dalat, and I was a graduate of West Point. We both were career infantry officers. After graduation, he had embarked on a promising military career, impressing all with whom he worked and quickly rising through the officer ranks to captain. He was identified as a "comer," one who would be groomed to rise to the most senior ranks in the Vietnamese Army. He spoke both English and French and was hand-picked to attend the U.S. Army's Infantry Officer Career Course at Fort Benning, Georgia. I attended that course in 1966. (Ironically, in 1961 we both were at Fort Benning at the same time, he attending the Career Course and I attending the Basic Infantry Officer Course and Airborne Training.) Upon his return to Vietnam, he was assigned to the Presidential Palace as the commander of the elite palace guard for President Ngo Dinh Diem.

Unfortunately, his fast-track career was interrupted on November 1, 1963, when a group of dissident Vietnamese generals, with the support of the U.S. government, mounted a successful coup, capturing the Presidential Palace and subsequently murdering President Diem and his brother. Captain Xuan was not personally injured in the struggle for the palace, but due to his obvious connection to the ousted Diem regime, his career was in ruins. He was allowed to remain in the army, but was relegated to insignificant posts at various training centers, where he languished for five years. Meanwhile the careers of his academy classmates continued to flourish, many rising to lieutenant colonel during this period.

Desperate for quality leadership, the Vietnamese government finally relented and brought Captain Xuan out of banishment in 1968, when he was assigned as the district chief of Dinh Quan. Because the position called for a major, Captain Xuan was hopeful for a quick promotion, but it didn't come. It seemed the Vietnamese generals had not yet totally forgiven him.

Captain Xuan's talent and potential were quickly recognized by all those Americans who came to know him. Both of my predecessors at Dinh Quan had recommended him highly for promotion, as did the U.S. province senior advisor. Still the promotion did not come. The Vietnamese Army announced its officer promotion list several times a year; when the large Tet (Lunar New Year) promotion list came out in 1969, Captain Xuan was crushed to discover that once again he had been passed over. My arrival in Dinh Quan came just a few months after this disappointing event.

On the day of my arrival, Captain Xuan was on leave, visiting his family in Saigon. He had chosen to leave his wife and three children there so that his children could attend French schools. He visited them periodically, and on special occasions they would come to Dinh Quan for a short visit. Our first meeting upon his return was polite and cordial. Sipping our cognac, we talked of many things, all the while sizing each other up. I was pleased with his command of English, knowing it would make things much easier in the months ahead. My Vietnamese language training had consisted of a few dozen hours of introductory instruction as part of the six-week MATA course at Fort Bragg, North Carolina. I could extend polite greetings, make rudimentary sentences, recite Vietnamese military rank, and count. If we were going to communicate, it wouldn't be through my Vietnamese! Despite Captain Xuan's reasonably fluent command of English, whenever we had an "official" meeting there was always an interpreter present—even though the captain generally spoke far better English than most of the interpreters! I never understood the reasons for this, but my suspicion was he used the interpreter simply to give him additional time in which to carefully phrase his responses.

It was soon apparent to me, as it had been to my predecessors, that Captain Xuan's talents separated him markedly from the other officers assigned to Dinh Quan. Approachable and friendly, he had a remarkably keen understanding of Americans—our strengths, our foibles, our customs, and our habits. I was impressed with him, both personally and professionally, and we developed an immediate rapport.

I was well aware of Captain Xuan's background, so near the beginning of June, I shared with him a letter I had written on his behalf. It was sent through the American chain of command with copies to the Vietnamese. The letter praised Captain Xuan, recounted his many talents, and strongly urged his promotion. He was grateful, but based on his previous experience and disappointments, afraid to be too hopeful.

When the next promotion list was announced in July, Captain Xuan was selected for promotion to major. I knew the bureaucracy well enough to be absolutely certain that my letter was still somewhere in the governmental maze and had played no part in his promotion—he had been promoted because he was deserving and because the Vietnamese Army could no longer afford to waste his considerable talents. He was convinced, however, that my letter had played a role in his selection for promotion, and our relationship was cemented, both at the professional and personal levels.

The district's other Vietnamese officers were generally good men, but far less talented. They were strictly "second team," cautious, conservative, and unwilling to take risks or stray far from established procedures. As a result, any decision of the slightest significance would be deferred to the district chief. Without exception, however, these officers worked well with members of the advisory team. In many cases, U.S. noncommissioned officers (sergeants) worked with and advised Vietnamese commissioned officers (lieutenants and captains); if sensitivities existed regarding rank consciousness—and they probably did—it was never apparent.

For the most part, Major Xuan dealt directly with me, or in my absence, with the other American officers on the team. Since his family lived in Saigon, he was, like me, a "geographical bachelor." He limited his fraternization with his junior officers and could be found most evenings in our team house enjoying the 16mm movies we regularly received. Our informal evenings together were times when we could discuss issues, exchange information, share ideas, and generally get the district's business accomplished. They were also when we discussed our families (we were nearly the same age and both had young children), our backgrounds, and our aspirations. We got to know each other on a personal level, and we became friends.

Over the years, I have discussed with others who served as advisors the challenges that we faced in dealing with our Vietnamese counterparts. Unfortunately, for many those relationships were frequently marked by frustration, mistrust, and deceit. I understand all too well the disastrous result such a relationship would have had on an advisor's effectiveness. I was blessed in that regard, and I believe the people of Dinh Quan were the better for it.

I am proud of what our team accomplished during our short stay. I believe our efforts assisted our counterparts and contributed to improved security, a stronger local economy, better education and health programs, and a strengthened local government. These results demonstrated to me the efficacy of the advisory effort. Even now, I remain convinced that the war for the hearts and minds of the Vietnamese people could have been won had both the U.S. and Vietnamese governments made the necessary commitments. Regrettably, the advisory effort never received the support it deserved, and despite the lip service, never got off the U.S. government's back burner.

Subsequent public release of North Vietnamese and Viet Cong documents speak pointedly of their deep fears of the successes that the Pacification, Chieu Hoi, and Phoenix programs were having at the time and the impact they might have on the outcome of the conflict. These successes were, however, too little, too late, and the programs were ultimately doomed by our unwillingness to stay the course.

PART THREE

The Culture

CHAPTER 10

The Clash of Cultures

The American presence in Vietnam brought about a clash of cultures. The fundamental cultural differences fostered misunderstanding, fed mistrust, led to contemptuous treatment of the Vietnamese, hindered development, limited cooperation with the Vietnamese armed forces, alienated the civilian population, provided ripe targets for Viet Cong propaganda exploitation, and played a significant role in the ultimate outcome of the war.

As an American advisor, some of the toughest challenges I faced were dealing with U.S. military units and trying to repair damage resulting from inappropriate conduct by Americans. I know these comments may not sit well with many of my colleagues whose service in Vietnam was exclusively in U.S. units. I certainly mean no offense, and my remarks are not intended to denigrate in any fashion the service of any U.S. unit or individuals. The truth is, however, that too often the trust and goodwill that might have taken an advisor months to build were instantly destroyed by a thoughtless act or comment by an itinerant U.S. officer or enlisted man.

I had served two previous tours in Vietnam: one with the U.S. Army's 120th Aviation Company, flying support missions out of Tan Son Nhut Airport in Saigon, and the second with the 2nd Battalion, 18th Infantry, 1st Infantry Division. I knew firsthand about U.S. units and the attitudes that were common in these units regarding the Vietnamese—distrust of the Vietnamese population, disdain for the Vietnamese military, and disrespect for Vietnamese women.

The "slope syndrome," for lack of a better term, is illustrative of the problem. GIs generally referred to the Vietnamese people as "slopes," "gooks," "slants," "zips," or "dinks." These disparaging terms tended to dehumanize the Vietnamese, thus somehow justifying inde-fensible attitudes and inexcusable conduct toward them. Regrettably, most American soldiers (of all races) considered Vietnamese men to be lazy, corrupt, and cowardly and most of the females to be whores. This attitude manifested itself in the often contemptuous and conde-scending treatment of the Vietnamese and, unfortunately, was equally prevalent among a great many officers and senior U.S. civilian offi-cials. There was little or no appreciation of the culture, nor any recognition of the cultural differences. "Different" inexplicably trans-lated into "inferior."

No U.S. military experience in the twentieth century had pre-pared American soldiers for the environment of Vietnam. In addition to the confusion wrought by the vast cultural differences, Vietnam also posed an unclear military environment. In contrast to conven-tional warfare, there were no front lines, no safe areas, and no one could be trusted. The enemy didn't always wear a uniform; therefore, you couldn't tell the enemy from the innocent civilian. Stories abounded of women and small children carrying bombs or tossing grenades into buses or cafes.

Perhaps best illustrating the bewilderment and disorientation this environment created for American troops is the fact that GIs referred to the United States as "the world." Typical comments from American soldiers included, "Hey, got a letter from my wife filling me in on what's going on back in the world," or "Only ten more days and I'll be on that 'Freedom Bird' going back to the world." To them, the whole Vietnam experience was something not of this earth—a differ-ent world that they couldn't comprehend.

Compounding the problem was the fact that the U.S. armed serv-ices did a poor job of preparing the individual soldier to operate in an alien culture and in an unconventional warfare setting. American soldiers were not by nature malevolent; there simply was nothing in their backgrounds or training that had prepared them to live and operate in an environment such as Vietnam.

Additionally, the very strong ethnocentrism intrinsic to the Ameri-can makeup was an obstacle to cooperation and the appreciation of another culture. We believe in the superiority of the American way, certain we have the best political system, best economic system, best educational system, best armed services, best religion, best lifestyle, and best values—in short, the best everything. Therefore, to be successful, others simply have to do things our way. Our attitude toward foreign languages is a manifestation of this superiority. Why should we learn a second language? America is the wealthiest, most powerful, and most successful nation on earth; others should learn *our* language.

As damaging to intercultural understanding and cooperation as American ethnocentrism was, it was unfortunately matched by the deep-seated xenophobia of the Vietnamese. This strong fear and mistrust of strangers, not unusual in oriental societies, hindered communication, undermined cooperation, and fostered mistrust. It not only damaged relations between the Vietnamese and their allies, but also hampered internal efforts at nation-building. The Vietnamese trusted few outside their immediate family. Neighbors neither trusted nor could be counted on to assist their neighbors. It was an attitude deleterious to the concept of community and nation-building, and created continuing problems for American advisors and officials at all levels.

However, it was the inability of U.S. personnel to speak Vietnamese that was perhaps the major contributor to misunderstanding—the two cultures simply could not communicate. This not only impaired the ability to work together, but also limited social contact, contributed to suspicion and anxiety, and reinforced in a perverse way the superiority complex. A simple thing like the pronunciation of the country's name became an irritant to the Vietnamese. Vietnam is correctly pronounced "Vee et Nahm," but many Americans, including President Johnson, carelessly pronounced it "Veet Naam," which in their language loosely translates into "sick duck." Language training was not provided to U.S. troops, and even those assigned to MACV for advisory duty frequently received only a cursory introduction to the language. I believe that nothing contributed more to the mistrust and lack of understanding than our inability to speak the language and therefore communicate in any meaningful way.

Another cultural difference that contributed to misunderstanding was the inherent impatience of Americans. We seek instant gratification and want instant results; we buy now and pay later, thrive on fast food and like our news in digestible soundbites. We avoid long books, long lines, and long movies. In short, we are an impatient people. The American (Judeo-Christian) culture perceives time on a linear spectrum, with progress measured by the milestones reached along the way. We went to Vietnam on a year's assignment. Our attitude was "Let's kick ass, take names, get the job done, and go home." U.S. commanders recognized that their accomplishments during their six months (or less) of command could make or break their careers. They had to get in and make their mark. There was no time to waste.

The Vietnamese culture contrasts sharply. It puts great value on patience and, influenced by Buddhism and other Eastern religions, conceptualizes time as recurrent or cyclical. What doesn't get done today can be done tomorrow, next month, next year, or even in the next life. There is neither need nor pressure to get things done quickly. This cultural trait was often interpreted by Americans as laziness, uncooperativeness, ineptness, or even cowardice. Second only to our inability to communicate, this contrasting attitude about time probably created the greatest difficulty in our relationship with the Vietnamese.

The contrast was equally sharp in the values each culture placed on a number of virtues, traits, and attitudes. Respect for the elderly and deference for authority are ingrained in the Vietnamese, while Americans are taught to question authority, and, regrettably, the elderly in our society are all too often neither revered nor honored. Vietnamese are quiet and self-deprecating—Americans are loud and boastful. The Vietnamese are subtle and evasive; preserving harmonious relationships is highly valued, and therefore "little white lies" are preferable to disagreeable truths. Americans are candid. The differences are nearly endless.

Likewise, cultural differences manifest themselves in physical gestures and facial expressions. While Americans make eye contact, the Vietnamese avoid it. To Americans a smile means amusement, pleasure, or agreement—to the Vietnamese it can mean the same, but it also can mean embarrassment, anger, fear, or disagreement. The simple smile was the source of a great deal of misunderstanding and frustration in Vietnam.

Americans, by nature, are touchers. We shake hands, pat one another on the back, and hug. Athletes pat each other on the fanny, we put our arms around our friends, and we tousle the hair of little kids. These gestures are perceived differently by the Vietnamese, and most of them, especially from a foreigner, are unwelcome and offensive. Public displays of affection between men and women are considered bad taste by the Vietnamese. Confucianism and Buddhism dictate discreet, modest, conservative behavior by women in public. Young GIs frequently violated these taboos by yelling sexual taunts, propositioning, and physically groping Vietnamese women. They also could be seen holding hands, hugging, and kissing their "girlfriends." This lack of respect for Vietnamese women alienated the larger population, challenged the manhood of Vietnamese males, and was successfully exploited by the Viet Cong in their recruiting and propaganda efforts.

On the other hand, it was not uncommon to see two Vietnamese men walking along holding hands. This was perfectly normal and acceptable conduct for male friends in Vietnamese society and carried no sexual connotation. It was not, as was widely interpreted by GIs, a sign of homosexuality. This simple act, so misunderstood and so offensive to the American GI, was a major contributor in convincing many American soldiers that the Vietnamese men were "faggots," inferior, unable to fight, and not to be trusted.

The marked differences in the standards of living were also a source of irritation. Wealth is a relative thing. Although the GIs' pay placed them on the lower end of the American economic spectrum, it was many times more than that of the average Vietnamese. GIs had money, radios, cameras, and other visible trappings of wealth. It would not be uncommon for an American soldier to squander the equivalent of a Vietnamese worker's monthly wages on a bar girl.

The huge disparity in living conditions also contributed to the difficulties. U.S. camps, especially those in the rear areas and most visible to the local populace, had (by Vietnamese standards) luxurious facilities: hot and cold running water, air conditioning, solidly constructed buildings, swimming pools, theaters, and post exchanges stocked with all sorts of luxury items. The lifestyle of these troops sharply contrasted with that of the surrounding Vietnamese people. This relative affluence and the resulting inflationary effect upon the economy naturally created resentment among the Vietnamese, compounding intercultural woes.

The American policy of isolating the troops from the civilian population was adopted for both security purposes and in recognition of the problems that hundreds of thousands of U.S. soldiers could create relative to Vietnamese sensitivities. Because American soldiers had money, their presence attracted the seedier profit-seeking elements of Vietnamese society. Not unlike the strips that can be found just outside major military installations in the U.S., areas adjacent to American camps in Vietnam drew prostitutes, drug dealers, illegal money changers, and black marketeers. For many GIs, this element was the only facet of the Vietnamese society with which they had any contact.

The U.S. high command was aware of the problems created by these cultural differences, but was unable to find a solution. The average soldier's enlistment period simply did not provide enough time for adequate training in the Vietnamese language and culture. Each soldier was given a small booklet that addressed some of the cultural differences, provided some "dos and don'ts," and contained a brief section of useful Vietnamese phrases. These booklets were distributed to GIs upon their arrival in Vietnam, but received little attention from soldiers overwhelmed with their new environment, in-processing, drawing equipment, and preparing to join their assigned units. Soldiers were also issued a card containing the Nine Rules, which they were required to carry in their wallets. These rules were intended to prevent American soldiers from offending the Vietnamese. It admonished them to respect Vietnamese women, to honor Vietnamese customs and law, to be courteous in dealing with the population, and to avoid being loud and boisterous. Ironically, the list cataloged the worst and most offensive GI behavior.

In retrospect, I believe that much of the misbehavior was attributable to the youthfulness of our soldiers, whose average age was nineteen. Vietnam was in some ways analogous to graduation week for high school seniors. Soldiers were away from home (many for the first time), were empowered, had money, had all that youthful energy, and were feeling their oats.

As an advisor living among and working with the Vietnamese on a daily basis, one experienced and learned to respect the cultural differences, tried to appreciate the different philosophical perspectives, and worked hard to learn and use the language. The Vietnamese appreciated the effort and were understanding when we frequently screwed up. Probably the most difficult problem for me was my own impatience. It was extremely frustrating to me to endure the excruciating delays in getting things done. I knew what needed to be done and what could be done, but could not always impart my own sense of urgency to my Vietnamese colleagues.

For the most part, our advisory team had excellent rapport with our counterparts and an equally good relationship with the people of Dinh Quan. One of my biggest problems was damage control resulting from the actions of other American units in the area. Examples included U.S. artillery or U.S. helicopter gunships firing indiscriminately and without proper clearance into areas occupied by friendly Vietnamese; U.S. military vehicles racing through villages, running Vietnamese vehicles off the road and terrorizing pedestrians; U.S. soldiers throwing cans and other items at Vietnamese from moving vehicles; soldiers yelling obscenities and soliciting Vietnamese girls; soldiers being loud and rude in public; and GIs openly flouting the authority of the Vietnamese police. As the U.S. presence in Dinh Quan increased with the arrival of elements of the 199th Brigade, so did the problems. Among the most damaging were the more subtle incidents involving U.S. treatment of Vietnamese military—trivializing the Vietnamese role in joint operations, reluctance to let Vietnamese officers participate in planning, failure to provide Vietnamese forces the same level of support provided U.S. units, and token efforts to provide training. Most troubling of all, these things not only generated resentment among the Vietnamese, but more tragically, failed to prepare them to assume the major combat effort after U.S. forces were withdrawn.

One particular incident that still vividly stands out even after all these years involved a brigade of the U.S. 1st Cavalry Division, which was operating in War Zone D in the northern portion of the district. Major Xuan and I had visited the brigade commander at the unit's temporary firebase to coordinate and to try to obtain supplies for our Vietnamese Regional and Popular Force units. We explained that we desperately needed everything: sandbags, radio batteries, concertina wire, Claymore mines, grenades, ammunition of all sorts, steel planking, and building materials—you name it, we needed it. The brigade commander, an American colonel, assured us that he would be glad to help us out and that when they were prepared to move out of the firebase in a few days, they would give us tons of materials that they would not have to move. It would be like Christmas in February! In preparation, we began to round up every available truck to haul out the precious cargo. Finally, after a number of days, word came that the American brigade was moving out. We assembled the convoy and moved cross-country to the firebase. When we arrived, we were halted by the unit's rear security element and held at bay while U.S. bulldozers ran back and forth, crushing, destroying, and bulldozing tons of materials and valuable equipment. When Major Xuan looked at me and asked why, I couldn't respond. I just shook my head. When I asked the same question of the U.S. major in charge of the rear detachment, he responded, "I've been ordered to have the site cleared by sundown and to ensure that these materials won't fall into the hands of the VC, and that is precisely what I intend to do."

I angrily replied, "Do I look like a goddamned VC?"

"No you don't major," he responded, "but how do I know that those 'slopes' on those trucks aren't VC?"

No amount of pleading or cajoling on my part could gain us access; we just sat and watched. I was pissed, embarrassed, and resentful—you can imagine how the Vietnamese must have felt.

By late afternoon the job was complete, and the security detachment and their equipment were lifted out, leaving us with 30 acres of bulldozed and scarred terrain. As soon as the last chopper pulled pitch and lifted out, we moved in and commenced our efforts to dig up and salvage what we could before nightfall. We uncovered cases of radio batteries that had been crushed by the dozers. Vietnamese units couldn't get replacement batteries; they were worth their weight in gold, yet these had been destroyed right before our eyes. We were able to recover several truckloads of salvageable materials before dark. We returned over the next couple of days and dug up enough to fill several more truckloads. Some items could be salvaged, but most could not. The Vietnamese never mentioned the incident again during my tour, but I knew all too well the message that had been clearly sent and clearly received on that memorable afternoon, and it bothered me tremendously.

I recently came across some journal notes I had written on July 29, 1969. The entry reads:

I must confess that I have mixed emotions about this war. I see all about me senseless killing and waste on an unimaginable magnitude. The attitudes of the U.S. units are appalling.

I hope to God I wasn't like that last tour. They talk of helping and assisting and joint efforts—but their deeds betray them. They are suspicious, ruthless, and possess a total lack of understanding of the problem. They are convinced that killing, destruction, and money can solve all. A VN would have to be naïve not to detect this. As for me, I'm caught in the middle—loyalties divided. My job requires my loyalties to be with the Vietnamese and my counterpart, but I'm also an American and have loyalties and responsibilities in that direction. Both sides point to me. I am the representative of each—what a burden.

Upon reflection, nearly thirty years later, I remain convinced that our failure to recognize and respect the cultural differences and to work within those parameters contributed as much to the U.S. failure in Vietnam as did our leadership's flawed strategy. You cannot win hearts and minds by imposing your will on others and openly showing disregard and disrespect for them and their culture. It is an attitude that historically has fostered revolt in colonies around the world. Americans, whose country was born of such revolt, should have known better.

CHAPTER 11

The Magic Red Seal

I want to tell you about one of the worst battles of the war. Not a battle in the conventional combat sense—I promised at the outset none of that—but a never-ending battle that was fought daily by American advisors in every corner of Vietnam: the battle with the blatant, mind-numbing Vietnamese bureaucracy. This is the story of one small victory in that struggle.

The French colonial era in Vietnam spawned a great many legacies. Saigon was appropriately nicknamed "the Paris of the Orient," and evidence of French influence was everywhere: architecture, dress, automobiles, language, commercial products, and restaurants. Even the layout of the city, with its wide treelined boulevards and characteristic traffic circles, mirrored Paris. The Vietnamese upper and middle classes had acquired many French tastes and adopted numerous French customs and habits. Most notably, they spoke French, sent their children to French schools, adopted Western dress and styles, developed a taste for French cuisine and French breads, and cultivated a love of cognac. Many adopted Christianity, embracing the Catholic faith. Other traditional Vietnamese, however, resented the Western influences and what they perceived to be the dilution of Vietnamese culture and values. I leave to others the debate regarding the pros and cons of the French colonial experience and its influence on Vietnam, but from my own limited perspective, the worst of the French legacies was the cumbersome governmental bureaucracy that they established and passed on to the Vietnamese.

Many Vietnamese government leaders of the sixties had served as middle-level bureaucrats in the French administration during the colonial era. The rigid French colonial civil service system—infamous for its corruption, inflexibility, bureaucratic layers, and frustratingly slow pace—was the administrative system in which the Vietnamese were trained. Unfortunately, they learned it too well and not only preserved the inherited deficiencies of the French system, but also managed to make it worse. The combination of the Vietnamese culture, so troublesome for Westerners, overlaid upon an archaic and inflexible Western bureaucratic administrative system, was deadly. The process was more important than the product; every action was painfully slow, requiring everything in triplicate illegible typewritten carbon copies; and every transaction required multiple reviews and approvals as it crept laboriously through the system. The entire process was designed to ensure that no one could be held responsible for any action with even the remotest chance of controversy. The combined worst traits of the Internal Revenue Service, the U.S. Postal Service, and your local Motor Vehicle Administration fail to come close to equaling the bureaucratic ineptness of the Vietnamese system.

Dinh Quan was no exception. The filing system at the district headquarters consisted of scores of oversized folders stacked on shelves lining the walls, each file containing hundreds of pages, many yellowed with age. The files deemed most important were kept in large wardrobe-like cabinets. Attempting to locate or retrieve something from any of the files was in itself an adventure. Nothing could be processed immediately, "expedite" was not in the bureaucratic vocabulary, and even routine actions generally required weeks to wind their way through the system. The fact that a war was going on did little to impart a sense of urgency. In fact, the war served merely as a convenient excuse for the inability of the system to function adequately.

American control of most of the material resources necessitated that many of the district's administrative actions be approved and co-signed by the American senior advisor. The processing of these documents was further slowed by the need to translate them into English so that the advisor could make a reasoned judgment on the merits of the request. Once signed, they entered the multi-layered system, and no step in the process could be bypassed. In most cases, the documents ultimately required action outside the district, so they faced a similar fate at the hands of the bureaucrats at province level and higher.

At various critical stages of the process, I noted that the Vietnamese ceremoniously stamped the document with an engraved metal stamp, leaving a red ink seal on the document indicating official approval. Once stamped, the document was dispatched to the next level in the process. Without the stamp, documents languished in never-never land and frequently disappeared into a huge administrative black hole, never to be seen again.

About two months into my tour, it occurred to me that what I needed was my own "official" seal. If I couldn't beat them, I would join them! Convinced this might somehow cause requests and other documents to move faster through the bureaucratic maze, I began to make quiet inquiries as to how I might get such a seal. I was pointedly and repeatedly advised that it was simply impossible, that such seals were the exclusive property and prerogative of the government, and that possession of an unauthorized stamp was not only illegal, but a serious offense to be dealt with harshly. The manufacture of these stamps was tightly regulated, and without approval—in triplicate and complete with multiple seals—from high in the Vietnamese government, authority to possess or have one of these stamps made was not possible.

Undaunted, I determined to press on. Since I had already experienced two months of frustration in dealing with the bureaucracy, I was absolutely certain there was no way I could go through proper channels to request and receive permission for such a device within the limits of my tour. There was only one recourse—the very efficient black market. I drew up a sketch of what I thought the seal should look like and tasked S/Sgt. Michels, our team medical NCO, with the job of getting the stamp produced. He knew just where to go and whom to see. For 2,500 piasters (roughly $21 US), he was able to produce not only a large metal stamp engraved expertly with our seal, but also a smaller one with my name and title—and a red ink pad. The entire process, which I had been repeatedly told was "simply impossible," took less than two weeks.

The stamp arrived late on a Saturday afternoon. I secreted it away in my desk drawer, anticipating with relish the reaction that I was sure would come. The following Monday morning, the first piece of mundane paperwork came to me for signature. As I recall, it was a request for a small number of sheets of roofing tin for distribution to some recently resettled families. The Vietnamese official who brought it to me waited patiently for my signature. He watched with some amazement as I pulled out my stamp, tapped it gently a couple of times on the red ink pad, and with a resounding *thunk* smacked it down on the corner of the document. As I removed the stamp from the paper, in its place was a bright red seal—the "official" mark of the Dinh Quan District senior advisor. Beneath it another *thunk* and another red splash with my name and title. I overwrote it with my signature, turned and, smiling broadly, handed it to the official. He literally shouted his approval and dashed out the door with the paper in his hand. Through the window in the radio room I watched him sprint across the compound to the district headquarters. I later learned that the paper with my new seal created a great deal of excitement and animated discussion in the headquarters. The Vietnamese weren't sure if this was legal or not, but they liked the idea—and none of the administrative bureaucrats were going to challenge a red seal!

From that moment on, nearly every order, request, or correspondence that passed through the district offices was brought to me for my stamp—even things that had nothing to do with U.S. resources and would not normally require an American signature. The stamp seemed to have a totally unanticipated magical effect, not only on my own little district band of bureaucrats, but also on those at province headquarters as well. It identified the documents as highest priority, causing them to emerge from the piles and receive unprecedented attention. Additionally, to our utter amazement, we discovered it expedited matters in dealing with *both* the Vietnamese civilian and military channels. Actions that used to take months now were completed in weeks, and those that used to take weeks were now completed in days. It was indeed a miracle. I often think the black market stamp may well have been my greatest contribution to the war effort in Dinh Quan District.

I have no way of knowing what became of the stamp—whether it is now lying in a box somewhere with someone's Vietnam mementos or was left behind and lost as the final advisory team packed up and left Dinh Quan in the early 1970s. I regret that I did not keep the stamp when I left the district in June 1970, but I chose to pass this magical instrument on to my replacement. I briefed him on the history of the stamp and carefully schooled him in the application of its magical powers. I am sure it served him well, as it did me.

In the years since, I have often wondered what might have been the outcome of the war if General Westmoreland had possessed his own magic red seal.

CHAPTER 12

"Dawk" and Other Delights

"An adventure" perhaps best describes the team's mealtimes in Dinh Quan. Whenever possible we took our meals at the team house, but the nature of our duties required us to frequently dine with our counterparts or other Vietnamese officials, often at a local eating establishment.

We were a long way from the abundantly stocked Saigon commissary that provided the tons of meat and other foodstuffs being consumed by those we lovingly referred to as the "Saigon Warriors." Our own daily fare often left a great deal to be desired. Fresh vegetables, fruit, and French bread were plentiful at the local market, but the problem was finding a safe and reliable source of fresh meat. Due to the Vietnamese's lack of refrigeration, purchasing meat at the local market was a risky undertaking at best. More than once, individual team members were halted by tainted meat as they were struck down by the intestinal affliction the GIs called "Ho Chi Minh's Revenge."

Periodically, I allowed team members to make the hazardous 112-kilometer drive down Route 20 and across Route 1 into Saigon for a brief R&R. An absolute condition of their overnight leave (and, in fact, the official justification) was that they take our shopping lists and make the run to the Saigon Commissary and the Post Exchange (PX). The jeep and its quarter-ton trailer would be piled full of goodies for their return to Dinh Quan. Chief among the booty would be a supply of fresh meat, packed with dry ice for the long, hot return trip. American soldiers are basically "meat and potatoes" men, and the return of the R&R jeep was always a treat because it meant charcoal-grilled steak and baked potatoes for supper.

Our team had a large freezer, so we were able to store the meats brought back from the city. A team of seven, however, which always seemed to have a variety of U.S. visitors living with it, can consume a lot of groceries in a short period of time. No matter how much was brought back, it never seemed to last long.

Although the lack of fresh meat was a major problem for us, we had a bigger problem in that we had no one who could cook. Never in my fourteen months did we have a team member with any culinary skills beyond boiling water or charcoaling a piece of meat. The evening meal was usually prepared by whichever team members happened to be available, and most of our meals came right out of the can—such gourmet delights as Dinty Moore stew, Chef Boyardee spaghetti, canned ham, chili, tuna, and what seemed to be a never-ending supply of Spam remain the most memorable! The most interesting thing about Spam was that, despite the claims of the Spam industry, no matter what you did to it or how hard you tried to disguise its taste, it was always the same. It was impervious to spices, condiments, or other food influences. Broiled, boiled, baked, fried, grilled, or sautéed—it still tasted like Spam!

The one fresh item that all of us were able to master was the egg. When all else failed, there was always the fried egg sandwich. Sandwiches of fried eggs and Spam smeared with a heavy layer of mayonnaise were the staple of the team's diet. You could almost hear the arteries clogging!

Our lack of cooking prowess made for some interesting creations. I recall Capt. Chuck Backlin once decided to make an angel food cake from a boxed mix someone had brought back from a Saigon shopping run. He carefully measured, weighed, stirred, and mixed. Watching him from across the room, I was reminded of a scientist engaged in serious lab work and on the verge of a breakthrough discovery. When he reached the point in the process requiring him to put his secret recipe in the oven, he discovered we did not have an angel food cake pan for baking. Rummaging through the cabinets beneath the counter in our kitchen, Backlin came up with a large 5-gallon capacity stew pot. In went the cake mix and into the oven (with some difficulty) went the pot. When the appointed time came, the team members, drawn by the enticing smell, gathered around. Out came the pot and there it was—a huge angel food cake, looking very much like a large watermelon! Despite the hoots and good-natured kidding, not a crumb of that cake survived.

My personal best culinary achievement was an apple pie. Although there wasn't a single fresh ingredient, from the reaction of my admiring comrades you would have thought it was fresh off a farmhouse window sill. Following its triumphant reception, there were frequent calls for a repeat performance in the months ahead. Peach, cherry, apple—my creations were limited only by the imagination of the canned pie filling manufacturers.

Lunch for the team was generally prepared by *Ba*. As the wife of the local village chief, she was herself a dignitary among the local Vietnamese. Despite working for the team as cook and housekeeper for several years, her English was limited to fewer than fifty words. We communicated through a combination pidgin English/Vietnamese and a great deal of animated pointing; when all else failed we turned to our Vietnamese interpreter, Sergeant Cuong. *Ba*'s lunches were interesting. Some would be Vietnamese fare, while others would be her best interpretation of American recipes, and frequently her meals were a combination of both. There would always be rice and most often French bread. Even *Ba*'s best efforts couldn't overcome the taste of Spam—it is resistant to tasteful preparation in both the American and Vietnamese cultures! Sometimes we would experience some mystery meat that neither *Ba* nor our Vietnamese interpreters would identify. We learned quickly that it was better not to inquire too insistently. We came to appreciate that old maxim, "Don't ask the question if you can't stand the answer!"

We knew from experience that the loggers who worked the deep forested areas that covered most of Dinh Quan District were always discovering and bringing in the carcass of some animal that had been killed by the routine nighttime H&I fire that both the Vietnamese and U.S. artillery frequented upon suspected VC camps, trails, and gathering points. These carcasses were sort of a wartime version of rural American roadkill. During my tour, such prizes included an elephant, a tiger, monkeys, water buffalo, wild pigs, something akin to a huge porcupine, incredibly large snakes, a variety of birds, and an assortment of other small game. These generally were available in the village marketplace and occasionally ended up in some disguised form on our table.

Another source of protein came from the various animals, birds, and fish that could be acquired from the Montagnards. Each day they would show up in the village with the game they had shot with their crossbows, snared in their traps, or caught in the local streams.

Fresh bread was a staple of each meal, and the Vietnamese made great French bread. It was available locally and it was cheap. The only problem was that the bread was always full of baked bugs that had infested the flour. No effort was made by the Vietnamese to filter out the bugs; they simply went on mixing the dough, and whatever bugs there might be went into the ovens with the dough loaves. American advisors quickly learned to simply pick the bugs out and get on with the business of devouring this otherwise incredibly good bread. It was always interesting, however, to watch unsuspecting visitors from U.S. units or those new to Vietnam the first time they broke open a piece of the French bread and came eye to eye with some baked bug carcass.

Care packages from home were always a special treat. In addition to cookies, cakes, candies, and the normal goodies that one associates with these packages, there were frequently specialty food items that simply were not available to us in the boonies—everything from smoked oysters to Jell-O. I recall receiving from my wife and daughter a complete package of all the necessary ingredients, including canned icing and candles, to make a birthday cake for my thirty-first birthday. Amazingly, it turned out well.

On special occasions we would invite the Vietnamese officers over for meals. They seemed to enjoy our cooking, or at least were too polite to give even the slightest indication that they didn't care for it. It was always amazing to watch them struggling with our flatware. Our dexterity with chopsticks certainly wasn't anything to boast about, but the fact that we had to master chopsticks or starve did require that we develop a modicum of skill. On the other hand, except for Major Xuan, the Vietnamese had neither the incentive nor the opportunity to practice, so they never improved. We had the only flatware in town! We would generally let them struggle for a while, then offer them chopsticks, which they always gratefully accepted. I recall we once got a small supply of frozen U.S. ground beef and decided to have a great spaghetti feast and invite our Vietnamese counterparts. The sauce, which was the secret recipe of Staff Sergeant Michels, simmered for hours, filling the team house with wonderful aromas and raising expectations of the meal to come. After great debate over just how to know when the noodles were done (someone recalled a test that required throwing a cooked noodle against the ceiling—allegedly if it stuck, the noodles were ready), the meal was served. It was terrific, and everyone dove right in. After a few minutes it was apparent that the Vietnamese were having a problem trying to eat spaghetti with a fork. Ever the thoughtful host, I offered chopsticks. It was even worse. In an Asian culture, a food such as rice or noodles would have been served in a bowl, which could have been held up to the lips so the food could be scooped into the mouth with the chopsticks. We served the spaghetti on plates, and the Vietnamese were trying to pick up the noodles and get them to their mouths. Some were holding their chopsticks at arm's length above their heads to get the end of the long spaghetti strands in their mouths and then nibbling their way toward the chopsticks. It took some stern stares from me to keep team members from chuckling aloud at the scene. Fortunately, our guests had a good sense of humor and were soon laughing at themselves. Although the party was a great hit, we later decided that spaghetti would not be on the menu or served to our Vietnamese comrades on future festive occasions.

Any difficulties the Vietnamese may have had with American cuisine paled in comparison to some of the experiences we had with Vietnamese food, which is usually chopped up into bite-size morsels that can be handled with chopsticks and is frequently covered with a sauce, making it difficult to identify what you are eating. Some foods, such as pork, could be recognized by their distinct taste and texture, but I frequently found I didn't have the faintest idea what I was eating.

I had been in Dinh Quan for about two weeks when Captain Xuan, the district chief, invited me to accompany him the next day on a visit to the northernmost villages and hamlets of the district. The trip was about twenty-five miles each way over a rather treacherous stretch of Highway 20. We drove by jeep, stopping from time to time to inspect a local militia unit or visit with a local hamlet chief. By noon we had arrived at our northernmost hamlet, located right on the II Corps border. Captain Xuan advised me that there was a great restaurant there, and he would treat me to lunch. The "great restaurant" was little more than a 12-foot by 12-foot hut with a dirt floor and no more than three or four small, rough wooden tables. I noticed that all the tables were full and that the floor was littered with bones and other food scraps, which the district chief pointed out as a sign of a good restaurant. Our unexpected arrival created quite a stir: great deference was shown, the whole family was paraded out to greet us, and the chatter from the other tables died away quickly. Another table and two chairs materialized from somewhere, and as we sat down, like magic the chatter erupted once more. Captain Xuan ordered for us in Vietnamese, and the owner went scurrying away. We each had a beer, and soon the meal arrived in a large bowl accompanied by a smaller bowl of rice. It had been a long morning, and we both were hungry, so we wasted no time in attacking the bowl. It was tasty, but the small chunks of meat were tough and bony, and I had no idea what it was. Near the end of the meal I asked Captain Xuan what the meat was. He responded in English with what sounded like "dawk."

I responded uncertainly, "Duck?"

He shook his head and said, "Dawk."

Again I said, "Duck?"

Again he said, "Dawk."

After several more such exchanges, I said, "Duck—quack, quack?"

He smiled a broad, impish smile and said, "No, no, Dawk—woof, woof!" I laughed along with him, but suddenly I didn't feel so good! After that, rarely did I inquire as to what I was eating. Captain Xuan loved to tell that story; in fact, the experience helped break the ice between us and was the beginning of a close personal relationship.

Capt. Bob Hughes was similarly set up at a dinner in his honor just prior to the completion of his tour. The entrée was sliced slivers of what he described as a rather tasty meat. Although everyone was eating, the Vietnamese officers watched him closely and joked among themselves throughout the meal. When it became obvious that the joke was on him and it had something to do with what he was eating, he mustered up enough courage to ask what he had just eaten. His hosts took great delight in telling him he had just devoured a roasted water buffalo penis!

On another occasion, during Tet 1970, a great banquet was hosted by the district chief at the district headquarters. Only the officers on my team were invited, along with the senior Vietnamese officers and the local village chief and elders. As the guest of honor, I was the first to taste the main dish, and a large covered platter was brought to me.

I lifted the lid and nearly jumped off my chair. Coiled in the dish was a whole, steamed 4-foot-long black eel. I felt like its eyes were staring at me! Once I got over the shock, I didn't quite know what to do with it. Major Xuan, sensing my problem, leaned over with his chopsticks and tore a huge chunk of meat from the eel. He placed it on a thin sheet of rice paper, added lettuce and nuoc mam (fermented fish sauce), rolled it into a small roll, and held it out for me to taste. It was terrific! I nodded to those at the table watching me and gave the universal signal—thumbs up! With that, the party began.

Later during the same dinner came the *pièce de résistance*. Major Xuan went to great lengths explaining to me what a delicacy the next course would be. This time when the cover was removed from the platter there were several little sparrows, whole but featherless, with feet and beaks intact, fried to a crisp charcoal color. It was a pitiful sight, and all of a sudden I knew I wasn't going to be able to handle this. Here I was, "Major Macho," a seasoned infantry officer with nearly thirty months' combat experience, backing down from a face-to-face confrontation with a shriveled-up sparrow! I had always prided myself on my ability to handle any of the food or drinks that confronted me. Once, while serving with the 1st Division on a previous Vietnam tour, I had participated in a Montagnard ceremony in which a goat was brutally slaughtered and its blood collected in a huge community bowl. The bowl was passed around the seated circle of Americans and Montagnards, each in turn sipping the goat blood through encrusted wooden straws. I had been able to handle that. I had eaten snails, snake, monkeys, dog, water buffalo, elephant, and all sorts of other unknown varmints, but I could not force myself to eat one of those little birds. I turned to Major Xuan and in my most polite manner said, "This is excellent, but I know what a treat this is, so I 'souvenir you' my sparrow." With that, I lifted the bird with my chopsticks and placed it in the chief's bowl. He thanked me, beamed, and in a single motion picked up the bird and bit its head off. Flakes of the charcoaled skin covered his teeth as I heard little bones snap and crack. I went for my cognac and did my best not to notice as the birds were consumed all around me. Nearly thirty years later the vision of that blackened bird lying on its back with its little fried feet sticking into the air still sends shivers up my spine!

CHAPTER 13

Spirited Adventures

"**D**estroyed" does not nearly do justice to Lieutenant Hughes's condition. It was his first week on the team, and he had fallen prey to the junior officers of the Vietnamese 18th Division. The Division's 43rd Regiment was operating in our district, and the regimental headquarters was encamped on the edge of the village about two hundred meters from our team house. The Vietnamese regimental commander, Lieutenant Colonel Nhut, was a friend and military academy classmate of Captain Xuan.

The occasion of Hughes's downfall was a party in honor of the new American senior advisor to the regiment. Sensing they weren't going to be successful in getting to the new, rather stiff and formal American lieutenant colonel, the junior officers turned their attention to the open, innocent, and gregarious Hughes. The technique was one often used against unwary Americans—a nearly unending series of individual toasts. One at a time, the Vietnamese would approach the victim and honor him with a toast. Of course, each toast required glasses to be emptied and held bottoms up to demonstrate to all the sincerity of the toast. It was not uncommon for the victim to be honored ten to fifteen times in an evening. The results were predictable—it didn't take many of these "honors" before the poor American would either be under the table or draped across it.

I watched with amusement as they methodically worked Lieutenant Hughes. At various points during the evening, I swear I heard them leading him in toasts to Elvis, baseball, and John Wayne! When I left the party, Hughes was standing unsteadily on a bench, loudly telling some tall tale with his "admirers" all gathered round. When the Vietnamese officers finally brought him home around midnight, he didn't know which continent he was on, much less that he was in the middle of a war zone. Sometime during that evening while staggering around barefooted, he severely cut his foot. Oblivious to the pain, he finally collapsed and was tucked away for the night. It was several days before he could even smile, much less return to normal. It took his foot a little longer to mend.

It would be an understatement to say that the Vietnamese loved to drink. As I think back, I am hard-pressed to recall any of my Vietnamese colleagues who didn't enjoy drinking. While cognac was the clear favorite, they enjoyed alcohol in any form: Scotch, bourbon, gin, beer—you name it, they would drink it! They also enjoyed drinking games and reveled in their ability to sandbag unsuspecting Americans. In addition to the "toasts" that did in Lieutenant Hughes, a particularly popular, but deadly, after-dinner game in Dinh Quan was one I named Spin the Beak. The rules were simple, in fact nearly the same as those of the American adolescent favorite, Spin the Bottle, except in Dinh Quan nobody got kissed! The Vietnamese version was played by placing a duck's beak on a plate, covering it with an upside-down bowl, and shaking it vigorously. The plate was then placed on the table and the bowl removed. The person at the table toward whom the beak was pointed won (or lost, depending on your point of view), but instead of getting a kiss, he had to chug-a-lug his drink. I harbored a deep suspicion, born of several severe hangovers, that the Vietnamese had mastered the art of controlling the beak, because invariably when I or one of my team members got drawn into one of these games, we seemed to "win" at a far greater frequency than our Vietnamese comrades!

The Vietnamese love of cognac was one of the vestiges of the country's many years as a French colony. Cognac was served on every occasion, generally with soda and lime. It was a middle- and upper-class Vietnamese addiction, especially for the officer class. It was so popular that quality cognac was better than currency for opening doors, greasing skids, and generally getting things done. There seemed to be no limit to the magic a bottle of Courvoisier could produce! This passion for cognac made gift shopping for Vietnamese friends easy. The PX in Saigon was stocked to meet the demand and always had a nice supply on hand at bargain basement prices.

The other alcoholic staples of life in Dinh Quan were the local beers: Bière Larue and Ba Muoi Ba, or "33." These Vietnamese brews were available in the village and considered appropriate for drinking at any time of the day or night. Team members religiously trekked down to a village restaurant on Sunday morning to enjoy a ritual breakfast of egg drop soup and a bottle of "33." What a way to start your day!

As I recall, Bière Larue (also called Tiger Bière because of the prominent tiger on the label) was the cheaper of the two, came in a larger bottle, and was considered the Vietnamese equivalent to a "red-neck" favorite. Ba Muoi Ba cost more, and to my unsophisticated taste buds, seemed better. Occasionally, you might come across a San Miguel from the Philippines, but these were in great demand and very hard to find.

On one occasion one of the team's NCOs returned from Saigon with several cases of Fosters Ale, which he had managed to acquire from some NCOs from the Australian Task Force whom he had run across. These beers took on a significance far greater than they deserved. You would have thought they contained elixir from the fountain of youth. Certainly the fact that they were pint size (25 ounces), instead of the normal 12-ounce U.S. beers, added to their attractiveness. They were carefully rationed and strictly accounted for. Each was consumed noisily with exclamations over its aroma, taste, color, and curative powers—some claimed it grew hair and cured warts! Despite the reverence bestowed upon them and their larger size, they didn't last long, and it was back to Bud and "33."

American beers were plentiful through the exchange system and were the general favorites of the team members, primarily because they only cost 10 cents a can. Our supply point for this staple was the small exchange in Xuan Loc. The lifestyle of the advisory team in Xuan Loc—air-conditioned trailer homes, a mess hall with fresh meat and real cooks, and physical security—was a far cry from life in the village of Dinh Quan. It was an interesting phenomenon that members of my team used any, often lame, pretext to get to Xuan Loc overnight to enjoy the luxuries, while at the same time members of the province advisory team loved to come up and spend the night with us to rough it and savor "real" advisory life. My favorite visitors were Maj. Bob Boyd, the province S-3 advisor, and George Laudato, a civilian USAID official. Bob and I had served together as captains in the 1st Division, both at Fort Riley, Kansas, and in Vietnam. Bob's interest wasn't in roughing it; he just wanted to get away from the province headquarters. George was a genuine character whose visits always brightened up the team.

For a brief period after my arrival, we had a liberal team policy regarding drinking beer. Team members could have beer at lunch and occasionally during the duty day. I figured that with the extreme heat and humidity, it couldn't hurt. I quickly learned the fallacy of that theory, as I discovered a few members of the team never knew when to quit. Thereafter, beer in moderation was only permitted after duty hours. There were, of course, exceptions to this policy, when special occasions called for team celebrations. Christmas, the 4th of July, Thanksgiving, Easter, and team members' birthdays were major events calling for special meals and parties. We were also often included in major Vietnamese holidays and celebrations. The Vietnamese took the best of all cultures and religions, celebrating Christian holidays, Buddhist holidays, and any others they could identify!

For the advisory team, however, the wildest occasions were the "last night" parties for any team member completing his tour and returning "to the world" or to the "land of the big PX," as the United States was referred to in GI slang. Prior to my arrival in Dinh Quan, some demented mind had established the tradition of getting the departing team member rip-roaring drunk, rolling him in the mud, and then hoisting him upside down to indelibly stamp his muddy footprint on the ceiling of the team house. This generally was preceded by shaving cream battles and food fights, leaving the team house looking like a scene from *Animal House*. (The Vietnamese had the good sense to find some pretext for leaving these parties early!) You've not lived until you've had a bunch of drunks dunk you in a 55-gallon water barrel, roll you in the mud, then try to hoist your slippery body upside down to put your footprint on the ceiling—all the while slipping and sliding about on a slimy concrete floor! That experience was more hazardous than going on an overnight ambush with one of the local Popular Force units, yet it was the one we all looked forward to with eager anticipation, because it meant you were on your way home!

PART FOUR

Team Life

CHAPTER 14

The Dinh Quan Surf and Raquette Club

The pride and joy, as well as the social heart, of the U.S. advisory team in Dinh Quan was, without question, the Surf and Raquette Club. Try as I may, I am unable to recall to whom we owed the credit for the establishment of this venerable institution. It may simply have evolved from the collective creativity of the team. However it began, early in my tour the idea of creating a "beach" in our backyard took root. Since the back of our team house was a notorious mudhole in the monsoon season, we had to carefully survey the landscape and select the appropriate site. In the center of our backyard was a slightly elevated area that sat astride a huge rock slab. This area drained well, was the right size (about fifteen feet by fifteen feet), and thus was selected as the beach location.

Sandbags were filled and laid out carefully to delineate the perimeter. We had previously noticed that the LaNga River, about ten kilometers to our southwest, where we frequently took our vehicles to wash them at a ford, had some beautiful white sand. We hauled several quarter-ton trailer loads of sand and spread it evenly about eight to ten inches deep within the sandbag perimeter of the beach. A hand-painted red-and-white sign was erected declaring this to be the Dinh Quan Surf and Raquette Club, naturally "For Members Only."

The beach was an instant hit. Every day from noon until about 2:00 P.M. team members would don bathing trunks, grab their towels, and head for the beach, about fifty feet away. We would stretch out on the white sand and luxuriate in the blazing Southeast Asian sunshine. It was glorious.

It is important to note, lest you believe we were the worst sort of slackers, that everything in Dinh Quan came to a screeching halt at noon. The Vietnamese, like many people living in very hot areas of the world, observed the sensible custom of taking lunch and then resting through the hottest part of the day. From 1200 to 1400 hours everything shut down, including the war. The village shops and marketplace were closed, and all commerce halted. The district headquarters likewise shut down; there was no one to advise, train, or assist. And in truth it was hot as hell! Even on combat operations, the Vietnamese would halt during this period of the day, light small fires for tea and rice, then relax in the shade till the heat of midday had passed. The war simply had to wait. For our team, it was simply a pause in the middle of the day that enabled us to catch up on paperwork, write home, read, or just lounge around. It somehow reminded me of my daughter's kindergarten naps, and I often thought how this very civilized custom would do a great deal to lower the stress in our hectic society.

The Vietnamese soldiers in our compound retired to their hammocks and spent a blissful two hours snoozing away in the shade. Not so for the Americans. We lounged on the beach, basking in the sun, listening to the radio (and the adventures of Chicken Man), and chatting away. The Vietnamese marveled at our craziness. While they truly believed that only mad dogs and Englishmen go out in the noonday sun, they quickly learned that Americans did also!

Life on the beach was good. Tales were told, and nearly anything was fair game for discussion. Many of the world's problems were resolved right there. Regrettably, no one was there to record these marvelous solutions. The beach was also a place where you got to know your teammates better. Folks opened up a bit while discussing their families, their past, and their hopes for the future. And of course, the beach was a good place to work on the perfect tan, a quest the Vietnamese never understood.

Many of us spent our time at the beach reading. Periodically, the team would receive a carton of thirty to forty paperback books of every variety imaginable: novels, how-to books, histories, biographies, you name it. These were read and passed around among team members until they literally came apart in the heat and humidity. Detective novels were always the most popular. Occasionally, some hardcore porn would find its way to our team. These generally were studied in greater detail, often requiring a second reading or even prompting the formation of an informal literary discussion group!

The reputation of the Dinh Quan Surf and Raquette Club and our pristine beach grew far and wide. Helicopters would fly in from all over the region just so folks could see, and often enjoy, the beach. I can't tell you how many photos were taken of that simple plot of ground! What had started out as a lark, born out of boredom, became an object of admiration and envy. In retrospect, I think the beach became the symbol for a lot more. It certainly represented American ingenuity and humor, and perhaps a little bit of home. I believe it also became a refuge in the midst of a war that was becoming more and more difficult to understand. Our team somehow sensed this, and the beach became an important aspect of our team life. And the fact is, there just wasn't a whole lot else to do.

The establishment of the beach also solved another problem that had begun to bother me. Prior to the construction of the beach, team members would head off at siesta time for their individual bunks in the team house; they would fall asleep, and because we frequently worked independently, their absence might go undetected for most of the afternoon. We were responsible for a large district, approximately 1,200 square miles. At best it was difficult getting to all the places we needed to go and being able to devote the necessary time and attention to the Vietnamese units and staff. The last thing we needed was to have team members sleeping away the productive afternoon hours. Shortly after arriving, I banned the practice of noontime beers. My second edict was no rack time during siesta. You could lounge on the beach, and even cat nap there. With apologies to Carl Perkins for tampering with his lyrics, "You could do anything you wanted to do, but uh, uh, baby, *no noontime snooze!*" As you might expect, those two rule changes were not initially popular with the team members; however, they did improve team effectiveness and ultimately the cohesiveness of the group.

ASIDE FROM DARTS, a little badminton, and horseshoes, there was little outdoor sports activity in which members of the Surf and Raquette Club could engage. On occasion, the Vietnamese 621st Regional Force company, located just across the highway from our compound, would challenge us to a friendly volleyball match. The first time this happened was during a Vietnamese holiday, and various units within the district were invited to participate in a volleyball tournament. I remember thinking this would be a duck shoot; three members of our team—Hughes, Kraft, and Kirkbride—were well over six feet tall, and the rest of us viewed ourselves as damn near Olympic-caliber athletes. We strung a net out front and for several days put ourselves through serious preparations for the upcoming event. With each practice, we grew more confident; there was even some talk about asking the *Stars and Stripes* newspaper to cover the event.

Finally the big day arrived, and at the appointed hour we marched confidently across the highway, through the gate, and into the RF compound—sort of our own little Olympic march. All that was missing was the flame! Just inside the gate was a carefully laid out volleyball court. I noticed the boundaries of the court were outlined with some gray powdery substance. I wasn't sure what it was, but it looked suspiciously like cement. The fact that the district warehouse, which coincidentally was inside this compound, had recently received several hundred bags of cement didn't escape me. Chairs had been set up along one side for the local VIPs, while on the other side a lone chair, from which the referee would rule, sat perched atop a raised platform. We were greeted warmly and introduced to our competition for the first round of the single elimination tournament. We had difficulty containing our gloating smirks as we noted that the tallest member of the RF company team was maybe 5 feet 5 inches! The net, which was set at regulation height (7 feet, 11 inches), towered over all of them.

Eight teams had entered, so we would have to win three matches to collect our trophy. Each match consisted of three games, and since it was a hot day, as we huddled just prior to the coin toss, we spent most of our time discussing how best to pace ourselves for the grueling nine-game afternoon ahead of us.

As team captain, I represented us and won the coin toss, so we served first. Our towering trio took their places on the front line, shook hands with their diminutive opponents directly opposite, and the game was underway. I drilled the first serve, and after a brief volley the first point was ours. As we celebrated, I remember Lieutenant Wingo smugly remarking, "Piece of cake!" As the game wore on, to our surprise it became a nip-and-tuck struggle—those guys were better than we had thought. After reaching a 14–14 deadlock, we eked out two consecutive points to emerge victorious 16–14. The second game was equally bitterly contested; however, the Vietnamese won with a late rally, 15–13. During the two-minute interval prior to the third and deciding game, we decided to quit messing around and to finish these guys off in quick fashion. Less than ten minutes later it was all over—a decisive 15–2 whipping! Not exactly what we had expected—they destroyed us! Their players, who in the first two games could hardly reach the top of the net, were now suddenly clearing it up to their elbows. Our "towering trio" thrashed about, arms flailing away, mostly in self-defense, as the Vietnamese rocketed shots at us (and off of us) from all angles. We were suitably humbled by the experience, but were reminded once again of the importance the Vietnamese placed on not losing face. Ever the good hosts, even in a volleyball competition, the Vietnamese did not want to embarrass their guests, so they had carried us for the first two games, even allowing us to win the first game.

We spent the remainder of the afternoon watching some real volleyball. The other seven teams were pretty evenly matched, but the 621st RF Company team, the one that had dismantled us, ultimately won the tournament. They had one player (about 5 feet 2 inches) whom we aptly nicknamed "the frog" because of his incredible leaping ability. At times, it seemed the entire upper half of his body was above the net.

In the months to come, we would play a number of matches against a variety of Vietnamese teams—and the outcomes were generally the same. Although we were allowed to come close from time to time, we never won a single match.

THE ONLY OTHER notable athletic event on my watch occurred during the celebration of Tet in 1970. There was a variety of entertainment: parties, dinners, music, and contests of all sorts. Naturally, we were eliminated early in the volleyball tournament, but the one contest that we hoped would redeem our reputation was the footrace from the base of Artillery Hill to the marketplace in the village—a distance of perhaps three kilometers (1.8 miles). Sergeant Miller, the NCO in charge of the engineer rock crusher detail temporarily occupying our bunkhouse, advised us that this was his event. He had some high school track experience some ten years earlier, which he was sure had prepared him for this event. We had no other volunteers, so

Miller was our champion. The course over which the race would be run was a straight shot up Highway 20, asphalt surface all the way. The first half-mile was slightly downhill, but from there to the finish it was as flat as a pancake. As the thirty or so contestants lined up, Miller was the picture of confidence in his cut-off fatigue trousers and his nearly new pair of Keds. Most of the Vietnamese ran in their boxer shorts, either barefooted or wearing sandals or combat boots. Major Xuan and I rode in the "official" jeep that would lead the runners at the start of the race then dash us to the finish line, where we and glory would await the winner.

At the crack of the starter's pistol, a .45-caliber automatic, the runners bolted from the starting line. True to his word, Miller pushed his way to the front and streaked down the hill. His strategy was simple: he would break fast, get the lead, and never look back. By the time he reached the bottom of the grade, he was nearly fifty yards ahead of the nearest runner. The crowd lining both sides of the road was cheering him on. It appeared the Dinh Quan record might be in danger. Once on the flat, Miller appeared to slow somewhat, and other runners soon were closing the gap. From my vantage point in the jeep about twenty yards ahead of him, I noted Miller's face had begun to contort and his stride had become a little erratic. At about the mile mark, he had been passed by about ten runners. As the pack overtook him, it became more and more difficult to see him. The jeep accelerated to the finish line so that Major Xuan and I could be there to greet the runners as they arrived. The last hundred yards was a sprint, with three runners vying for the 500-piaster cash prize, the equivalent of about $4 U.S. Within seconds, all the other runners had crossed the finish line, but no Sergeant Miller. Then I noticed the jeep that had been following the runners. It was driven by S/Sgt. Michels, our team medic. Draped unceremoniously across the back seat was a pale green Sergeant Miller. With about a quarter-mile to go, he had collapsed into a drainage ditch, thrown up, and nearly passed out. Michels had policed him up and dumped him into the back of the open vehicle. As the jeep slowly made its way through the crowd at the finish line, Michels knowingly nodded to me, grinned and, without stopping, quietly took Miller home and put him to bed.

The team was uncharacteristically kind to Miller in the days that followed. There was a little ribbing, but not the rash of shit that normally accompanied such misadventures. *Ba*, however, couldn't resist. She thought his performance was the funniest thing she had ever seen. She would point at him, say "Meeler," pump her arms furiously as if running, then stagger against the wall and cackle wildly. Miller, unamused, remained silent through it all.

CHAPTER 15

The Sauna

The team members gathered around the table in the dining area stared at each other incredulously. Was he serious? A sauna? He wanted to build a sauna?

Captain Hughes had struck again! Sometime after Christmas 1969, this idea, which was destined to expand the amenities of the Dinh Quan Surf and Raquette Club, began to take shape. The beach by this time was a legend at the peak of its popularity. As the team members, who all served as the board of directors for the club, listened to Hughes's idea, we were, to say the least, less than enthusiastic. The initial reaction was a rather disdainful dismissal of the whole concept. There were snickers and some unflattering references to his failed attempt to construct a croquet court.

Hughes was somewhat taken aback at the overwhelming resistance that greeted his sauna idea; the facts that we were experiencing daily temperatures well over 100 degrees and that the humidity was already extremely high didn't seem to factor into his thinking. His unabated enthusiasm and persistence, however, finally wore us down, although a healthy skepticism remained. He and Lt. Ray Wingo set about designing this new addition to the Surf and Raquette Club.

Enlisting the help of the nearby U.S. engineer company, Hughes and Wingo came up with a conex steel shipping container roughly eight feet by eight feet and six feet high. They constructed wooden benches inside along the left wall and cut away the lower right rear corner with an acetylene torch. A metal box approximately two feet square was constructed and welded into place inside the conex, filling the hole that had been cut out. When completed, it looked like a metal cube sitting in the corner of the sauna. On top of this cube, smooth stones from the river bed were piled. From the outside it appeared that a square bite had been taken out of the right rear of the conex. The bite was the location of the charcoal-fueled fire that we would light every day. It burned beneath the corner, turning the metal cube inside red hot, which in turn heated the stones. The smoke from the fire, prevented by the tight welds from entering the conex, merely drifted away.

Using the sauna was simple. We would douse the extremely hot stones with water, generating steam and raising the temperature and humidity within this steel container—already sitting out in the blazing sun—to incredible levels. Conditions inside became unbearable in record time. The routine consisted of a leisurely session on the beach followed by the purification rite of the sauna. At death-defying levels of heat and humidity, it became a macho thing to see who would fold first. The first person to bail out would swing the wide metal door back and forth, evacuating the steam which had built up inside, and then we would start all over. We had no way of measuring the heat, but it was of hellish proportions—it's a wonder it didn't kill us all! When no one could stand it any longer, there would be a race for the cold showers. The whole experienced left us absolutely drained. If the Vietnamese, who made every effort to get out of the sun and heat, thought the beach was a crazy idea, you can imagine their reaction to our sauna!

While the sauna was a success, Captain Hughes's earlier attempt to add to our amenities—the ill-fated croquet course—was not. In the fall of 1969, right after the monsoon season had passed, Hughes came up with the idea of constructing a croquet course in our back-yard, just beyond the beach. Everyone thought this was a marvelous idea and volunteered their own suggestions as to how best to do it. A plan was drawn up that would initially lay out a small court, one that could be expanded in the future. We all had a vision of the Dinh Quan Country Club, with croquet substituting for golf—a perfect companion to the Surf and Raquette Club! Hughes wrote his wife in Panama City, Florida, and had her ship him a croquet set—mallets, balls, wickets, and stakes. Now all that we had to do was construct the course. Shovels, picks and rakes were borrowed from the engineers, and we were set to go.

The following Sunday morning, work commenced in earnest. All of us worked feverishly throughout the day, shoveling, raking, breaking up rocks, filling up holes, lining up materials, chopping brush and weeds, hauling dirt and sand, and so forth. At day's end, exhausted, we paused to admire our work. It was a disaster! The ground wasn't level, the area was too small, there was no grass, the soil was full of rocks, and the ball wouldn't roll straight. In fact, with all the rocks the ball would hardly roll at all. We realized that in the enthusiasm of our planning we had somehow overlooked the critical fact that croquet was intended to be played on a large, smooth, level, grassy area. The area we had selected was neither large, smooth, level, nor grassy; it was an absolute mud hole during the rainy season. Despite Hughes's urging that it only needed a little more work to be world class, we threw down our tools, abandoned croquet, and turned our attention to badminton. For the next couple days Hughes worked on his own, determined that he would show us all. Despite his efforts, there was little improvement, and slowly even he came to grips with the futility of this undertaking. Quietly and unceremoniously, work on the croquet court stopped. In deference to Hughes, there were no "We told you so's"; until the sauna idea surfaced, the disaster was hardly mentioned. The sauna's ultimate success, however, redeemed Captain Hughes and restored his reputation.

The sauna also secured our place in the advisory team hall of fame, had there been one. We were now folklore, and even other Americans began to think we were all crazy! Their curiosity, however, generally got the best of them. A visit to our team invariably meant participating in a ritual lounge on the beach and a steam bath in our sauna. Had there been a late-night talk show in Vietnam, we surely would have been guests every evening!

CHAPTER 16

Outhouse #2

The explosion, though nearly half a mile away, shook the school building where I was teaching my high school English class. The blast had come from the vicinity of the team house. My heart stopped. I could see a huge cloud of dust and smoke rising from the compound. I ran from the building, leaped into my jeep, and raced at breakneck speed back down the highway toward the compound. The only thing I could think of was that somehow the VC had gotten a satchel charge into our team house. I knew that all the team members were in the house when I left, and I shuddered at the thought of what I might find. As I was to discover, this incident had its origin in a problem that had plagued the Dinh Quan Surf and Raquette Club for some time.

The beach was our pride and joy, our daily refuge. Unfortunately, the limited confines of the compound did not afford it either the airy spaciousness or the seclusion we would have liked. To the contrary, the beach was surrounded by the other facilities necessary to support the team house: to the right rear was the generator shed, the infamous sauna was to the right front, and to the left front were the supply shed and shower facility. The biggest complaint, however, for obvious reasons, was that the team's outhouse was directly adjacent to the beach.

The outhouse was a homemade wooden structure similar to those I had known during my youth in West Virginia, even down to the obligatory crescent moon painted on the door. The only discernable difference was that the upper half of our outhouse was made of screen wire in deference to the heat and humidity. Inside was a holder for toilet paper and a small rack for the obligatory magazines. Painted dark green, with a metal pitched roof, it was, in the vernacular, a typical "one holer," except instead of the deep hole in the ground beneath the seat, ours contained a concrete slab upon which sat a large metal container made of a 55-gallon drum that had been cut in half.

In the heat and humidity of Vietnam, this facility required daily attention. If ignored for even the slightest amount of time, it emitted a smell that was indescribably ghastly, polluting the air of the entire compound. Therefore, one of the most critical but least desirable duties shared by team members was the daily burning of the collecting barrel. The barrel was dragged from under the seat, thoroughly soaked with diesel fuel, ignited, and allowed to burn for several hours. The ensuing smoke and foul smell were always a source of irritation to the Vietnamese living on the compound, but they never said a word. I guess they figured that smell was better than the alternative!

Right beside the outhouse and next to the beach was the "piss tube," a simple steel cylinder about four feet long and eight to ten inches in diameter in which artillery ammunition had been shipped. This tube was buried nearly vertically about a foot into the ground. The open end, which extended about two and a half feet into the air, provided a near perfect urinal. Unfortunately, it didn't take long for the ground in which the tube was buried to become supersaturated. The accompanying smell was enough to make your eyes water and considerably reduced the pleasure of the nearby beach users. The problem was that the beach and outhouse rested directly over a huge slab of rock only about ten inches beneath the surface. Numerous attempts to penetrate this slab so that the tube could be buried deeper in the ground had failed, and while this was a frequent topic of discussion among the beach dwellers, the hours and hours of creative debate failed to produce a workable solution. The obvious alternative of relocating the tube had been considered and rejected. In order to avoid the rock slab, the tube would have to be located at least twenty feet farther away from the team house. The inconvenience of having to travel twenty additional feet to take a leak was absolutely unthinkable! And so the problem remained.

SFC Robert Kirkbride, the senior NCO on the team, came in one afternoon carrying a large box and declaring that he had the solution to the piss tube problem. He explained that he had just come from a visit to the U.S. engineer company, which was working on a major project to improve Highway 20. On this particular day the engineers had given Sergeant Kirkbride a 40-pound shape charge! To put this in perspective for those unversed in the area of explosives, a quarter-pound stick of explosives will blow up a car and completely destroy a small building. Kirkbride proposed using this 40-pound explosive charge to blast through the rock slab beneath the outhouse, a spot approximately forty feet from the back of our team house and no more than sixty feet from adjacent Vietnamese buildings.

When Captain Hughes and I raised some concerns about the wisdom of using such a large explosive device, Kirkbride responded with undisguised disdain that we obviously didn't understand the concept of the shape charge. He explained that the device was shaped like a cone, and as such, the force of the explosion was precisely directed to a small area directly beneath the cone. According to Kirkbride, the explosive device would deliver a smashing blow to the slab and allow us to dig through it, thus solving our piss tube problem forever! To allay our concerns, he agreed to place plywood sheets next to the outhouse to protect the screen wire from any errant stones that might be tossed up. I remained skeptical and told him that before he proceeded I'd like some expert advice from the explosive specialists assigned to the engineer company. Obviously offended by our doubts, Kirkbride went to bed that night grousing to himself about "officers" and our apparent inability to comprehend something as simple as a shape charge.

The next morning I was scheduled to teach my English class at the Dinh Quan High School, a two-room building that served the sixty-plus kids who were able to attend. It was one of just a few schools in the district, but, despite the remoteness of many of the hamlets, the lack of transportation, a shortage of teachers, the rural attitudes and suspicions of many of the Vietnamese, and the war itself, most of the youngsters in the district had the opportunity to attend. Those who did were enthusiastic and eager to learn. I taught several times a week and always enjoyed working with the kids. They readily accepted me, and I was frequently invited to attend special functions at the school.

On this particular day, I had finished my classes about noon and was standing on the front porch of the building lighting up a cigar when the explosion occurred. It rattled me so much that as I raced back toward the compound, I unknowingly drove right through a concertina-wire barricade the National Police had erected across the road as part of a vehicle checkpoint. (Weeks later we were still trying to get the wire untangled from beneath the jeep.)

As I rounded the corner of the compound, I was greatly relieved to see the team house still standing, but *Ba*, our housemaid and cook, was in front of the building crying and wailing, and the Vietnamese in the compound were running in every direction. I skidded to a halt in the gravel parking area, leaped out, drew my pistol, and ran for the team house. As I sped by *Ba*, I noticed something strange: she wasn't wailing, she was howling with laughter. Tears were streaming down her face, and as she staggered around, all she could do was point toward the house and laugh!

As I ran through the front door, I tripped, nearly killing myself, on the debris that littered the floor. The fluorescent lightbulbs had fallen from the overhead lights, shattering all over the floor, and the screen wire and curtains around the upper half of the house were blown away. The upright water cooler was knocked over and water was everywhere. Pictures, mirrors, the clock—everything had been knocked off the wall. All the canned goods had been blown off the shelves and were rolling around on the floor. Chairs and small pieces of furniture were turned over and strewn about, and a heavy dust cloud hung in the room. No one was in the team house. I raced out the back door, a maneuver made easier by the fact that the screen door had been blown off its hinges and was lying askew in the kitchen area.

As I ran into the backyard, I was confronted by a large smoking hole in the ground where the outhouse used to be—not a shred of it remained! Gone also—apparently vaporized—were the plywood sheets that Kirkbride had carefully placed next to the outhouse to protect the screen wire from "errant pebbles."

I noticed that all the team members were there and laughing their asses off. Only then did it sink in as to what had happened. While I was off teaching school, Kirkbride had decided to surprise me by blasting the rock and fixing the piss tube. It would all be completed by the time I returned, and he could smugly say, "See, just as I told you. Nothing to it!"

My first reaction was one of immense relief. I didn't know whether to laugh or throw up. My relief quickly turned to anger, however, and

I started looking for Kirkbride. There he was, ashen-faced, totally shaken by what had occurred. "Don't worry, sir," he stammered, "I'll have a new one built before dark!" At that point I came unstuck, and the relief combined with the absurdity of the moment took over. I started laughing uncontrollably and had to lean against the team house for support.

When we regained our composure and began to survey the surrounding area, we quickly discovered that the blast had also inflicted serious damage on some of the other buildings in the compound, including our supply shed. Window screens were blown away, metal siding was ripped off exterior walls, and dirt and dust blanketed everything. Even the sandbags defining the beach were shredded. Miraculously, no one was injured.

We spent a great deal of time explaining what had happened, agreeing to repair damages, and simply apologizing to the Vietnamese, particularly to the National Police, our nearest neighbors. The blast had likewise wreaked havoc on their family housing located about sixty feet away. No one had thought to advise the Vietnamese, so no one in the compound was expecting the explosion. Like me, they had thought the worst. If there had been doubters previously, I was certain that this last act must have convinced them all that Americans were crazy.

Sometime later that afternoon, a Vietnamese villager appeared humbly at our door, carrying the toilet seat from the outhouse. It had been blown several hundred yards but somehow had remained intact!

All through the afternoon and evening we could hear feverish hammering and sawing noises coming from the back of the house. Sergeant Kirkbride did not even come in for dinner. True to his word, by daybreak, Outhouse #2 stood proudly on the spot previously occupied by its predecessor, complete with the half-moon painted on the door. Later, in a ceremony rivaling the British coronation, the surviving toilet seat was restored to its rightful location atop the box in the new outhouse.

In the hours and days that followed, the telling and retelling of the events that had occurred in my absence grew funnier and funnier. Lieutenant Wingo had taken a series of photos of the event, managing to capture the instants before, during, and after the blast. These photographs remain some of my treasured possessions.

Sergeant Kirkbride's outhouse exploit became a legend among the Vietnamese and the other U.S. advisory teams in the III Corps area. I would be remiss, however, if I did not report that despite the destruction inflicted on the compound by Kirkbride's blast, the rock slab was undisturbed! It remained solidly intact, and the piss tube problem was never solved.

CHAPTER 17

The Inferno

If the Vietnamese thought we were crazy, we certainly did little to persuade them otherwise. The beach, the sauna, the blowing of the outhouse, and our general antics, when viewed objectively, would cause anyone to look askance. I think some of the Americans who dealt with us likewise thought we were a click or two off windage.

At this point I must confess my own notable contribution to that reputation. Shortly after construction of the beach, I noted that the right half of our backyard was overgrown with a tall tropical grass. It ran from the generator shed along the rusty barbed-wire fence that separated our compound from that of the National Police, up to within several feet of our team house—about sixty feet—and extended about twenty feet into the compound. The grass was about seven feet tall and was tough, thick, and razor sharp. Earlier efforts to cut it back from the beach area had been difficult and were soon abandoned. Over the years the grass had accumulated a lot of trash, and I was certain it was the nesting place of all sorts of unpleasant varmints, most notably an uninvited snake visitor that had terrorized our team house.

In what could only be described as a fit of brilliance, I concluded that burning was the solution to our perplexing grass problem. It was all so simple that I was amazed no one else had thought of it. The following afternoon I assembled the team out back and briefed them on my plan. They, like me, thought it was a great idea. We rounded up rakes and shovels to help us control the fire and filled some buckets with water—just in case we needed them. We had decided to direct the flames from south to north so that the fire would burn away from the team house. With the calculated precision of professional forest-fire fighters, we carefully lit the grass.

I don't know what I had envisioned, but what happened next clearly wasn't it. Within seconds flames were leaping 15 feet in the air. The fire was raging and totally out of control! The heat was so intense you couldn't get near it, and tossing our meager buckets of water on it was like spitting into a forest fire. At the same instant that I realized the fire was running wild, it occurred to me for the first time that sitting squarely at the far end of the fire's path was the generator shed holding ten 55-gallon drums of diesel fuel. This terrifying thought was suddenly interrupted by the screams and shouts coming from our National Police friends, pointing out one other slight oversight. The family housing for the National Police, a cluster of small wooden buildings, was right up against the single-strand barbed-wire fence that was the only barrier between the wall of flames and them. The grass, in fact, grew right up next to these buildings. I remember thinking, "Oh my God! I'm going to burn down the whole fucking compound!" There wasn't a thing we could do. We watched helplessly as the flames soared on until, in a clear demonstration of the old adage, "God takes care of drunks and fools," divine intervention took sway. Whatever breeze had been blowing suddenly ceased. The flames roared up to the fence line but miraculously did not cross. (Of course, the fact that the entire population of the police compound was throwing water on the houses to wet them down may have contributed somewhat.) Meanwhile team members had frantically hacked away at the grass nearest the generator shed so when the flames reached that point they merely burnt themselves out. It was all over in a matter of minutes. We proceeded to stamp out and water down any remaining embers. Fortunately no one was injured, and the police housing amazingly escaped serious damage. It took quite a while longer for my heart to stop pounding!

My "great idea" had terrorized ten families, totally pissed off the National Police, nearly blown up my own generator shed, and threatened to burn down the entire compound—not the sort of actions that instill trust and promote the rapport necessary for an advisor. It took a heap of apologies and an offer to pay for any damages to calm our neighbors down.

Of course, it did get rid of the grass and any resident critters, and it allowed us to clean up that section of our compound. There was, however, an unanticipated cost—a major loss of privacy. We hadn't realized it before, but the grass screened the outhouse, the open-air piss tube, and the beach from the National Police housing. With the grass removed, the view from their back windows now encompassed it all. We slowly let the grass grow back, and my subordinate team members wisely and tactfully refrained from ever mentioning this misadventure in my presence.

CHAPTER 18

The Shower and Bath House

Showers! Americans love showers! The ingenuity of U.S. soldiers for fabricating showers out of odd scraps of war refuse is legendary, and their inventiveness in this pursuit during the Vietnam War only served to enhance the legend. Not only the heat, dirt, and humidity, but also the ever-present potential for disease and infection in Vietnam, made the shower not a luxury, but an absolute necessity. It cleansed, cooled, disinfected, and refreshed not only the physical being, but also seemingly the emotional being. A "whore's bath" out of your steel pot (helmet) in the field might suffice temporarily, but there was nothing like a good hot shower. It was no surprise then to discover that wherever U.S. soldiers were found, a homemade shower was not far away.

When I arrived in Dinh Quan in April 1969, the shower stall behind the team house was a small coffin-sized box enclosed on three sides, with a raggedy piece of target cloth hanging in the doorway providing only a modicum of privacy. Water was stored above the shower in a salvaged aircraft wing tank that had been cut in half; the tank held at best 30 gallons of water. A showerhead was crudely affixed to a pipe extending downward from the tank with a device on it that allowed the water to flow when a chain was pulled. The water was heated by the sun during the day.

The "showeree" stood on a wooden pallet that allowed the water to pass through and drain onto the ground. The setup worked, but had several limitations. Although we had liberally scattered gravel around the area, the ground immediately surrounding the shower was always muddy. But the main problem was that the capacity of the tank limited the amount of time you could spend soaking. The established standard operating procedure for showering was: get wet, turn off the water and soap up, then turn on the water and quickly rinse. It was a great concept for conserving water, but everyone, myself included, ignored it and soaked away. With seven team members, plus our normal ration of visitors, the tank required constant refilling, a chore in which water would be pumped from the compound's well into 5-gallon "jerry cans," which were then carried up a ladder and emptied into the container. Since the sun was the only source of heat for the water, the time of the refill dictated whether or not the person showering would enjoy a hot shower.

It wasn't long after the beach was established and the sauna constructed that our attention turned to the inadequacies of the shower. We also thought there should be a better arrangement for washing and shaving. At the time, each of us had a tin bowl that was placed on a rack behind the team house. The rack was sheltered by a lean-to–type tin roof attached to the rear of the house. The area was also used by *Ba* and the two girls to do the laundry and some of the food preparation. Every time someone wanted to wash up or shave, he got his pan and filled it with water from either the 5-gallon cans lined up alongside or the 55-gallon drums that collected rainwater off the roof of the team house. When he was finished, he simply threw his water out on the ground. Because there were no walls, when it rained, water blew in under the roof, getting everything and everyone wet. The entire arrangement left a great deal to be desired.

One evening after Hughes had run out of water mid-shower and was cursing profusely about having to climb up the ladder to refill the tank (wrapped only in his towel, with his ass hanging out for the world to see), we decided it was time to act. An elaborate plan was devised: a large shower, privacy, lots of water, sinks with running water, hot water for shaving, shelter from the elements, and electric lights. Understand, this was to be a convenience that could respectably grace the cover of *House and Garden* magazine.

It was incredible to watch the team in action. With the help of the local U.S. engineer company, we erected a massive wooden tower atop which we secured a large metal container in which an aircraft engine had been shipped. A couple of the team NCOs pulled off some deal in Saigon to get the container. It held more than 400 gallons of water! The necessary pipes were rigged, and then came the bath house itself. A large wooden building was constructed, with a corrugated metal roof, ventilated wooden clapboard walls, and 3 feet of screen wire at the top to provide additional ventilation. The shower stall, a luxurious 4-foot square, was built on the end directly adjacent to the water tower. The water flow was controlled by a knob that you could actually open and leave on without having to hang on to a chain. Running the length of one interior wall was a wooden framed counter that held three sinks; above each was a mirror and an electric light. The water flow from the tower to the shower and sinks ran through glistening white porcelain cabinets that were, in fact, small electric water heaters. All the comforts of home!

As with the water tank, the plumbing parts and other building materials were scrounged from all over. The NCOs appeared to be miracle workers, because critical parts just seemed to magically appear! (I prudently did not inquire too deeply into the source of these treasures.) The electric water heaters were my major contribution, and I came by them legitimately. These heaters were widely used at province headquarters in Xuan Loc, and after considerable "guilt sowing," I was able to shame Dick Hretz, the province civilian deputy, into giving us several of them.

Water resupply, the biggest bugaboo with our old shower, was solved by getting the engineers to stop by weekly with their tanker truck. In order to keep the dust down in the dry season, they used the tankers to wet the road where they were working. They'd simply pull up by the tower and pump in 400 gallons fresh from the La Nga River. (We also persuaded them to wet down the main street of the Dinh Quan village. With all the truck traffic back and forth between Saigon and Dalat, wetting the road vastly improved living conditions for those living or working alongside it.)

The final touch on the bath house was an extension of the drain pipes so that water was carried off into a nearby drainage ditch. Life was good. Predictably, showers got longer, and it was not at all unusual to hear the less than melodic sounds of some happy soul singing loudly off key while enjoying the benefits of this latest contribution to team comfort and necessity.

CHAPTER 19

Hollywood Goes to War

Bells clanged and the villagers screamed as gunfire exploded and the body count rapidly mounted. No, we weren't under attack; it was simply another night at the movies, and Clint Eastwood was blazing away on the big screen.

One of the few but probably the most appreciated "perks" enjoyed by U.S. advisory teams in Vietnam were the 16mm movies. The Department of Defense, in conjunction with the Hollywood movie industry, had established a program that provided a wide variety of movies on 16mm film. These movies, which ran the gamut from the worst of the B movies to the latest first-run films, were available on a rotating basis to U.S. units all over Vietnam. Advisory teams were no exception, and each team had been issued its very own 16mm Bell and Howell projector. For the advisory team in Dinh Quan, one of the week's highlights was the arrival of the chopper from Xuan Loc with its cargo of military supplies, mail, and five to seven movies for the week. Considerable effort and debate went into determining the sequence and schedule for the showing of these movies, with each team member arguing for his particular choices.

Normally, we would show one movie each evening after dinner. The team member assigned radio duty for the evening would position himself just outside the radio room, where he could monitor radio traffic yet still be able to watch the movie. Since advisory duties required each team member to be out in the evening from time to time, it was necessary for each of us to master the idiosyncrasies of the temperamental projector. Additionally, the film frequently had numerous breaks, chewed-up guide holes, and less than perfect soundtracks as a result of hundreds of showings and rough handling. Considering the environment, I guess it's amazing that they worked as well as they did! Nonetheless, woe to the poor operator if the film broke or jumped track during a critical scene. I can still recall one evening when I held a flashlight for nearly two hours when the soundtrack activator bulb on our projector burned out. It was "showtime," and in that situation rank did not matter. By carefully aiming the light into the machine, I was able to provide the necessary light beam to activate the soundtrack. The slightest movement on my part resulted in interruption of the soundtrack and brought an immediate disgruntled response from my teammates. Believe me, the next day I was on the radio to everyone within a 75-mile radius trying to locate a replacement soundtrack bulb!

A major spin-off benefit of having the movies was that they afforded me an opportunity to invite Major Xuan, the Vietnamese district chief, over each evening. Major Xuan had left his family in Saigon so that his children could attend French schools. A traditionalist, he did not like to fraternize with his junior officers. So nearly every evening he would take advantage of my standing invitation and come over for the movie. He and I would sit on the sofa, sip a brew or two, and take in the latest cinematic offering. I quickly discovered that these informal sessions were the most productive portion of the day. It strengthened the personal relationship between Xuan and me, enhanced communication, and fostered cooperation in all aspects of district activities. Many a plan was hatched and problem solved while John Wayne or some other Hollywood icon was blasting away on the white sheet that we hung on our wall to serve as a screen for these occasions.

It was not unusual for us to show the same movie twice in a single evening. The better flicks required an encore, and frequently team members who had been out attending to duties would arrive late and demand a rerun for their benefit. Strangely, it seemed that often some of the worst B movies actually got better with a second showing—or maybe it was just the beer!

Sometimes we received advance "movie reviews" from other teams via the radio network. If the reviews were especially good, we would run two or more separate movies in a night rather than wait for their scheduled appearance later in the week. As bad as some of these films were (and some were atrocious), I don't believe we ever had a movie that we didn't enjoy—even if our enjoyment came from the hilarious ridicule being heaped on the film!

The construction of our team house resulted in a far greater audience each night than we anticipated. The team house walls were wooden from the concrete floor up to about four feet, and from there to the ceiling they were simply screen wire to allow the ventilation necessary to deal with the heat and humidity. I came to note, with some concern, that each night as our movies got underway, scores of faces would appear at the screen wire, peering in to watch the movies. Generally these would be soldiers or national policemen who would stand for hours transfixed by the action taking place on our makeshift screen. This obviously created a security concern among team members. It would have been easy for someone to toss a grenade into the darkened room or to place a satchel charge against the wall of the building. I am absolutely convinced that among our phantom audience were bona fide members of the local Viet Cong organization. We were easy targets in that situation, but as everyone soon learned, when serving on an advisory team, you are constantly vulnerable. It was an occupational hazard that was just part of the job. There never were any movie-related security incidents during my tour, and to the best of my knowledge none before or after. In retrospect, perhaps the movies made us more secure. An attack on us would have eliminated the major source of entertainment in Dinh Quan District!

Recognizing the interest created by our movies and acknowledging our faithful phantom audience, I decided to build an outdoor screen. Inspired by my teenage experience with drive-in movies, we erected a large 6-foot by 10-foot screen made of white target cloth on two large poles in front of our team house. One benefit, which we didn't anticipate but soon recognized, was that the movie image was equally visible from both the front and back of the screen. We now had a back-to-back theater! Since Dinh Quan was a very rural district, very few of the Vietnamese spoke English, so it really didn't matter if they could hear the dialogue or read any text that might appear on the screen. The outdoor movie was a tremendous hit. Crowds would frequently exceed a hundred or more inside the compound, with scores of others gazing through the concertina wire 20 yards away that separated us from Highway 20.

The Vietnamese audience was a lot more vocal in its reaction to the movies than the typical American audience. They seemed to enjoy each and every movie no matter how bad it was, often pleading with us to back it up to "instant replay" a particular piece of action or to rerun the entire movie. They particularly enjoyed action movies, especially Westerns. The plots were simple, you could always tell the good guys from the bad guys, and you didn't need to understand English. Clint Eastwood's spaghetti Westerns were popular in the United States at that time, and eventually all of them reached us. The Vietnamese went wild over them! We must have shown each one more than a half-dozen times. They kept elaborate score, shouted, cheered, rang bells, and generally celebrated each time Eastwood dispatched another of the villains.

Near the end of my tour, I managed, through some "horse trading" with an American unit, to get a copy of John Wayne's *The Green Berets*. I thought the Vietnamese would really love it. Here was a film showing the Vietnamese to be courageous, tough fighters in noble defense of their country against the treacherous Viet Cong. I was especially excited, because as a captain on the Infantry Center staff at Fort Benning, Georgia, I had been personally involved with John Wayne in selecting sites for shooting the movie. In addition, a number of my friends appeared as extras in the film.

Word of the movie spread through the district, and when the time for the showing came hundreds of spectators were on hand. I must admit that the anticommunist/anti-VC slant of the film caused me to be far more concerned about security than usual. I discussed it with Major Xuan, but other than increased vigilance, there was little we could do. I very discreetly wore my pistol under my jungle fatigue jacket that evening, although the protection it provided was more psychological than real.

The movie started with a great deal of excitement and expectation, but once the scenes in the film shifted to Vietnam, the enthusiasm dampened, and clearly something was amiss. Even the district chief seemed upset. I asked him what was wrong. At first he politely denied that anything was wrong, but the longer the movie ran, the more his agitation became apparent. Finally, choosing his words carefully so as not to offend, he told me what was wrong. It turned out he was angry and disappointed—here was the great Vietnamese war saga, and the actors playing the parts of the Vietnamese in the movie weren't Vietnamese! They were Chinese, Japanese, Koreans, and Asians of all sorts, but they clearly weren't Vietnamese, and their attempts at the Vietnamese language were for the most part atrocious. The Vietnamese in the audience were likewise offended and disappointed, but were too polite to walk out. They sat through the movie, applauding quietly from time to time, but clearly my big entertainment treat was a total bust!

OCCASIONALLY, SOMEONE WOULD come up with an XXX-rated movie from Hong Kong or elsewhere. Although the troops generally referred to these movies as "training films," for the record these were not on the Department of Defense official circuit. These films were generally of horrible quality, black-and-white, and grainy, with no plot and no soundtrack. Nonetheless, these little jewels, judiciously not shown outside, really created a stir as everyone felt obligated to comment on all aspects of the performances! The Vietnamese officers were little different from the Americans in their reactions to these films. Invariably, there would initially be some embarrassed giggles, but before long they would be pointing and howling with laughter. It was not unusual for them to urge a second or third showing of these films—just like their American counterparts.

I recall on one occasion being invited to dinner at the field headquarters of the 43rd Regiment of the 18th ARVN Division. The 43rd Regiment was conducting a military operation in War Zone D, a major portion of which was in Dinh Quan District, and had established its command post in a Buddhist temple about a quarter-mile from my team house. When Hughes and I arrived, we were escorted into the temple, where the regimental commander, a Vietnamese lieutenant colonel, and his senior staff, as well the senior members of the U.S. advisory staff assigned to the regiment were assembled, enjoying their cognac prior to dinner. After an excellent dinner, with more cognac, of course, the lights were extinguished, and to my shock and utter amazement a series of the seediest XXX movies one can imagine were thrown up on the temple wall. "Pornographic" fails to do justice to the scenes flickering across the makeshift screen. While everyone was caught up in the cinematic drama, I was overcome with a sense of uneasiness. I wasn't sure if Buddha had mastered lightning bolts or not, but Hughes and I kept exchanging nervous glances, half-expecting one to come tearing through the roof at any minute!

CHAPTER 20

The Dinh Quan Power and Light Company

"**A**w shit!" It was happening again—we were losing power; the picture was dimming; the projector was slowing, causing the action on the screen to approach slow motion; and the voices on the soundtrack were increasingly distorted. Howls of disapproval rose as the generator, once again coughing and sputtering, slowly succumbed. There were few things sacred to team members, but among the most coveted were their mail, their privacy, and the evening movie. Any interference brought a unified torrent of protest. Whatever the source of this problem, it was occurring with greater frequency and had become a perplexing nuisance for the team.

Dinh Quan District was a very rural area roughly seventy miles northeast of Saigon. Its more than 16,000 inhabitants were primarily farmers, although there was a thriving logging industry as well. There was, however, none of the infrastructure in place that we in the United States take for granted. There was no electricity, no telephone system, no running water, and no sewage system. Conditions were, by most standards, rather primitive.

The advisory team depended on a neighboring U.S. engineer company for potable water. Although there was a well in the compound, the team opted to use it only as a last resort since the water treatment chemicals left an unpleasant aftertaste. Team garbage was buried and sewage burned daily. Communication with the outside world was provided by tactical military radios. Propane fueled the kitchen stove, and electricity for the team was provided by diesel-powered generators that ran continuously.

Initially one, then two 5-kilowatt generators provided ample power for the team house, as the electrical demand was very basic.

Power was required for lights, refrigerator, a large freezer, communications equipment, fans, and a multitude of electric household appliances such as the coffee pot, toaster, mixer, and electric skillets. The generators were alternated so that power was continuously available and preventive maintenance and repairs could be completed during each generator's scheduled down time.

My efforts to get Dinh Quan included in the Rural Electrification Program had not been successful. The electrification program was slowly working its way throughout the countryside, but we were a little too remote and our population a little too sparse to receive any priority. Plus there remained the problem of security. The electric power lines erected during the French colonial era, which were shown on the map paralleling national Highway 20 across the district, had long since been destroyed by the Viet Cong.

The team's needs were more than adequately met by the generators. The district headquarters had its own generator, but to conserve fuel it shut down early each evening. My predecessor, as a gesture of good will, agreed to extend electrical services to the district chief's house and the other three buildings in the compound so they could have uninterrupted power. From time to time, the larger load on the system would lug down the generators so that lights dimmed and appliances ran slower. This was especially noticeable during the evening movies when the soundtrack slowed down, slurring the dialogue to an undistinguishable growl. Being in a foreign country, in a combat zone, and living in primitive conditions a long way from civilization, advisors by nature learned to be pretty tolerant. But any interference with the evening movie was a matter of highest concern.

We accommodated as best we could. We cut off unnecessary lights and appliances and fine-tuned the generator's engine, yet the problem not only continued, but appeared to get worse. It seemed that the generator was just maxed out by the demand, and there was little we could do.

Sometime during the middle of my tour, two of the team's NCOs (discretion requires me to omit the names of these bona fide heroes) returned from a supply run and gleefully announced that our electrical problem was solved. They had "acquired" a new 15-kilowatt generator for the team. Since I could clearly see the U.S. Air Force markings stenciled all over the crate, I tactfully declined to inquire about the source of this new treasure. Officially I had to be concerned, but deep down inside I didn't care! Our problem was solved: 15,000 watts! In my mind that was enough to power a small city. Surely that would be enough power to meet our simple needs.

The new generator was terrific; it ran smoothly and efficiently, sending electricity surging through our team house. No more dim lights, no more slowed motors, no more slurred soundtrack. Life was good. We ensured that the larger generator was online during the early evening hours, our peak load period. The 5 kilowatts could handle the non-peak loads during the day and late at night.

As time wore on, though, it seemed to me that occasionally I would detect a slight lugging down of the 15-kilowatt generator. I generally dismissed my concerns by attributing the aberration to water in the fuel or some mechanical maladjustment. Over the weeks, these occurrences grew more and more frequent and more and more pronounced. We adjusted carburetors, tinkered with the timing, inspected the fuel source, and did everything we knew to do, yet the problem persisted. We asked for and received assistance from province headquarters in the form of a small-engine mechanic and sought help from our U.S. engineer neighbors. Still the larger generator labored and struggled along. As the situation continued to worsen, I started to think that perhaps the problem wasn't the generator, but the load on it. But what one earth could be using that much power?

One night after dark, and during the peak load period, I climbed up on a large rock formation behind our team house from which I could observe the entire compound and most of the surrounding village. I directed SFC King to man the generator and on my command to shut off the power. When I gave the word, King threw the switch and, as expected, the team house, the district chief's house, and the other few buildings in the compound went dark. Something was wrong, however, and at first I couldn't put my finger on it. I signaled Sergeant King to put the power back on. As he did, the entire village blazed to life! At my direction, off and on went the power switch, and off and on went the lights throughout the village. I couldn't believe my eyes—we were supplying power to the whole damned village! No wonder our generator was struggling under the load.

The very next day we began to trace the intricate electrical network that had grown up around our generator. We discovered that at first the Vietnamese officers who worked at the district headquarters but lived outside the compound had taken it upon themselves to quietly run lines from the compound to their homes in adjacent compounds or in the village. These lines were then tapped into by relatives and neighbors, and their lines tapped into by their families and neighbors, and so forth. The network expanded geometrically like a network marketing scheme. We even discovered that the village barber had tapped into the network and was selling hookups from his barber shop! We further discovered that every sort of wire imaginable was hooked into the grid. Commo wire, electrical wire, baling wire—you name it, we found it hooked up. God only knows how much of the power supply was consumed in wire loss.

When we reported the piracy to Major Xuan, the district chief, he was appropriately shocked and apologetic. Although he displayed his anger at his subordinates for permitting this and directed them to immediately disconnect all illegal power sappers, the truth was that of the more than 9,000 people who lived in the village, the only seven who didn't know all about the electrification of the village were the seven Americans on the advisory team!

The directive to disconnect the illegal hookups was certainly not a popular one in Dinh Quan. There was a noticeable change in the haze above the village as oil lamps once again were pressed into service. As a compromise, we did allow the adjacent military compounds to keep their hookups. Life in the team house returned to normal, but a week or so later when I went to get a haircut, I noticed that our enterprising barber had not been deterred. He had purchased (probably from the money he made from our generator) a small generator of his own, which he had running out of his barber shop. Several adjacent homes glowed with lights powered by his generator. Although the advisory team got out of the public power business, I believe that with our entrepreneurial friend the barber, we spawned the beginnings of the Dinh Quan Power and Light Company.

CHAPTER 21

Snakes Alive

Snakes? You bet your sweet ass! Vietnam was a country brimming with an abundance of all sorts of wildlife. During my three tours I encountered birds, reptiles, and animals of all types—tigers, elephants, giant lizards, water buffalo, wild boar, deer—you name it, they were there, as were some of the most ferocious man-eating insects on the face of the earth. Just ask any "grunt" about the mosquitos and the notorious fire ants! But there were also snakes. Snakes of all types—big snakes, little snakes, harmless snakes, and deadly snakes. One particularly nasty snake, an extremely poisonous viper, was dubbed the "two-step snake" by the troops. Rumor had it that this snake was so deadly that if you got bitten, you were dead before you could take two steps!

There is a scene in the movie *Raiders of the Lost Ark* in which Indiana Jones is confronted with a tomb full of snakes. His response is to cry out in a wavering voice, "I hate snakes!" That is precisely my personal reaction to snakes—they absolutely terrify me! I've handled them in training, I've killed them, and I've eaten them, but that is all a macho thing born out of peer pressure. The truth is they give me the willies. No book about Vietnam, however, could be complete without at least one snake story. I have three.

The first is the mystery snake. I returned to the team house late one afternoon to find everyone in a state of panic. *Co* Houng, the youngest of the house girls, had seen a snake in the house, and all she could tell us was that it was small, maybe two feet long, and green. She thought it was a "bad" (poisonous) snake. When she saw it, she ran outside screaming, so she had no idea where the snake had gone. Armed with rakes, machetes, and axes, we conducted a feverish search but failed to turn up the reptile. The obvious conclusion was that the snake had also panicked and fled outside. There was some joking about the snake, but I believe each man was secretly convinced that the snake was still in the house and probably hiding in his room! *Ba* and the girls left for home early that afternoon, admonishing us to find that snake. All through the evening I couldn't help but notice that everyone was distracted. They kept glancing furtively around the room, apparently expecting the creature to spring at them out of the shadows. Another ominous sign was the conspicuous absence of the Vietnamese officers who came over religiously every night to watch our evening movie. I also noted that during the movie every single member of the team quietly found a box or chair to rest his feet off the floor. In addition, not all the lights were extinguished during the showing of the movie as they normally were. As the movie ended and the evening wore on, I sensed an unwillingness on the part of team members to retire to their rooms. I confess I wasn't too excited about the prospect either.

Generally after the movie people drifted off to their rooms to write letters, read, and listen to their favorite music, but not that night. The dining room table was lined with letter writers, while the readers occupied the sofas that lined the walls. The interpreters found reason to excuse themselves early and headed away from the team house. Even the dogs, AWOL and Baron, seemed agitated. Our earlier attempts to have them sniff out the snake had met with no success, yet they remained restless. The dogs' agitation only heightened the team's anxiety.

About midnight we realized that we were going to have to confront our fears and go to bed. Trying to be macho and nonchalant about the snake, we all reluctantly trudged off to our rooms. For the next fifteen minutes there was a silent choreography in every room as we cautiously and carefully stripped our beds, moved furniture, shook out boots and shoes, and generally searched our areas, each secretly hoping that someone would find the snake, but praying it wasn't going to be him. We all slept fitfully that night, half-expecting the snake to climb into our bunks to get us. Thankfully, the night passed without incident.

The following morning, after subjecting *Co* Houng, the only eyewitness, to an intense interrogation about when and where she saw the snake (the CIA would have been proud), we set about the task of snake-proofing our house. Springs were tightened on the screen doors to ensure that they closed quickly and tightly, and all holes in the walls or screen, no matter how minute, were carefully plugged or patched. It took a few more days for the whole incident to blow over and things to return to normal, but every time the snake story was told to a visitor, the snake grew bigger and more deadly. By the time I left country, it had grown to a venomous 10-foot salivating man-eater!

I had experienced several other unpleasant run-ins with snakes during my previous Vietnam tours. In the summer of 1965, I was serving as the headquarters company commander in the 2nd Battalion, 18th Infantry, of the U.S. 1st Infantry Division ("The Big Red One"). After several months of occupying a mud hole that we called a firebase in Long Binh, the battalion was given orders to relocate to an area at the southern tip of the Long Binh triangle.

When the battalion had first arrived in Vietnam several months earlier, Long Binh was a deserted combination of scrub brush and jungle, much like parts of the III Corps area. We carved out a firebase and set about securing our area of operations. The buildup that was to turn the area into a massive logistical complex would come later. As U.S. administrative and logistics units arrived and began to blacktop the entire area, the combat units were displaced farther into "Indian territory." The analogy with the cavalry's role in opening the West in the 1800s was not lost on me.

After receiving orders to relocate the battalion, Lt. Col. Jack Hougen, our battalion commander, directed me, as headquarters commandant, to reconnoiter the proposed new area and physically lay out the new base camp. The area chosen had been a Japanese ammunition supply point during World War II, and from the air you could still see the outline of those earlier roads. Armed with a map, compass, wooden stakes, and miles of white engineer tape, I set out with a fifteen-man detail to mark the perimeter and lay out the street network of the new camp. After several hours of sweaty work, we had the outline in place. As we were walking back to our vehicles about a hundred meters away, I noticed some movement in a clump of bamboo about fifteen feet ahead of us. As I approached cautiously, suddenly about ten feet in front of me a cobra rose up out of the knee-high grass. Its hood was expanded, and it was slowly weaving its head back and forth as it watched me. Attempting to deal with my self-confessed fear of snakes, I found myself staring into the cobra's eyes.

Somewhere in the back of my mind I remembered once hearing that cobras often spit venom into the eyes of their victims, blinding them before the kill. I wasn't sure how far a cobra could spit, nor was I sure how fast it could move, so, resisting the urge to run, I moved ever so slowly away from the snake. Simultaneously, I unsnapped the flap on my holster and removed my .45-caliber pistol. When I had backed up about twenty feet from the weaving snake, I became aware that the men in the detail had all moved a respectful distance away and were just standing there watching me. My inclination was to run like hell, but I was an officer and expected to set an example. Also, down deep I felt a little foolish about being backed down by a snake. I certainly didn't want that story circulating around the camp when we got back, so I decided I would take out this VC snake. I had qualified as expert with the pistol, so I thought it shouldn't be too hard. I had a mental picture of driving back to the battalion firebase with this monster VC cobra draped over the hood of my jeep.

Screwing up my courage, I edged carefully closer, took aim, fired—and missed! I fired twice more, missing both times. With each shot the snake seemed to creep closer, still weaving hypnotically back and forth. The men in the detail began to move farther back toward the vehicles. Determined to kill this thing, I took another step forward and emptied the remainder of the clip at the snake; the snake kept inching forward. Impossible—I couldn't have missed from that range! By this time the detail was in full retreat. I was fumbling with the pouch on my pistol belt, trying to retrieve another clip of ammunition for the pistol, when I glanced up at the snake. He was still coming and getting uncomfortably close, so I did what any red-blooded American soldier would have done: I shouted, "Oh shit!" and ran like hell for the jeep!

By late that evening, word around the firebase was that I had fired several hundred rounds and thrown two grenades in my futile efforts before being routed by the snake. My version of the story was much better, proclaiming that in recognition of the snake's courage and its mystical actions in dodging my bullets, I had generously decided to spare its life. I was disappointed to learn that nobody believed my version.

I was to experience yet another memorable close encounter of the reptilian kind in April 1966. Still with the 2nd Battalion of the 18th Infantry, I was now commanding B Company. We had been out for several weeks on a large division search-and-destroy operation. My company had covered a lot of terrain, experienced a number of successful skirmishes, and was dog-tired. As a reward, we were lifted by helicopters back to the 2nd Brigade field command post to serve as the brigade reserve. This would give us a chance to get cleaned up, get some hot chow, receive our mail, and most importantly, hopefully get a couple days of rest.

Arriving at the command post late in the afternoon, we were assigned to a very large bamboo thicket about a hundred meters square, the only shady spot in the immediate area. We formed our own company perimeter and dug in for the night. In keeping with my established routine, while I was out walking the perimeter and reminding the troops that we were still deep in "Indian country," so it was necessary to maintain noise and light discipline and not relax too much, my command group dug in and established communications with all concerned. Meanwhile, my artillery forward observer coordinated all the nighttime defensive mortar and artillery concentrations.

Returning to the company command post in the center of the perimeter, I strung my hammock just a few inches off the ground and directly over my hole. In case of incoming fire, in less than a heartbeat I could roll right out of the hammock into the foxhole. We had arrived too late for hot chow that evening, so I polished off a C-Ration pork and beans, doctored with onions and Tabasco sauce, and a can of peaches before flopping into my hammock. The radio/telephone operators (RTOs) had dug their hole about six feet away, and though they had the volume turned down, in the dead silence of that bamboo thicket I could still hear both radios—the company communication net and the brigade net. It was a moonless overcast night, and visibility was poor. Inside the bamboo thicket it was, as the saying goes, like the inside of a cow—black! Even starlight scopes, those night-vision devices that amplify ambient light, were useless; there was no light to amplify. I asked the RTO on the company net to remind all platoon leaders to strictly enforce both noise and light discipline. This was no time to get careless. Having completed my chores, I settled in for the night. I was totally exhausted and looking forward to a good night's sleep.

I was quickly fast asleep. Sometime around two in the morning I was awakened by a voice coming over the company net. This was a frightened voice. Fear transmits unmistakably, and I had heard it many times before: trembling voice, change of pitch, and rapid breathing gasps—it was all there. I shot up like a bolt.

"6 Tango, this is 3 Tango, over," came the call.

My RTO replied, "This is 6 Tango, go."

The voice came back instantly, "6 Tango, there is something big moving in the bamboo just in front of my position!" My RTO knew that 3 Tango was the RTO of the 3rd Platoon leader and that his position was inside the perimeter approximately fifteen meters behind his platoon. He tried to assure his frightened counterpart that the company was all around him, that he was secure, and that nothing could have penetrated the perimeter to get to him.

The 3rd Platoon RTO came back immediately, "No, there is something and it's big, and it's right in front of my position!"

Other units had used the bamboo thicket before us, and there was quite a bit of litter about. My RTO responded, "There is a lot of trash around. You are probably hearing a rat or some other small animal foraging around for food. Over."

A very frightened voice responded, "You don't understand! It's right in front of me!"

By now I could hear some rustling as other radio operators on the net who had been listening in started waking up their leaders. The voice continued, "I'm gonna turn on my flashlight." Before we could respond, the stillness was punctuated with a bloodcurdling scream!

The hair went up on the back of my neck. I leaped into the RTO's hole, grabbed the handset, and shouted, "3 this is 6, what the hell is going on?" By now the entire company was wide awake. I could hear people fumbling for their weapons in the blackness.

The 3rd Platoon RTO was still on the radio, screaming hysterically. "A SNAKE! A GIANT FUCKIN' SNAKE! I TURNED ON MY LIGHT . . . IT WAS RIGHT IN MY FACE . . . OH GOD, IT MUSTA BEEN TWENTY FEET LONG!"

I responded, "3 Tango, this is Buffalo 6. Now calm down! Where is the snake now?" There was a short pause, then, forgetting all radio procedure, he gasped, "I don't know, sir! It ran!"

I responded, "3 Tango, this is 6. Which way did it go? Over." Every radio operator in the company was listening and waiting for the answer.

The voice came back, "I don't know!"

There was a moment of silence as the realization of the situation sunk in on all those listening. We were dug in in a circle. You literally couldn't see your hand in front of your face in the darkness. A huge 20-foot-long snake was somewhere inside the circle trying to get out. Suddenly, all hell broke loose as 150 men simultaneously sprang noisily out of their holes. Lights came on everywhere. Every single one was certain that monster snake was headed straight for him. Light and noise discipline be damned! VC be damned! Getting shot was one thing, but being eaten in the dark by a monster snake was more than anyone bargained for.

I was struggling to regain control. My fear was that someone would find the snake and, in an attempt to shoot it, accidently kill or wound others in the company. It took a major effort by the platoon leaders, but we finally got things under control, and everyone bedded down.

Of course, no one slept for the rest of that night. At the slightest noise, lights blazed and equipment rustled. At first light we scoured the area, but there was no sign of "Mister No Shoulders." We never found that snake, but in the months ahead anytime we encountered snakes of any size in the bush, 3 Tango would invariably receive the expected ration of shit from his comrades.

CHAPTER 22

Going to Saigon

Despite the war raging around it, Saigon was a beautiful and exciting city. Evidence of French influence was everywhere, from the wide boulevards, traffic circles, and architecture, to the restaurants and language. It was the Paris of the Orient. It was therefore no surprise that soldiers in the field relished any opportunity to visit for a few days, and Advisory Team 49 was certainly no exception.

About every four weeks it would be necessary for the team to mount an expedition into Saigon to acquire essential goods and provisions. Selection for this "perilous" journey was highly coveted among the team members. The trip amounted to our own little version of R&R—thirty-six hours to get the goods, see the sights, and indulge in whatever form of relaxation suited your particular desires. It was all there—from the most elegant French restaurants to the seediest whorehouses. The most celebrated of the latter were the "steam bath and massage parlors," affectionately known to the troops as "blowbath and steamjob parlors" or "steam and creams."

Saigon's notorious black market, which operated openly in the streets, was the source of almost anything you wanted and could always guarantee you an exchange rate for piasters several times better than the official exchange rate. It was therefore not difficult to secure volunteers each month for the trip.

There was no particular process for selecting who would go, although there would always be at least two members of the team. This not only provided security on the trip, but also ensured that the team members didn't forget that they were due back in Dinh Quan the following day. No roster was kept, but it seemed to work out pretty equitably, with all team members going from time to time. I

117

could always count on SFC King and SFC Kraft to point out that we were running low on some essential staple and suggest that perhaps we needed to send some folks into town. They also were the first to volunteer each and every time. No matter which team members went to Saigon, there were always incredible adventures that got replayed over and over to team members and other visitors. I wish I had kept a journal.

Once a date had been set for the next trip, elaborate "want lists" were produced by each of the team members and money was collected. Lists included food items from the commissary, cleaning and household supplies, individual toiletries, and personal shopping needs. We each contributed to the food fund each month, and from that we would purchase necessary foodstuffs. Lists and money in hand, and briefed personally by each member regarding his personal wishes, the designated shoppers headed off in the morning as soon as word was received that the highway from Dinh Quan to the La Nga River bridge was open.

The trip to Saigon was by jeep, southwest down Highway 20 to Highway 1 and then due west to Bien Hoa and Saigon, approximately seventy-five miles. Barring any unusual delays along the way, a jeep pulling a trailer could make it in slightly less than three hours.

The most hazardous part of the trip was down Highway 20. It crossed about one-third of Dinh Quan District and all of Kiem Tam District before intersecting with Highway 1. There were a number of isolated stretches that represented real danger areas for single, lightly armed vehicles. All you could do was be alert, drive fast, and hope for the best.

Generally the trip itself was uneventful. Frequently the shoppers made a hurried stop at the Kiem Tam District compound to drop off movies or other inter-team correspondence. Once you hit Highway 1 west of Xuan Loc, traffic picked up, as did the frequency of populated areas. Although this area was not really any more secure, somehow the presence of other people made it feel so. Soon came the swirl of Bien Hoa and the maddening traffic of Saigon with its bicycles, pedicabs, lambrettas, cyclos, trucks, hordes of blue-and-yellow Renault taxis, and old Citroëns that always reminded me of a 1930s gangster film. Compounding the confusion were thousands of U.S. military vehicles. Exhaust fumes were often so thick that they choked those walking along the streets. It was not uncommon to see pedestrians wearing surgical masks.

On one occasion, I was driving the jeep, and while trying to pull into a rare parking place I was hit broadside by a cyclo (a motorbike with a rickshaw-like two-wheeled passenger seat on the front). The woman passenger in the cyclo was carrying a huge basket of fish, which flew out and landed all over the jeep. While we tried to help the woman by bandaging a pretty nasty cut on her forehead and gathering her fish, the cyclo driver, unfazed by the whole affair, calmly picked himself up off the street, bent the front platform of his machine back into a semblance of its previous shape, loaded the woman and her fish, and raced away with a deafening roar amid a suffocating cloud of blue smoke.

ONCE IN THE city, the visitors' first task was to find accommodations for the evening. There were a number of sleazy hotels catering to GIs, complete with a noisy bar on the first level, a half dozen or more small rooms upstairs, and hot- and cold-running prostitutes. The bars were loaded with the standard-issue bar girl trying to hustle the soldiers through that time-honored ritual seasoned soldiers quickly learned to avoid—the infamous "Saigon Tea" ploy. Unwary GIs would succumb to a bar girl's plea to buy her a drink. He would then be charged an inflated amount for the girl's drink, which was nothing more than tea. A skilled bar girl could get unsuspecting troops to buy scores of these drinks for her during the evening, all while he drank himself under the table on beer or other hard drinks. During the entire evening the bar girl would be physically all over the victim, and at some point she would suggest that the soldier buy her from the bar owner—a lesser fee for a short time and a much larger amount for all night. Despite being forewarned, the prospect of having a female to talk to and getting laid was simply too tempting, so GIs willingly handed over their money and made a lot of Saigon bar owners wealthy men.

The Saigon tea routine frequently led to misunderstanding and not infrequently to violence, as young and inexperienced troops in town for the first time believed they were entitled to something more after spending considerable sums on Saigon tea. They learned quickly that the purchase of those drinks got them only the attention of the bar girl—nothing more. Things sometimes got ugly, and with everyone carrying a loaded weapon, barroom showdowns could take on the flavor of the Wild West.

I found myself in the middle of such a scene early in 1970. I had made the Saigon trip this time with SFC Kraft. As a rule, I stayed with George Laudato at his villa when I was in town. George was an officer with the U.S. Agency for International Development (USAID) and frequently worked with us in Dinh Quan. The advantages to be gained by accepting George's hospitality and open invitation were many—good food, pleasant surroundings, good company, and access to Saigon's finer things—but this time I had gone with Kraft to the hotel of his choice. About eleven o'clock that evening we were in the hotel bar having a drink and being entertained, if I can use that term loosely, by a four-piece Vietnamese band, complete with oversized speakers and echo chambers, trying its best to sound like an American rock group. I also noticed that they were generally being ignored by most of the people in the bar.

Wily veterans that Kraft and I were, we avoided the Saigon tea routine, which in turn meant the bar girls had nothing to do with us. From our vantage point, a table in the far corner of the bar, we were able to observe the absurd theater being played out before us.

Suddenly an American buck sergeant from the 173rd Airborne Brigade, whom we had observed huddling and cuddling with several bar girls and buying them drinks all evening, was on his feet, screaming, cursing, and threatening the bar owner and the girls. He had spent nearly $100 on drinks for the girls and felt that entitled him to get laid at no additional cost. He had one of the girls by the arm and was forcibly trying to drag her up the stairs. His other hand waved his loaded M16 rifle, and he threatened to shoot the owner if he tried to stop him. Every one of the thirty or so people in the bar sat transfixed, watching this little drama play out. I was the only officer there (and most likely the only one who had ever been in that bar). I looked at Kraft—he nodded knowingly, grunted, and we got to our feet. By now the sergeant had the scared and crying girl on a stairwell landing about six steps above floor level.

We moved cautiously toward him. He growled in disapproval at our approach. We tried to talk to him, but he wasn't listening. He continued to scream threats at the Vietnamese bar owner, who by now was in a total state of panic. As we started slowly up the steps toward him, he noticed my major's insignia for the first time. His expression changed from anger to confusion. He was drunk, but he was sober enough to recognize a major and realize the possible consequences of his situation. I said in the calmest voice I could muster, "Sergeant, I think maybe it's time to turn in. You've had a lot to drink, and I think you need to sleep it off. Let the girl go before you get yourself into some serious trouble. Sergeant Kraft here will help you get up to your room."

His eyes shot back and forth between the bar owner and me, and after a long moment he released the girl, uttered one final threat to the bar owner, careened against the stairwell wall, and started up the steps. Kraft followed him upstairs, got him to his room, and talked to him to calm him down. Meanwhile the normal mayhem of the bar started right up again. After a few moments Sergeant Kraft reappeared, smiling; our 173rd comrade had passed out on his bed.

The bar owner came rushing over to express his undying gratitude. He must have thanked us a hundred times. The bar girls were suddenly friendly, and there was not a single, "You buy me one Saigon tea?" At the end of the evening, as Kraft and I were getting up to go to our rooms, the owner came across the room, beaming, with five or six bar girls in tow. As a reward for our heroics, not only was there no charge for our drinks, but he was offering us our pick "on the house" for a short time, and for just a few piasters they would be available all night. I wanted to laugh, and when we didn't immediately respond, he must have thought I was insulted because he blurted out, "No, no, for you major. No short time, all night—no Ps [piasters]!" I heard Kraft mumble something to himself that sounded vaguely like, "I know rank hath its privileges, but this is goddamn ridiculous!"

I ALWAYS TRIED to spend part of the first day in Saigon looking up friends who I knew were assigned there. With two previous tours in Vietnam, one of them based in the Saigon outskirts at Tan Son Nhut Air Base, I knew my way around the city pretty well. I also tried to spend a little time at the Saigon marketplace, an intriguing maze of stalls and vendors and a smell (not offensive) that can only be described by a westerner as "Asian." I always emerged with some treasure after haggling intensely with the shopkeeper. In addition, we all took the opportunity to try to place telephone calls home. All the serious shopping took place on the second day.

The second morning was reserved for the Saigon PX and the commissary, a large grocery store. Trips to both were in themselves an adventure; you never knew what you would find or not find. Since these facilities serviced the thousands of Americans, both civilian and military, serving in Saigon, as well as the thousands like us who came there from the outlying areas to shop, entire stocks could be consumed overnight. On one trip to the PX, a shipment of cameras from Japan might have just arrived, setting off a feeding frenzy among shoppers. The next trip it might be stereo components; you just never knew till you got there. It was always like sale day in Macy's bargain basement—no place for the faint of heart! Parking at these small inner-city compounds was a nightmare. Let me rephrase that—just getting near these facilities was a nightmare! Shopping at the commissary was much the same. I recall one time not being able to find the basic canned vegetables that were on our list, but finding a shelf with hundreds of boxes of lemon Jell-O. You just know there was a big demand for that!

In any event, the routine called for hitting the PX first, then the commissary, where the perishables and frozen foods were the last items picked up. We'd pack them in ice, load them in the quarter-ton trailer, and sprint the 75 miles back to Dinh Quan, arriving around suppertime. High on the shopping list each month were steaks and other meats and fresh potatoes for baking. We had an oil drum sliced vertically in half that we had fashioned into a grill. Chunks of locally fired charcoal were available in the local marketplace, so while the steaks and chops lasted, we'd fire up the grill and barbeque away.

Getting the groceries home intact wasn't always an easy chore. On the same trip that SFC Kraft and I had our "drunk in a bar" incident, we had finished shopping, loaded the jeep and trailer, and were winding through the Saigon traffic headed home when Kraft, who was driving, noticed in the his side mirror that two young Vietnamese men on a motorbike were riding beside the trailer and trying to steal bags of our groceries. He shouted at them, and when they abruptly turned away with a pilfered bag of our groceries in hand, Kraft executed a U-turn in the middle of a traffic-laden intersection and lit out in hot pursuit. Wherever they went, Kraft, the jeep, the trailer, and I went—in and out of traffic, up alleys, and across sidewalks—horn blaring! Thanks to Kraft's kamikaze driving skills we were gaining on them. When we had closed to about ten yards, it occurred to me, "What are we going to do when we catch up?" From the look in Kraft's eye, I was sure his plan was to run over them. I wasn't so sure this was the best plan, but before I had time to protest, they suddenly slowed, leaped from the motorbike, dropped the purloined bag of groceries, raced off on foot, and disappeared into the crowd. We skidded to a halt and leaped out, but they were long gone.

A crowd was starting to gather as we collected the giant cans of green beans and other commissary treasures that were scattered on the street. We repacked the trailer, this time tying the canvas cover down securely so intruders could not get at our stash. We stood there for a moment looking at the motorbike lying in the gutter. What a waste, we thought, to leave this abandoned machine lying in the street, and what fun it might be to have such an acquisition for our team in Dinh Quan. Advisors on motorbikes—we might start a whole new approach for the advisory effort. Unfortunately for us, both the back of the jeep and trailer were jam-packed from our recent shopping efforts, so there was no place to put a motorbike. Just as I was trying to figure out how we could strap it to the hood of the jeep, the White Mice (the local police) arrived. We decided to turn the motorbike over to them, but explaining what had happened was another story. Try as we might, we could not communicate the events leading to the abandonment of the bike. Finally, I just gave up and said to the more official looking of the two, "Biet souvenir?" (Do you understand the word "souvenir"?) His face lit up and he nodded affirmatively. With a greatly exaggerated gesture I said, "I (pointing to me) souvenir you (pointing to him)," and rolled the bike over and presented it to him. He was beaming as I shook his hand and saluted. He smartly returned the salute. He saluted once again as Kraft and I jumped back into the jeep and gunned it toward Highway 1 and Dinh Quan. Looking back, I saw him proudly showing it to his fellow policemen. What he did with it I'll never know, but I suspect he took it home to his family, expounding on the generosity of those wealthy Americans and his good fortune at being in the right place at the right time.

PART FIVE

The Battle for
Hearts and Minds

CHAPTER 23

Pacification

Over the course of the last forty years, President John Kennedy's 1960 analysis of the Vietnam War has come to be accepted as conventional wisdom. "In the final analysis, it is their war," he said. "They are the ones who have to win it or lose it. We can help them, we can give them equipment, we can send our men out there as advisors, but they have to win it—the people of Vietnam."

It did not, however, represent the view of the senior American military at the time. They held to the traditional military view that the key to victory was to seek out and destroy the enemy forces. In contrast, those of us sent as advisors quickly recognized that in order to win the war, the South Vietnamese government would first have to win the support and loyalty of the people. This struggle for hearts and minds was the pivotal piece of the entire war, and the instrument for winning this struggle was the pacification program.

As officially defined by MACV, the pacification program was:

> the military, political, economic, and social process of establishing or re-establishing local government responsive to and involving the participation of the people. It includes the provision of sustained, credible territorial security, the destruction of the enemy's underground government, the assertion or reassertion of political control and involvement of the people in government, and the initiation of economic and social activity capable of self-sustenance and expansion. The economic element of pacification includes the opening of roads and waterways and the maintenance of

lines of communications important to economic and military activity.*

In layman's terms, pacification meant extending the influence of the government into the rural areas of Vietnam and winning the support of the people. In order to accomplish that, two components were necessary: physical security and economic development.

As a district senior advisor, I was neck deep in each of those areas. The security component, which provided the necessary umbrella under which all pacification efforts operated, was critical and consumed a great deal of our time and effort. However, without the economic development and improvement in the quality of life that pacification promised, the government could not demonstrate its viability and win the support of the people.

For that reason, in 1967 President Lyndon Johnson created Civil Operations and Revolutionary Development Support (CORDS), an organization to coordinate and oversee the efforts of the multiple military and civilian agencies that were involved in pacification efforts. It brought together as one team the Agency for International Development, the U.S. Information Agency, the State Department, the Central Intelligence Agency, and the U.S. military advisory efforts under the command of Robert Komer, appointed civilian deputy to General Westmoreland.

The CORDS organization extended downward through a deputy for CORDS at each of the four corps headquarters, through a combined civilian-military advisory team at each of the forty-four provinces, and ultimately to an advisory team in each of the nation's 256 districts. The district teams were the action arms of CORDS. We were, so to speak, "where the rubber met the road." Pacification, so critical to the war's ultimate success, was more than the primary mission of province and district advisory teams. Quite simply, it was our *raison d'être*. Surprisingly little has been written about this aspect of the Vietnam experience; yet if the war in Vietnam was to be won, it ultimately had to be won here.

Winning the struggle for the hearts and minds of the people was the core objective of pacification. And while pacification was a Vietnamese

---

* Harry G. Summers, Jr., *Vietnam War Almanac* (New York: Facts on File, 1985), 276.

government program, the United States played a major supporting role through its advice, assistance, and material support. The communists clearly understood that the people were the key to winning the war, but this simple truth was seemingly difficult for many senior American officers to comprehend. Their fixation remained on more traditional combat methods to destroy the enemy. "Grab them by the balls and their hearts and minds will follow," a slogan oft repeated in U.S. units, illustrates the lack of appreciation of this most fundamental aspect of the war and explains the unfortunate secondary role relegated to the advisory effort in Vietnam.

Unfortunately, the upper echelons of the Saigon government, taking their lead from their American counterparts, also placed pacification in a secondary role to the military struggle. This manifested itself in many ways. There was no Vietnamese organizational equivalent of CORDS, thus coordination and control continued to be fragmented; personal political interests and loyalties often determined the scope and depth of Vietnamese commitment; military officers and civilian officials of lesser ability were generally assigned to province and district organizations; little or no action was taken to remove corrupt or inept officials; and lower priorities, thus fewer resources, were assigned to pacification programs.

SHORTLY AFTER MY arrival in Dinh Quan, "The 1969 Accelerated Pacification Campaign" was launched by Prime Minister Tran Van Huong. This campaign defined the areas of concentration and established goals, both nationally and at the province level. The areas of concentration included improving village and hamlet security, strengthening village and hamlet government, neutralizing the Viet Cong Infrastructure (VCI), increasing participation in the People's Self-Defense Force (PSDF), resettling refugees, administering the Chieu-Hoi Program, coordinating information and propaganda programs, and stimulating the rural economy.*

This plan was intended to be more than a mere extension of the earlier Pacification and Development Campaign already in place and

---

* Circular 924 PThT/BDXD/KH, "Phase II Goals of 1969 PD Plan," Office of Prime Minister, Central Pacification and Development Council, Republic of Vietnam, 26 June 1969 (U.S. National Archives).

containing the same eight national objectives. The accelerated plan, by raising the bar, was intended to reflect the urgency of these objectives, as the newly elected Nixon administration had promised the American people that the U.S. presence in Vietnam would be gradually phased out. The threat of American withdrawal served to increase pressure on the Vietnamese and provided advisors a little more leverage in dealing with counterparts. As a result, there were significantly increased efforts at both national and local levels to move forward with the plan's objectives.

The advisory team in Dinh Quan was involved in pacification activities across the spectrum. In addition to our military advisory and training activities, security activities, and intelligence role, team members were involved in assisting in the improvement of the administrative processes of the district government, supporting local elections, providing support and credibility for village and hamlet elected officials, enhancing the image of the district government, and supporting the programs and activities of the Vietnamese national government. We were, in effect, helping in the struggle for the hearts and minds of the local people.

We actively assisted in a broad array of public health programs. For example, we provided training and medical supplies to local medical facilities and assisted with medical emergencies by providing direct medical treatment. We also arranged for evacuation of the seriously injured and requested emergency medical assistance from U.S. units in the province. Although the Vietnamese are by nature a clean people, Dinh Quan was a rural area without the advantages of many of the sanitary and medical measures that Americans take for granted. To assist in this regard, we imported U.S. military doctors to conduct clinics and promoted projects to eliminate insects, enhance sanitation, and improve wells, water drainage, and sewage disposal. Working closely with the local government, we were successful in the establishment of a small but greatly needed district hospital. S/Sgt. Michaels (*Bac-si*) also worked closely with both the new district hospital and the local military hospital providing training, assistance, and medical supplies.

We worked with local officials and U.S. unit commanders to help curb inflation and prevent the monetary instability that could result from the presence of U.S. units in the area. In addition, we worked to sensitize U.S. troops to the Vietnamese culture in efforts to reduce the "ugly American"–type incidents so common when the two cultures mixed.

We helped to get schools repaired, scrounged classroom materials, and visibly supported all educational activities. U.S. units were especially good in this regard. Once we were able to convince a U.S. unit to undertake a project, such as a school repair, they would descend upon the facility with all the necessary manpower, materials, and resources, and almost miraculously a renovated structure would appear. We also made special efforts to involve ourselves in the activities of the schools, participating in ceremonies and visiting frequently. I was recruited by the headmaster to teach English twice a week in the local high school, an experience I always looked forward to and enjoyed.

Team members were heavily involved in a wide variety of economic development programs: constructing village marketplaces, improving farming techniques, providing building materials, borrowing heavy equipment courtesy of our engineer friends, and implementing the many developmental programs sponsored by USAID.

Dinh Quan was a district of refugees and resettled hamlets, so efforts to assist refugees and resettled communities were of ongoing concern. Resettled families were issued bags of cement, sheet metal for roofing, a six-month rice allowance, and 5,000 piasters (roughly $44).

Team members were also involved in several efforts to improve communications, such as placing television sets in the village marketplaces and distributing transistor radios. We were involved in efforts to improve official radio communications by scrounging equipment and batteries, and by providing a secure net on which the district chief was able to communicate and discuss sensitive information with the province chief.

For each of our activities, we were able to get assistance from other U.S. agencies outside the district. In fact, the liaison and coordination that we effected among the many U.S. agencies and the local Vietnamese officials were principal roles of the team. In addition, we promoted liaison visits between the district staff with neighboring districts and U.S. units in the area.

Finally, we were closely involved in the major ongoing efforts to improve transportation in the area. Chief among these was the ongoing project to improve National Highway 20 (QL 20). This reconstruction was unquestionably the most significant project in the district throughout the fourteen months of my tour. QL 20 ran southwest to northeast, dissecting the district into roughly equal halves. The overall project was to straighten, widen, rebuild, and resurface the highway from its origin, its intersection with National Highway 1 near Xuan Loc, to the city of Dalat in the central highlands, a distance of approximately two hundred kilometers. In Dinh Quan District, the project ran from the La Nga River Bridge in the west to the II Corps border in the east (Lam Dong Province, Bao Loc District), a distance of 40 kilometers. A U.S. engineer company (Company D, 169th Engineer Battalion) had a base camp at the La Nga River Bridge from which they ventured out each day to work on the highway in both Kiem Tam District to the west and Dinh Quan. They had a rock crusher operation in Dinh Quan village, and when they were operating the crusher, the small detachment stayed overnight with us in the bunkhouse. The granite boulders that were Dinh Quan's signature landmark were perfect for the highway project. Just one of the boulders, when blasted and crushed, produced enough gravel for 8 miles of a double-lane roadbed. When operations first began in Dinh Quan, the engineers encouraged the Vietnamese to collect rocks and stones of all sizes and pile them alongside the road. Each morning, members of the team would drive by and leave piasters to pay for the rock pile. The larger the pile, the more piasters. Subsequently, an engineer truck would come by, pick up the stones, and haul them to the crusher site, where they would be reduced to gravel. It didn't take the Vietnamese long to figure out this system, and soon the engineers discovered that the large piles of rocks appearing alongside the road and for which they were paying were in some cases large piles of dirt covered over with a layer of rocks. So much for the honor system! After that, the rock piles were probed with a long stick before payments were made.

Another U.S. engineer company was located on Highway 20 in Bao Loc District, which bordered Dinh Quan on the east. This company was to rebuild the highway in Bao Loc and to complete the easternmost portion of the highway in Dinh Quan District, although during my tour they never worked in our district. This company, whose designation I am unable to recall, was a National Guard unit that had been called to active duty and shipped to Vietnam for a one-year assignment. During the last two months of their tour, they ceased work on the highway and concerned themselves only with their own security. They were determined to take no more casualties and to get everyone home safely. For us, those last sixty days were an incredible windfall. They would give us anything that we wanted and could haul away. Supplies, materials or equipment—you want it? You got it!

The section of the highway that ran through the easternmost portion of the district was especially prone to being washed out during the monsoon season by the water cascading down from the bordering highlands. When that occurred, a major effort would be undertaken (normally by the Vietnamese engineer battalion stationed in the province capital) to get the road repaired or at least passable for the hundreds of trucks that ran daily through the district en route to Saigon.

The entire population of Dinh Quan District lived along Highway 20. Earlier resettlement programs had moved the Vietnamese people from remote villages and hamlets in the district to new hamlets constructed alongside the highway. This was an effort to deny the Viet Cong access to the population and to resources (taxes, food, recruits, and supplies) and to improve security along the highway. In addition, Dinh Quan had several new hamlets occupied by refugees resettled from other parts of Vietnam. These new hamlets were likewise located astride QL 20.

As the construction progressed up Highway 20, the underbrush and jungle were cut back from the highway, the road straightened, and the roadbed built up and widened. The surface was crowned to facilitate drainage and then blacktopped. The finished product was a two-lane highway built pretty much to U.S. highway standards at that time.

For Dinh Quan, the highway improvements were a godsend. Security was improved along the highway and vehicle traffic increased. The economic benefits were readily apparent. The village of Dinh Quan was a major stopping place for the trucks shuttling back and forth between Saigon and Dalat. Drivers ate at local restaurants and stayed overnight there, vehicles were repaired there, and the local marketplace benefited by having the fresh fruits and vegetables from the Dalat region available for sale. This project contributed significantly to the improved quality of life of the people of Dinh Quan.

In sum, despite the secondary role it was given, I believe the pacification program was succeeding, both in Dinh Quan and in the other districts across Vietnam. Progress was visible, the quality of life for the people was improving, and every measure showed that the Vietnamese government's influence was being strengthened and expanded further into the countryside. Concurrent efforts to improve security and to eliminate the local Viet Cong infrastructure were likewise succeeding. North Vietnamese documents released after the war reveal that they similarly felt the pacification program was effective. These acknowledged successes ultimately led the North Vietnamese to basically abandon both the Viet Cong and their earlier guerrilla war strategy, and to pursue a conventional war strategy to achieve their ends. The U.S. military withdrawal and the inability of the South Vietnamese armed forces to stem the tide alone resulted in the North Vietnamese victory in 1975.

Buddha—or Lady Luck—smiled down on the author, Maj. Ron Beckett, during his third tour of duty in Vietnam.

The Dinh Quan district headquarters compound was home to the American advisory team house. The compound also housed the District Intelligence Operations Coordination Center (white building in center), the district chief's house (shuttered building on the right), and the district headquarters (white building behind truck). Note the Regional Force outpost atop the rock formation in the background.

Home Sweet Home—the advisors' team house. The small addition on the left housed the radio room and an additional bedroom.

Maj. Ron Beckett with Baron, one of the team's mascots.

Staff Sergeant Joseph *Bac-si* Michels, the team's medical advisor.

Sergeants Cuong
(standing) and Suong,
two of the interpreters
who made it possible for
the advisory team to
accomplish its mission.

The author with his Vietnamese counterpart, Maj. Tran Thanh Xuan.

NINE RULES

1 Remember we are guests here: We make no demands and seek no special treatment.

2 Join with the people! Understand their life, use phrases from their language and honor their customs and laws.

3 Treat women with politeness and respect.

4 Make personal friends among the soldiers and common people.

5 Always give the Vietnamese the right of way.

6 Be alert to security and ready to react with your military skill.

7 Don't attract attention by loud, rude or unusual behavior.

8 Avoid separating yourself from the people by a display of wealth or privilege.

9 Above all else you are members of the U S Military Forces on a difficult mission, responsible for all your official and personal actions. Reflect honor upon yourself and the United States of America.

NINE RULES

FOR PERSONNEL OF US MILITARY ASSISTANCE COMMAND, VIETNAM

The Vietnamese have paid a heavy price in suffering for their long fight against the communists. We military men are in Vietnam now because their government has asked us to help its soldiers and people in winning their struggle. The Viet Cong will attempt to turn the Vietnamese people against you. You can defeat them at every turn by the strength, understanding, and generosity you display with the people. Here are nine simple rules:

DISTRIBUTION — 1 to each member of the United States Armed Forces in Vietnam

The Nine Rules Card, which every American serviceman in Vietnam was required to carry.

RONALD L. BECKETT
MAJOR, INFANTRY
DISTRICT SENIOR ADVISOR

The author's red seal had a magical effect on expediting paperwork through the bureaucracy.

Capt. Bob Hughes celebrates the survival of the roll of toilet paper in the aftermath of SFC Robert Kirkbride's "Outhouse Massacre."

SFC Kirkbride scrambled to construct a new outhouse. Several buildings were damaged by the blast—including the storeroom directly behind him—but the rock slab survived intact.

The new bath house held sinks with hot running water, lights, mirrors, individual storage cubicles, and a real shower—all the comforts of home.

From left to right: Captain Hughes, Lieutenant Wingo, and the author trying to repair one of the team's three generators that supplied all the power for the team house and other buildings in the district compound.

Children from Dinh Quan and the surrounding area attend the local school.

Two local farmers decked out to show off their cow, part of a USAID cooperative project.

Lieutenant Colonel Nhut, commanding officer of the 43rd Regiment, 18th ARVN Division, is seated at the head of the table, with Lieutenant Colonel Bryan, senior advisor to the 43rd Regiment, standing nearby. The regimental command post was located at Dinh Quan during operations.

The author at the 25-meter rifle range built to help train Vietnamese Popular Force troops on the M16 rifles distributed under the Accelerated Pacification Campaign. Note the obvious oversight in not considering proper drainage during monsoon season!

Specialist 4th Class John Houston, the team's radio/telephone operator, with First Lieutenant Dat at the beginning of a local Regional Force Company operation. Dat was the district operations officer.

Capt. Bob Hughes and SFC Robert Kraft with Dinh Quan's Provincial Reconnaissance Unit.

This U20 Beaver was impaled on tree stumps after crashing at the difficult Dinh Quan airstrip.

The burned-out fuselage of the U20 Beaver following the crash. The pilot and four passengers survived the crash and were rescued by advisory team members.

Capt. Bob Hughes being decorated by Maj. Tran Thanh Xuan, the district chief.

CHAPTER 24

USAID

"Twenty-seven Americans were killed today in heavy fighting against North Vietnamese main forces northeast of Saigon. Enemy losses were estimated to be in the hundreds." Such reporting by Walter Cronkite and other television news anchors flooded the evening newscasts playing in homes across America. Unlike previous wars, where success was measured by terrain captured, in the Vietnam war success was measured by body count—an unreliable number, too often inflated by commanders wanting to make themselves look successful. These numbers told little about the progress of the war and nothing about the achievement of U.S. goals in the war. Unfortunately, since the war against the North Vietnamese/Viet Cong being conducted by regular U.S. and Vietnamese armed forces was the overwhelming focus of the news from Vietnam, this statistic became the news. Lost on most Americans was the fact that the major combat operations represented only one prong of the two-pronged strategy designed to win that war.

The second and far less visible prong was the pacification program described in the last chapter. The concept of this program was simple: by improving the lot of the Vietnamese people through enhanced security, economic development, infrastructure improvement, and a heightened sense of community and loyalty to the government, the program would discourage support of the Viet Cong and result in ultimate victory for the South Vietnamese government. Such an undertaking was an incredible challenge. Not only were there frequent setbacks at the hands of the VC, but also far too often the allied military efforts were in direct conflict with efforts on the nation-building side.

A primary player in the pacification effort was the United States Agency for International Development (USAID). Under the CORDS concept, USAID had a major role: it was tasked with the responsibility for the economic development, public health, public administration, and education programs. From my narrow field perspective, it appeared that the career bureaucrats in USAID were in hog heaven. Funds seemed limitless and any program, no matter how outlandish, could attract a sponsor. More programs and projects translated into more staff and larger budgets—empire building was alive and well. I concluded that USAID loved the war in Vietnam. I don't necessarily mean they loved the war itself, but they sure loved the opportunities it offered. And they especially loved Dinh Quan District.

When I was in graduate school at the University of Alabama, I took a course on U.S. politics in which we learned that demographers had identified Cuyahoga County, Ohio (the greater Cleveland area), as sort of "America in microcosm." It mirrored in remarkable detail the overall ethnic, social, and financial makeup of the entire nation. Therefore, television programs and marketing campaigns that were successful in Cuyahoga County could be counted upon to be equally successful across the country. Political pollsters trying to get a feel for the pulse of America in the 1940s, 1950s, and 1960s could always rely on this small slice of Ohio. "So goes Cuyahoga County, so goes the USA," was the conventional wisdom of the time.

In similar fashion, demographers had discovered that Dinh Quan District markedly mirrored the rest of South Vietnam. Dinh Quan had the right proportion of Catholics, Protestants, and Buddhists; of Vietnamese, Chinese, and Montagnards; of rice farmers, small merchants, and other workers, and it was all very accessible since it sat astride National Highway 20. It was rural in outlook and relatively backward in development. It was Vietnam in miniature, and so it seemed to follow that whatever would work in Dinh Quan would work in all of Vietnam. Having made such a discovery, the game was afoot.

During my tenure as senior advisor in Dinh Quan, we were visited by scores of "experts" from Washington and Saigon. They all had programs they were promoting or ideas they were certain would fuel development efforts. These ran the gamut from political to health to economic development. Most of these ideas were sound, well-conceived, and based on the needs of the Vietnamese. They generally proved to be successful and, in fact, contributed to the development and the well-being of the citizens of Dinh Quan. Some programs, though well intentioned, failed to consider the Vietnamese culture and values and therefore proved to be abysmal failures. Others simply were ill-conceived or, as it seemed to those of us charged with implementing them, harebrained! I always found it suspect that though we offered hospitable, albeit Spartan, accommodations, few of these folks spent the night. They invariably scurried back to the comfort and security of Saigon before nightfall.

I don't wish to paint USAID as simply an organization of careerists and opportunists who dashed in, dumped their latest empire-building creation, and dashed out. It was not, but some of the programs suggested to us by these junket bureaucrats seemed to reinforce our worst suspicions in that regard. In stark contrast were the USAID personnel in the field. They were hard-working, dedicated professionals. Based in Saigon or in the provincial capitals around the country, they visited frequently, were responsive to our requests for assistance, stayed with us for days at a time, shared our lifestyle, and worked with us and the Vietnamese to implement and oversee the various development projects. They were welcome guests and considered members of our team. I wish I could recall all their names and give them the appropriate credit for their numerous contributions to our development efforts. Unfortunately, time has not been kind to me in that regard.

However, there is one character from that bunch that no passage of time could make me forget—George Laudato. George was a career officer with USAID who had served on several continents in some pretty unglamorous locations. He was a dedicated professional who could always be relied upon for support and who had earned the admiration and respect of both the advisors and the Vietnamese. George was in his thirties, short in stature, outgoing, and had a terrific sense of humor. (He always reminded me of sort of a senior elf.) George made major contributions in helping to put into place a number of reforms and successful programs in Dinh Quan and other areas of the province. He also shared our frustrations as we struggled to implement and manage some of the ill-fated programs cited in the following chapters.

George's popularity with the team was enhanced by the fact that he shared a villa in Saigon with several other USAID colleagues, and the welcome mat was always out for members of our team who managed to get into Saigon. For those of us living in "the boonies," a trip to George's was akin to the country mice visiting the city. Life there was good—delicious food, all the creature comforts, good company, and the use of the villa as a base while enjoying the offerings of Saigon: restaurants, entertainment, shopping, and other diversions.

George and his friends had mastered the intricacies of the Saigon black market. Whatever the requirement, for a price anything was possible, whether it was currency exchange, repair parts, or military equipment. On one occasion we were trying desperately to get some sandbags through the normal supply channels, but none were available anywhere. We had even attempted to barter with some nearby U.S. units, but they were likewise having difficulty getting them. We were assured by everyone that there was a theater-wide shortage. Through the black market contacts, as I recall, they were delivered within an hour. U.S. logisticians could have learned some lessons from those guys!

When the war ended, Laudato was kind enough to assist me in my efforts to locate Major Xuan and his family. Refugee camps had been established in Thailand, the Philippines, and Guam. These camps processed the refugees, assisted them through the red tape of the immigration procedures, and helped them resettle in the continental United States. I had advised George that I would be willing to sponsor Major Xuan and his family should they come through the program. He advised his colleagues operating the camps in Thailand and Guam to be on the lookout for Xuan, but despite our combined best efforts, we were never able to locate him.

I maintained contact with George for a number of years after the war, but unfortunately, like too many of the folks you meet during a service career, you lose contact due to the frequent moves. He visited my family and me when we lived in Wilmington, Delaware, in the early seventies; my daughter, Natasha, loved him. We lost contact with George sometime after he was posted to Egypt, but my memory of him is irrevocably bound to a sense that George represented the best of USAID.

While we experienced a great deal of success in Dinh Quan in implementing programs that enhanced economic development and the well-being of the people, we also experienced some singularly memorable failures. Some of these have earned their place in my collection of unbelievable but true tales.

CHAPTER 25

Chicken Man

"Goooooooood morning, Vietnam!" blared the voice on the radio. It was another morning in Vietnam, and Armed Forces Radio was on the air. The Armed Forces Radio and Television Network was the single most popular entertainment medium in Vietnam. In the eighties it would be popularized in this country by Robin Williams's movie *Good Morning, Vietnam.* During the 1960s and early 1970s, AFVN broadcast twenty-four hours a day, could be received anywhere in Vietnam, played the most popular music, and was the source of the latest news. It seemed every GI in Vietnam had a small portable radio, so wherever you went, the familiar voices of AFVN could be heard. Armed Forces Radio was also popular with the Vietnamese, not only for the latest U.S. music, but also because listening to it was an excellent way to learn English. And being able to speak English meant having the ability to communicate with Americans and opportunities to work in high-paying American jobs.

During 1969–70, AFVN carried a serial of sorts dramatizing the daily adventures of a fictionalized superhero by the name of "Chicken Man." Chicken Man was a giant chicken capable of thinking, speaking, and, within his "chickenly" limitations, physically acting as a human being. Much like Superman, Captain Marvel, Batman and Robin, Spiderman, and all the superheroes who preceded him, he fought corruption and evil wherever he found it. Unfortunately, his style and abilities more closely resembled Inspector Clouseau of the *Pink Panther* movies than the other superheroes. His exploits were hysterical and legendary. The troops loved him, and I, likewise, was among his dedicated listeners.

In the spring of 1969, I unwittingly became the Chicken Man of Dinh Quan. As with many of the real Chicken Man's adventures, it all started innocently enough. One morning a helicopter arrived with a contingent of USAID officials from Washington and Saigon. They had come to share with me in most excited terms their latest project for economic development. They wanted to pilot their project in Dinh Quan and then, when it proved to be a success (as they were sure it would), the program would be expanded nationwide.

The objective of this latest scheme was to develop a thriving new industry in Vietnam—a chicken industry. Frank Perdue I am not, so I found it difficult to share the same level of enthusiasm and confidence exhibited by my highly paid visitors. Their plan was simple. The generous citizens of the United States, through our government, would deliver approximately 2,000 baby chicks into the care of the farmers of Dinh Quan. In addition, chicken food and instructions for raising the chickens would be provided at no cost. All the farmers had to do was agree to not eat, sell, or trade the chicks until they had reached maturity; then they could dispose of a percentage of their flock, keeping the remainder to produce the next generation. This would provide food for their tables and profit from sales, but most importantly it would produce a class of chicken entrepreneurs that would add to the economic well-being of the country.

My role was to ensure proper distribution of the chickens, supply appropriate quantities of chicken feed, oversee raising of the chickens, ensure compliance with the rules, and provide frequent status reports to "Chicken Central" in Saigon. Simple enough, you say? Unfortunately, not.

First, I remind you that Dinh Quan District covered more than 1,200 square miles, contained more than 16,000 people in fourteen separate villages and hamlets, and was located smack dab in the middle of a war. In fact, as I've mentioned, the northern third of the district composed the southern portion of the infamous War Zone D. The large intelligence map that adorned the wall of our radio room ran red with grease pencil symbols representing the vast numbers of VC and North Vietnamese Army (NVA) units that were reported to be moving across or located in our district. The Dinh Quan Advisory Team, on the other hand, consisted of seven lightly armed Americans, two interpreters, two dogs and several one-lunged jeeps. It would have been difficult to meet these administrative requirements if we had been living in Alabama—in Dinh Quan it was damn near impossible!

Nonetheless, late one afternoon a small convoy pulled into the compound. Its cargo was hundreds of baby chicks and several tons of chicken feed. To the dismay of the onlooking Vietnamese, scores of the chicks had not survived the long flight from the eastern U.S. and the subsequent heat, lack of ventilation, and rough handling that greeted them in Vietnam. Their little dead bodies were sorted and toted away.

I confess that after all these years, my memory is a little fuzzy regarding exact numbers, but to the best of my recollection, the U.S. distribution plan, carefully thought out in Washington, was to provide twenty-five to fifty chicks to each of fifty farmers. The farmers would have to volunteer to participate and agree to abide by a number of rules regarding the care and disposition of the chickens. Those selected were supposed to represent some equitable distribution pattern among the district population. Everyone agreed that the American plan was generous, fair, and well-conceived. We weren't in America however, we were in Vietnam—a different culture with a different set of rules. The Vietnamese distribution plan, and the only one that was going to be followed, was to allow the district, village, and hamlet chiefs to decide who got the chickens and how many they received. When all the dust settled there were roughly seventy families, each with ten to forty chicks, depending on the family's blood ties to officials, influence in the village, loyalty, and support of the existing governing structure. It was a not-so-subtle reminder that the concept of patronage is neither a creation, nor the unique possession, of American politicians.

USAID had tasked us to report weekly on the progress of our chicken industry. The forms we were to use required individual inventories for each of the participating families. Additionally, we were to account for any missing chickens—X number died, Y taken by the VC, Z mysteriously disappeared, and so on. Some of the outlandish excuses we were provided to account for missing chickens rivaled those offered by schoolchildren who failed to do their homework—even including, "my dog ate it"!

The participating families were spread over the length of the district, and, unfortunately, in many instances we weren't even certain who they were. In order to try to gather the necessary information, team members had to break up and operate singly or in pairs. As a rule, we made every effort to avoid operating alone outside the immediate village of Dinh Quan. It was just too dangerous. It was, in fact, dangerous in most parts of the district to even be operating in pairs, yet we had no choice if we were to effectively do our jobs, chickens notwithstanding. U.S. units in our area required vehicles to travel in convoys with heavy security before they were permitted on Highway 20. They would see us running about in a single jeep, no helmets, no flak jackets, and armed only with pistols and rifles, and shake their heads in utter disbelief. Despite the fact that the reporting requirements put us in physical danger, threatened our sanity, and drove the Vietnamese wild, we gave it our best shot. The reports in the first two weeks were diligently prepared and sent on their way to Saigon to be examined and then passed on to USAID in Washington. I could just envision the proud smiles on the faces of those bureaucrats who had created this program as they reviewed the reports.

Sometime early in the fourth week, the chickens started mysteriously dying. As we would roll up to count the flock, we would be greeted by an excited farmer who would describe in animated detail what had happened to some of the young chickens—often demonstrating the quivering and shaking motions that preceded the deaths of his birds. The chickens would go into convulsions, shake violently, roll over on their backs, quiver, and die. Unknown to us at the time, some sort of deadly virus was attacking the birds. Casualties at first numbered in the scores; by week's end hundreds were dead. I urgently radioed the situation to province headquarters, and they in turn sent the alarm up the chain of command. Thereafter we were pestered on what seemed an hourly basis for the latest "body count." As expected, we were soon invaded by a hoard of experts. They poked and prodded, interrogated the farmers, examined the chicken feed, and questioned us at length. Finally, we were directed to gather up a number of little chicken corpses, pack them in dry ice, and ship them off to Washington for analysis. Through it all the body count continued to mount, and within another week, all 2,000 chickens were dead.

I wasn't prepared for the startling reaction of the Vietnamese. It was neither sorrow nor disappointment as you would expect, but sheer anger. They vehemently blamed us for giving them inferior chickens. They had cared for these birds, worked hard, sacrificed, played by our rules, and for what? The chickens had died. Forget the fact that we had supplied the chickens and the chicken feed, and the program had not cost them a single *xu* (a Vietnamese coin worth less than a penny); they were convinced they had been cheated!

After several weeks, we received word from Washington that the American-bred chickens had fallen prey to some rare strain of Asian poultry virus for which the U.S. birds had no natural immunities. This was a prospect none of the experts had considered.

Months later, USAID attempted another chicken project, this time on a much smaller scale with no fanfare, and this time using a tougher breed of chicks from Taiwan. The earlier failure, however, had dampened enthusiasm among both the Americans and the Vietnamese. In addition, these birds were not nearly as desirable, as they were much skinnier and tougher. The participating families simply ate them or sold them with no effort to perpetuate the flock.

Thus the great Dinh Quan chicken caper quietly faded into memory. For members of the team, however, it was difficult to eat a piece of fried chicken or listen to the radio episodes of Chicken Man for weeks after without breaking up. Years later, while driving near Philadelphia, I experienced a brief flashback when I heard a replay of one of the Chicken Man tapes with its signature cry of "bak-BAK! bak-BAK!" on a local radio station. Instinctively, I turned in at the nearest Kentucky Fried Chicken.

CHAPTER 26

Miracle Rice

The diversity of the American diet makes it is difficult for us to understand and appreciate the importance of rice in Vietnamese culture. Not only is rice the very heart and soul of their diet, it has religious significance as well. It is the main staple of every meal, estimated to make up 60 percent of the Vietnamese diet. In fact, many meals in rural Vietnam consisted of rice, nuoc mam (a fermented fish sauce), and perhaps a few vegetables. Vietnamese soldiers going into the field carried cooked rice balls stuffed into socks and tied to their backpacks.

Vietnam has always been one of the world's largest rice producers. Even during the war, when a great deal of arable land went untended, Vietnam still ranked among the world's top ten rice-producing nations, raising more than 16 million tons. However, despite its ranking, Vietnam was unable to produce sufficient rice to feed even its own population during the war years.

Rice-growing techniques in Vietnam had not significantly changed in centuries. It was traditional, primitive, and back-breaking work. Throughout Vietnam only a few tractors were used for rice farming. There were no tractors in Dinh Quan District—not surprising since the farmers were generally poor and could not afford them—and the farms were very small and separated by built-up dikes that made it difficult for tractors to operate effectively. In Dinh Quan, as with most of rural Vietnam, the water buffalo was the beast of burden. It was used to pull a wooden plow-like implement that turned the soil and prepared it for seeding. The water was drained, and the rice seeds were spread over the muddy paddy. Once the seeds had taken root, the paddy was reflooded and the plants allowed to grow.

After growing for about a month, the seedlings were removed by hand and replanted in flooded paddies. Throughout the growing season, the entire family worked to help weed and fertilize the crop. At harvest, the rice plants had grown to about waist-high, bending slightly under the weight of the rice kernels. When the plants were mature, the paddies were drained and the plants were cut and threshed, a process that physically knocked the rice grain off the plant. The harvest, like the planting, was hard work, again done by hand. The plant itself was used for animal fodder, woven into mats, and sometimes made into rice wine. Little was wasted.

Due to the central role that rice played in Vietnamese life and the fact that the Vietnamese were unable to produce sufficient rice to meet their own internal requirements, it was inevitable that the folks at USAID would become involved. In 1969, IR8, a hybrid strain of rice noted for its extremely high yields, was introduced into Vietnam. IR8, also known as "miracle rice," was developed by the International Rice Research Institute. The program was introduced in several areas of the country, including Dinh Quan. I have read Thomas Hargrove's *A Dragon Lives Forever*, his account of the successes of the IR8 program in Chuong Thien Province in the Mekong Delta. Unfortunately, the IR8 experience in Dinh Quan was markedly different.

In Dinh Quan, the miracle rice project was announced with the usual fanfare. From my perspective, this program seemed to make a lot more sense than many of the others we had experienced. This new strain of rice would produce far greater yield per hectare, allowing farmers not only to provide amply for their family's rice needs, but also to profit. The participating families were carefully selected and trained on how to grow their crops to maximum yield. There was a great deal of interest across the district in the daily progress of this program, and everyone watched carefully as the crop was planted, transplanted, and allowed to mature. The results were incredible. Paddies yielded 150 to 200 percent more grain than with previous strains of rice. People were astounded at the bumper harvest produced by the miracle rice program.

Just when it looked as if the USAID folks had finally scored with a big one, the bottom fell out. The Vietnamese didn't like the rice; they found it to be too coarse and to have an undesirable taste. They judged it to be inferior and wouldn't eat it, and no one wanted to buy it. Our intelligence sources even advised us that the VC tax collectors would not take it. Perhaps to Western taste buds there was little difference in the quality of the rice, but the Vietnamese, much as wine connoisseurs distinguish among fine wines, identified differences that were distinct and significant. Ultimately, the rice was fed to the animals, and the following season local paddies were returned to traditional rice crops.

Like many other well-meaning projects before it, the IR8 program in Dinh Quan failed, but not in its promised yield—in fact that had exceeded all expectations. The project itself failed because it did not meet the taste requirements of the local Vietnamese. Had there been famine and hunger, I am sure people would have gladly eaten the IR8, but in Dinh Quan food was not scarce, and given a choice, the people rejected it.

I have learned that subsequent varieties of miracle rice were able to maintain the high yields with vastly improved quality and taste. These new varieties will surely play an increasingly important role in the race to keep up with and feed the burgeoning populations of many third-world countries. Though the experiment in Dihn Quan was a disappointment, I like to believe that the lessons learned there and in other parts of Vietnam contributed to these later successes.

CHAPTER 27

This Little Piggy Went to Market

It wasn't long after the Dinh Quan chicken program fiasco that someone came up with an equally brilliant plan involving raising hogs. Again Dinh Quan was chosen to be a test site, and once again the entourage of experts appeared on our doorstep.

This time the concept was an economic development project intended to foster a sense of cooperation and community among Vietnamese families. In doing so, this project would address a major Vietnamese social and cultural characteristic that was a principal obstacle to efforts to build a cohesive nation. This obstacle, discussed in an earlier chapter, was the typical Vietnamese's deep-seated xenophobia, a suspicion and mistrust of those outside their own family—especially strangers. The focus of the Vietnamese nuclear family was inward; help and support was to be found within the family, not outside. Families were suspicious of their neighbors and especially suspicious of their government. The more rural the environment, the stronger this suspicion. In Dinh Quan the problem was compounded by the fact that most of the families there were relatively new to the area, having been resettled from other locations within the past few years. If they were suspicious of their neighbors, you can imagine their attitude toward these strange programs being promoted by "foreigners."

However, if Vietnam was to survive the war, shake off its colonial dependencies, and become a viable democratic nation, it would have to find ways to overcome this fatal obstacle and build in its people trust and loyalty to their community and to their government. The hog project and a similar cow project were being championed as having the potential to become one of the major programs that could be implemented nationwide to assist in developing this new spirit of trust and cooperation. Pretty heady expectations!

The hog project was basic and the implementation simple. Pigs were to be given to selected groups of families for joint ownership. The families would share the responsibility for raising the animals and the meat and profits that the animals would generate. A specified portion of the profits would be used to acquire new piglets, the rest would be pocketed by the participants, and the cycle would then repeat itself. This mutual interest and responsibility would ideally foster cooperation and become the foundation for nation-building. Additionally, this program would contribute to economic development. It certainly appeared to be a win-win undertaking for all concerned.

Using a process similar to that used in the chicken project, the families were selected by the district, village, and hamlet chiefs. Agreements were drawn up, spelling out in great detail the rights, rules, and responsibilities for the participating families. Pigs could not be butchered or sold until maturity, and participating families would share equally both the profits and the responsibilities.

In a number of hamlets, three or four families whose homes were adjacent were grouped and assigned joint responsibility for two or three pigs. Pens were built on carefully selected sites that gave participating families equal access. The interfamily squabbling that accompanied the site selection for the pens should have alerted us to the problems ahead, but somehow, it didn't.

Tons of feed were imported at U.S. expense and stockpiled in the district warehouse to be provided free to the families as required. USAID field agents worked diligently with the families, instructing them on the care and feeding of swine. Again, as in the chicken project, participation did not cost the families anything but their time and effort.

The scope of the hog project was considerably smaller than that of the chickens, so management and reporting from our team's perspective was much simpler. In all, there were roughly fifty to sixty pigs shared among approximately forty families. At our insistence, the families were selected from villages and hamlets nearer to the district capital of Dinh Quan. Thus for our advisory team, oversight was easier and a lot safer.

The big day finally arrived, and several trucks rolled up carrying their squirming, squealing cargo along with the initial supply of feed. The pigs and feed were issued, and after a great deal of controversy, schedules were developed assigning responsibilities among the families. In general, each family was to be responsible for the care and feeding of the animals for a week at a time. Responsibility was to rotate among cooperating families with the changeover being at sun-up every Monday morning.

The following Monday morning—and every Monday morning thereafter for the next four months—there was a line of farmers outside the interpreters' office, which was an attachment to our team house. They were there to complain to the *Thieu-ta* (major), which was me, about the horrible mistreatment being foisted upon the pigs by their lazy, incompetent, and totally unreliable neighbors. Much of the criticism dealt not with actual mistreatment, but anticipated mistreatment! It became a comedic routine, every family ratting out the other families every week. There were frequent reports of actual fights between families, and the local police even had to intervene on several occasions. The Vietnamese officials, from the district chief down, were inundated with complaints. Instead of building cooperation among families and fostering a sense of community, exactly the opposite was happening. What little harmony had previously existed between neighbors was being rapidly destroyed as a result of this well-meaning program.

All efforts to mediate the disputes or to find a solution to the dilemma failed. Nothing seemed to work. Again the experts came to assess the situation and offer their advice. Despite the handwringing, the experts had no better solutions to the problem than we did. There was general dismay all around as the realization finally sank in that the project was not only a failure, but also doing a great deal of harm. Grudgingly came the capitulation; in order to prevent further mayhem, it was decided to dismantle the hog project.

In the days that followed, settlements were negotiated with each group of families. The settlements ended the program and attempted to equitably distribute the pigs or the profit from the sale of the pigs among the participating families. Needless to say, in that environment, negotiations were difficult. In some instances, the district chief had to impose a settlement. Such was the ignominious end of the Dinh Quan hog industry.

The similar cow project, which came later and tried to incorporate lessons learned from the pig failure, fared only slightly better and was likewise abandoned after the first year.

These projects were a disappointing setback for the suits in Washington; well-intentioned programs that looked good from their distant perspective had completely failed to consider the social and cultural realities of rural Vietnam. It was a lesson that was demonstrated again and again during the Vietnam War, but somehow never quite sank in. American ego or ethnocentrism—however you wish to describe it—just wouldn't allow us to come to grips with the fact that the American way wasn't always the best way for succeeding with other peoples and other cultures. It cost us bitterly in Vietnam, and it's a lesson that we still seem not to have learned.

As for me, the intervening years have softened my frustration and disappointment, but I truthfully cannot watch a Porky Pig cartoon without a flashback to 1970 and the Monday morning lineup.

CHAPTER 28

TV Comes to Dinh Quan

There it was, a black-and-white Sylvania with a whopping 17-inch screen! By July 1969, I had hoarded sufficient team funds to acquire a television set for the team house. When it came time for the next shopping trip to Saigon, Captain Backlin was entrusted with the money and told to bring back a television set from the PX. It arrived with great ceremony, and we immediately mounted it high on the wall in the living/dining room area. We stuck an antenna on the roof and sat back to enjoy our new convenience. Since we were 75 miles from the transmitter in Saigon, our reception left a great deal to be desired. I knew that airborne transmitters mounted in fixed-wing aircraft provided coverage for many parts of Vietnam; I was never sure of the source of our signal, but whatever it was, reception was fuzzy at best.

There were only two channels: the Vietnamese National Channel and Armed Forces Television. Both operated only during limited hours each day. The Vietnamese channel was government-controlled and, as you might expect, highly propagandized. The American channel wasn't much better. We could find the military-censored version of the news, some sports reruns, and the weather (which was either hot or rainy and hot, depending on whether or not it was monsoon season) sprinkled among reruns of old U.S. sitcoms and game shows.

As it turned out, the TV wasn't such a big hit with the team after all. The quality of the programming, the poor reception, and the TV's prime-time competition, our 16 mm movies, all combined to reduce its attractiveness. The daytime preference was the Armed Forces Radio Network with its lively DJs and steady stream of the latest American music.

The big impact of television came later, and it wasn't on the team members. In January 1970, under the auspices of the Revolutionary Development Program, I was approached about the possibility of locating a television set in the central marketplace so that the local Vietnamese could have access. After consulting with the district chief, and he, in turn, with the local village chief, it was decided that the village of Dinh Quan would be the recipient of this first public television set. Subsequently, television sets would be provided to the other villages in the district. When the word got out among the villagers that television was coming, it caused quite a stir of excitement and anticipation.

A large pole, approximately six feet high, was erected on the north side of the marketplace, and atop the pole was constructed a large wooden cabinet. The television set, a black-and-white 21-inch model, arrived and was ceremoniously placed in the cabinet. The antenna was placed atop an even taller pole behind the television set. Power was supplied by a small generator housed in a nearby shed.

Control of the TV set was jealously guarded. Although there was only one Vietnamese channel, no one other than the village chief or his personal designee was allowed to touch the controls on the set. The TV station in Saigon only transmitted at certain times of the day, primarily in the early evening hours. Thus, every evening after supper, the villagers would gather around, hunkered down in their peculiar style, to await the arrival of the village chief, who would unlock the cabinet, swing the double doors wide open, turn on the set, and carefully adjust and readjust every control until he was satisfied that it was just right. Sometimes the unveiling of the TV would be preceded by a short speech of some sort. Promptly at 10:00 P.M., the ceremony was reversed: the TV was turned off, the doors closed, and the box carefully locked.

The village TV set suffered from the same marginal reception as did the team's set due to our distance from Saigon. As a result, the picture would sometimes have ghost images, at other times fade in and out, and frequently the picture would start to roll. These technical problems would be accompanied by grunts of discontentment among the viewers and always spurred the designated controller into frantic action to correct the problem.

If Armed Forces Television programming was bad, the Vietnamese National Channel was ten times worse. Vietnamese music, patriotic stories and songs, megadoses of propaganda extolling the virtues of the Saigon government and its programs, messages exhorting the populace to resist the Viet Cong, and highly filtered news were the staple of each evening. Hardly the stuff of which Emmys are made, but for the villagers in a very rural area of Vietnam it was entertainment, and at that time it was the only show in town.

The village TV was an instant success; however, like every other new gizmo, after a while the novelty began to wear off. In addition, the painfully boring programming took its toll. The evening crowds started to dwindle somewhat. Early on, each evening brought out a hundred or more villagers, but after a couple of months, that figure was more like twenty to thirty each evening. I also noticed that the village chief showed up less and less often to turn on the set. That honor was now the responsibility of his designee.

A final and significant factor that contributed to the decline in attendance was that we, by this time, had erected our outdoor movie screen beside the team house and were showing first-run Hollywood movies every night. The growth in our attendance closely paralleled the loss in the marketplace. Somehow a Vietnamese farmer riding a tractor and singing patriotic songs on a fuzzy 21-inch black-and-white TV screen could not compete with Clint Eastwood blazing away in living color on our 60-square-foot screen!

CHAPTER 29

Security Operations

The annihilation of enemy main forces, the isolation of the VC cadre and militia from the people and resources (recruits, taxes, foodstuffs, and supplies), and the identification and elimination of the Viet Cong infrastructure through the Phoenix Program constituted the military strategy that was to provide the essential security umbrella under which the pacification program would work.

The role of engaging the main force units fell to U.S. and ARVN units, although in 1969–70 the brunt of the effort was being undertaken by large-scale U.S. operations. American strength in Vietnam was at its peak, and the military pressure on the enemy main force units was having the intended effect.

In Long Khanh Province, the major territorial security task lay with the ARVN 18th Division and the U.S. 199th Light Infantry Brigade. Their mission was to keep the NVA and major Viet Cong units at bay, permitting the Regional Force and Popular Force units to deal with the local guerrilla units. In Dinh Quan, this worked well. The 199th had established several firebases in the province from which they mounted operations against the main force units. During the latter half of my tour, the 4th Battalion of the 12th Infantry, 199th Brigade, constructed a firebase in Dinh Quan District about a half mile northeast of the village of Dinh Quan. They operated continuously to our north in War Zone D. On occasion, other U.S. and Vietnamese units also operated in the region. During my tenure, the U.S. 1st Air Cavalry Division, the U.S. 11th Armored Cavalry Regiment, and the elite Vietnamese Airborne Division all conducted operations in the district.

The Vietnamese 18th Infantry Division was likewise active in security operations in Long Khanh Province. Dinh Quan District was the area of operations (AO) for the 43rd Regiment of that division. The 18th Division had originally been formed as the 10th ARVN Division, but was redesignated the 18th Division, due to the stigma associated with being "number ten." The number ten signified the worst of anything to the Vietnamese, with the number one being the best. (Kids in Saigon seeking handouts from American soldiers quickly learned that "VC numbah 10, GI numbah 1" provided an effective entrée into the GIs' pockets.) Despite its redesignation, the 18th Division continued to have a poor reputation primarily due to the inept but politically favored generals appointed to command it. My experiences, however, working with the division's regimental and battalion commanders were by and large favorable. The 43rd Regiment, commanded by Lieutenant Colonel Nhut, was a particularly well-led and effective unit. In the bitter last days of the war, the 18th Division (then under new leadership) was to distinguish itself by defeating four North Vietnamese mainline divisions before finally being overwhelmed in its heroic last stand at Xuan Loc.

Local security in the district was provided by the Regional Force (RF) and Popular Force (PF) units in the area, the "Ruff-Puffs." The regional forces, sort of a National Guard equivalent, served only in their home province. They were generally less effective than the ARVN units, lacking in equipment, training, and leadership. They also were generally less aggressive in their military operations.

The Popular Force platoons recruited from Dinh Quan's hamlets and villages were even less effective. Equipped only with World War II vintage small arms and receiving only minimum training, their role was to provide local security to their hamlets and villages.

Finally there was the People's Self-Defense Force (PSDF). These ragtag units made up of old men and young kids were to provide internal security, supplementing the role of the Popular Force units. They were poorly armed and trained—many of these individuals did not even have weapons. The primary contribution of these units was their enfranchising role, making their members and their families part of the official structure, thus strengthening the hamlet's and village's ties to the national government. As you might expect, their military effectiveness was nearly nonexistent; however, they were a good source of intelligence on VC activities in their respective hamlets.

At each succeeding level, the quality of the leadership, training, weapons, and equipment dropped significantly. The role of these local forces was to provide security within their specific areas of operations and to deny VC cadre and militia access to the people and vital resources. These local forces were also frequently the targets of Viet Cong attacks, and as such, suffered considerable numbers of casualties.

Only once during my fourteen months was there a major NVA/Viet Cong attack upon installations or hamlets within the district. In May, shortly after my arrival, a Viet Cong main battalion attacked Artillery Hill, a fortified hilltop position containing two sections of a Vietnamese 105mm artillery battery and the 177th Regional Force Company. The attack overran the hill, destroying the artillery pieces, but at a great cost to the attackers, as they were illuminated by the parachute flares and subjected to the deadly fire of the Gatling guns of the "spookies," airborne gun platforms mounted in C-130 aircraft. We retook the hill at daybreak the following morning in what was to be my first tactical operation as an advisor. The artillery pieces were soon replaced, and thereafter for the next three months we had two members of the team atop the hill each night. We later learned that the attack was a diversion to neutralize the artillery and cover the movement of the NVA's 9th Division as it crossed Highway 20 farther west in the district.

One other major battle did occur, but it didn't involve any local units. The 18th ARVN Division and elements of the Vietnamese Airborne Division had a meeting engagement with elements of this same NVA division about five kilometers southwest of Dinh Quan village. The early evening contact developed into a major battle astride Highway 20 until the NVA broke contact in the early morning hours. These major engagements so near our location served as a clear reminder of the vulnerability our close proximity to War Zone D created. We were fortunate, however, that while main force VC and NVA units traversed our district en route to other locations, they chose not to come after us.

Locally, within the district, were the 60th Regional Force Inner-Group headquarters (sort of a mobile battalion headquarters commanding several RF companies), five regional force companies, and nine popular force platoons, as well as the village self-defense forces. In addition, a Vietnamese 105mm howitzer battery (six guns) from the 18th Division was located in the district—the four guns atop Artillery Hill and two guns located about fifteen kilometers to the east. My team was augmented by four mobile advisory teams (MAT), five-man teams assigned to train and assist the RF units. These teams lived in small defensive compounds alongside their Vietnamese counterparts, in conditions that were both primitive and dangerous. As the district senior advisor, I was responsible for these teams, so to the extent possible we tried to integrate them into our team. We visited them frequently, provided support and assistance, included them in our communication network, and developed contingency plans to assist in the event they came under attack. They were also frequent visitors, coming to partake of the splendors of our team house. We assisted them materially as best we could.

The MAT teams made us realize that opulence is a relative thing. Those of us in Dinh Quan perceived life in Saigon or Long Binh as the ultimate in decadent living—physical security, air conditioning, movies, clubs, pools, bowling alleys, miniature golf courses, fresh food, and all the material goods and pleasures one could hope for. Not far behind were the living conditions at province headquarters in Xuan Loc. But to the MAT teams, our living conditions, Spartan as they were, were next to heaven compared to theirs.

The district advisory team played a major role in all aspects of security and local military operations. First was our training role. Though training of local forces was the responsibility of the Vietnamese, team members, as well as our attached MAT teams, had a significant assisting role. We participated in classes from rudimentary first aid to weapons training to small-unit tactics. We steered clear, however, of the obligatory political, or propaganda, classes that were part of the Vietnamese training regimen.

Of particular note in our training efforts was our rifle range. Two converging concerns led me to approach Major Xuan about building a rifle range on the outskirts of the village adjacent to the helicopter landing pad: first, as a result of the Accelerated Pacification Campaign, we were starting to receive M16 rifles for our PF units; and second, we had noted that in a number of small engagements at close range, the VC had apparently escaped without casualties—a testament to the sad state of the local marksmanship. Poor marksmanship should not have been a surprise. Local units received little training; ammunition was scarce, so practice was nonexistent; and the size and weight of their weapons, which were designed for the American soldier, were poorly suited for the shorter, smaller Vietnamese. In many cases a soldier who properly placed the butt of an M1 or M14 rifle in the hollow of his shoulder was unable to reach the trigger due to the length of the stock. The under-the-arm adaptation used by most eliminated effective use of the weapon's sights and wreaked havoc with any accuracy.

My plan was simple. We would call upon our engineer friends to bulldoze the area, creating an earthen berm for firing platforms and a large berm backstop behind the target area to stop the rounds from projecting out into the adjacent rice paddies. We could construct the target frames ourselves and get targets through supply channels. We would undertake to scrounge ammunition from U.S. units, and we could operate the range and conduct the training. PF units receiving the M16 rifles would rotate through; receive training on care, maintenance, and operation of the weapon; receive marksmanship training, and get real practice on a 25-meter range. We could also cycle the RF companies through for refresher training.

Major Xuan jumped at the plan. It not only helped him solve a major problem, but he could happily report to the province chief his plans to distribute the M16s and describe how he was going to provide the training. He included some Vietnamese cadre on the team of trainers, authorized the construction of the range, and had his S-3, Lieutenant Dat, establish the training schedule. The engineers came, surveyed the site to ensure correct distances, and brought in their equipment. In less than a day the rough work on the range was completed. We scrounged the targets and built and installed the target frames. From somewhere, SFC Kirkbride produced a large red range flag to fly from a pole when the range was in operation, warning passersby and farmers in the paddies to stay out of the line of fire. I approached the U.S. 199th Brigade and they willingly provided the ammunition we needed to get the range operation underway. Major Xuan and I fired the ceremonial first rounds, officially opening the range, and the first PF platoon commenced its training.

The range was an instant success, but the M16 was an even greater success. Its shorter stock fit the Vietnamese, its lighter weight made it easier to handle, and its smaller, lightweight 5.56mm ammunition meant soldiers could carry more rounds. But best of all, the M16 could deliver accurate and deadly automatic fire. The PFs not only felt they were being recognized, but also that at last they had a weapon that could compete with the Viet Cong and their Kalashnikovs, the AK47 Russian-made automatic rifle. In addition, the older weapons turned in by the PF units could now be redistributed to the People's Self-Defense Force members, many of whom previously had no weapons at all.

There was only one small problem with our range, and it resulted from a rather large oversight on our part. The range was constructed during the dry season on land that had previously been rice paddies. We had neglected to consider drainage, so when the monsoon season came the dikes kept all the water contained. Except for the firing platform and targets, our range was completely underwater. It was still usable, but soldiers being trained on the range would have to wade through the knee-deep water to get to their targets. Nonetheless, the PF soldiers were so happy to get their new weapons and to have an opportunity to fire them that no one ever complained.

U.S. UNITS WERE also charged with assisting in training the Vietnamese. Gen. Creighton Abrams, who had replaced General Westmoreland as COMUSMACV, emphasized the importance of this mission to his field commanders. Unfortunately, these efforts rarely manifested themselves at the district level. U.S. commanders lacked enthusiasm for this role, mistrusting the Vietnamese and viewing the requirements to train them as a distraction from their mission of seeking out and destroying Viet Cong/NVA units and their quest for body counts. Thus the training provided in many cases consisted of "joint" operations in which the Vietnamese commander was excluded from the planning and the Vietnamese units were generally relegated to some secondary role. In most cases even this was limited to ARVN units and seldom included RF or PF units. In Dinh Quan we did manage to coordinate some smaller unit operations with the 199th Brigade. There were a few joint operations including our RF companies and even some ambushes that included local PF units. Overall, however, U.S. support for local training was superficial, and most times it was nonexistent. Even our attempts to provide U.S. support to local operations often resulted in disappointment. On more than one occasion, based on pretty good intelligence, we had planned an airmobile operation within the district in which U.S. helicopters would be used to transport the local RF units. We would deploy the troops for pickup at the appointed hour, only to discover after waiting several hours in the hot sun that the helicopter support had been diverted elsewhere and that no one had bothered to advise us.

Local security operations took many forms, ranging from multi-company raids on suspected VC locations to platoon-sized operations to provide security for loggers to squad-sized ambushes at night on trails leading to the various hamlets. As a general rule, team members participated in these operations to the extent that their counterparts participated. For example, if Major Xuan personally commanded the operation, I accompanied him. If he remained at the forward command post, I remained with him. If he delegated the operation to one of his subordinates, I generally did not go on the operation. The same rules applied to the other members of the team. One cardinal team rule was that no team member ever went on operations alone with the Vietnamese. We always sent a minimum of two advisors.

Aside from the nightly ambushes, cordon and search operations were the most frequent type of operation in the district. Several team members would participate in each of these operations, which occurred often. A RF or PF unit would cordon off (surround) a hamlet, allowing no one in or out. Another unit accompanied by the National Police and members of the intelligence staff would search the hamlet, checking identification papers and looking for "strangers," known VC, or draft dodgers. Sometimes these operations were accompanied by speeches, entertainment, and some propaganda efforts with the assembled residents. On occasion, American units would provide the cordon and participate jointly with the search element. American participation generally meant an accompanying "medcap" (medical clinic with American doctors to treat the villagers) and often the division band to entertain.

Another form of security operation common in Dinh Quan was the roadside checkpoint. The National Police would frequently establish a checkpoint on Highway 20, checking papers of travelers and cargoes of the hundreds of trucks that traveled the highway daily.

LATE ONE AFTERNOON in March, Major Xuan sent a soldier over to tell me that a North Vietnamese officer had taken refuge in Loi Tan hamlet, about four kilometers northeast of Dinh Quan. The house he was hiding under was surrounded by the local PF platoon. Major Xuan and I, accompanied by Captain Xinh and a platoon from the 312th RF Company, raced to the scene. Our plan was to try to get the NVA officer to surrender. His capture would provide valuable intelligence and certainly be a feather in Xuan's cap.

Arriving at the scene, we found the hamlet residents all gathered in a group on the perimeter of the hamlet, talking excitedly about the situation. The PF platoon was in a circular array surrounding the house. The platoon leader reported that the officer, apparently very sick, had walked out of the nearby jungle and into the village seeking help. When discovered by the local PF, he had taken refuge under a house. While many of the houses in the hamlet had dirt floors, some had wooden floors at ground level, and a few had wooden floors elevated about three feet above the ground. The space beneath the house was enclosed and used for storage. It was beneath this type of house that the officer had taken refuge.

When the NVA officer had initially been approached by the hamlet chief and PF platoon leader, he had fired his pistol, sending them scrambling to safety. Over the next forty-five minutes, various attempts were made to coax the officer into surrendering. He was promised he would not be harmed, that he would receive medical attention, and that he would be treated as an honorable prisoner of war in accordance with the provisions of the Geneva Convention. All the while, the RF soldiers who had moved into place around the house worked themselves closer and closer. Aware that the noose was tightening, the trapped officer shouted a warning to come no closer. The district chief responded that this was to be his last warning—either the officer could come out on his own or he would be killed. After a long moment the silence was shattered by a muffled explosion from under the building. The RF soldiers moved in quickly and ripped away the thatched siding that enclosed the crawl space. Two soldiers cautiously entered, and seconds later they shouted excitedly. I couldn't understand what they were saying, and without explanation Major Xuan took off at a trot toward the house. Instinctively, I followed. There was still dust in the air as we ducked under the house. There, in the far corner, was the lifeless body of the NVA officer. Rather than be captured, he had pulled the pin and rolled over onto a hand grenade. I remember thinking, "What a senseless act.

What sort of propaganda had this middle-aged man been exposed to that would drive him to this? No doubt he had believed the stories he had been fed of the torture and mistreatment that befell those captured by the Americans or South Vietnamese." His body was dragged from under the house and carefully searched for items of intelligence value. The search turned up a map with markings that the intelligence types would love, a small notebook also of intelligence value, a small amount of North Vietnamese money (a bill and two coins worth perhaps $1.50), and a weathered photo of a woman and two children, presumably his family. Major Xuan, disappointed that he had not been able to convince the officer to surrender, removed the Chinese-made K54 pistol from the officer's belt and, turning to me said, "*Thieu-ta*, a souvenir for you. Perhaps you will remember this day." In the intervening years, I have often remembered that day and pondered the futility of that event.

THE OTHER MAJOR roles that team members played in local operations were fire support coordination, medical evacuation, communications relay, and helicopter and fixed-wing air support. Responses to requests for this kind of support through U.S. channels were not only far quicker than those passed through Vietnamese channels, but also could be confidently relied upon. If an American was on the ground with the operation and in need of support, the response was even more rapid. Except for local artillery support, which could be provided by the ARVN battery stationed in the district, Vietnamese response in these support areas was spotty.

The area of fire support was the most contentious and problematic between the advisory team and the Vietnamese. Any artillery, helicopter gunship, or airstrike in the district required the prior clearance of the district chief. He had the singular and absolute authority in this regard. This process was intended to ensure that friendly units, civilians, and friendly hamlets were not accidentally fired upon. The district headquarters, and specifically the operations officer, First Lieutenant Dat, had the responsibility of acting in this regard for the district chief. Dat would know the location of any local units that were operating in the area, and loggers and other civilians were required to clear through headquarters before going into the jungle. He could then check the map coordinates of any intended targets to ensure that no "friendlies" were there. Lieutenant Dat's job was made more difficult by the fact that the loggers, Montagnards, and others didn't always bother to seek clearance from district head-quarters before entering the jungle. This meant that he could never be absolutely sure if the potential target was a VC tax collector or some Montagnard out hunting without clearance. The exception to this procedure was War Zone D, a designated "free-fire zone," which constituted the northern half of the district. Anything or anyone there was fair game—no clearances were necessary. Not infrequently, however, this free-fire mentality spilled over, causing problems in the other parts of the district as American commanders or pilots would fire at targets in the controlled-fire half of the district without clear-ance. The consequence of this "shoot first, sort 'em out later" attitude was a number of incidents in which local RF/PF units or friendly civil-ians were fired upon. Regardless of whether the attack was accidental, due to mis-orientation, or a deliberate disregard for the rules of engagement, it resulted in my having to respond: first, to an alarmed call to have us contact the offending units to direct a cease fire; sec-ond, to the anger of the Vietnamese officials that once again the process had been violated; third, to the outrage that innocent people had been injured or killed; fourth, to the requirement to deal with and provide reparations for the families of those killed or injured; and lastly, to the immeasurable cumulative effect that these incidents had on the local people and their attitudes toward Americans. The VC never missed an opportunity to exploit these incidents.

Conversely, there was frequently a problem getting Lieutenant Dat to authorize fire in a timely manner. A legitimate target would be spotted and a call made for clearance to engage the target, but because of Dat's uncertainty as to the whereabouts of unauthorized innocents, he would be hesitant to give the necessary clearance, adding to the frustration of Americans and frequently resulting in their ignoring the clearance process. It was a catch-22—Dat's hesita-tion and cautiousness in trying to ensure that no innocents were injured resulted in encouraging Americans to ignore the process, thus endangering more innocents.

This hesitation and paralyzing cautiousness resulted in an unfor-tunate incident between Lieutenant Dat and me that had a lasting impact on our working relationship. A platoon-sized operation, accompanied by Sergeants Kirkbride and King, had been mounted about eight kilometers southwest of the village of Dinh Quan. The operation was targeted upon a squad of VC tax collectors who were reported to be collecting taxes from the loggers operating in that area.

About midafternoon contact was made, and the firing was intense. Kirkbride called, reporting that the situation was getting hairy and requesting artillery support. He gave us his map coordinates and, allowing a margin for error, requested the first rounds be placed 500 yards to the rear of the VC. Once the first round impacted, he could adjust subsequent rounds and walk the fire forward onto the enemy position. I personally ran across the compound, met Dat outside the operations center, and gave him the request. I needed clearance to fire, and the ops center would have to direct the ARVN artillery designated to support the operation to fire. Dat said he wasn't sure—there were many loggers in the area. Meanwhile Bob Hughes had brought over a PRC 25 radio so I could communicate directly with Kirkbride and King. When I finally got them back on the net, they reported that the situation was getting worse, that they were engaged with something larger than a squad of VC, and that they needed help. I could tell from Kirkbride's breathing and tone that the situation was pretty serious. I turned to Dat and said, "Get the fire *Trung-uy*!"

Again he hesitated. "I'm not sure," he stammered.

I pride myself on being a man slow to anger, but at that point I lost my cool. "Well, goddamnit, I'm sure," I screamed at Dat as I slammed the folded-up map in my hand down on the hood of the jeep we were gathered around. The map ricocheted off the hood, hitting him squarely in the face. He just stood there stunned, the blood draining from his face. I reached over, spun the dial on the radio, and called the U.S. 155mm artillery section at the engineer compound, gave them the coordinates, and directed them to fire the mission. They ask about clearance, and I responded, "I just gave you the goddamn clearance. Fire the mission."

"Roger, sir," came the reply, "rounds are on the way!" I turned and looked squarely at Dat, tossed the radio handset to Hughes, and walked back to the team house.

As soon as the first rounds impacted, the VC broke contact with the RF platoon and disappeared. The platoon regrouped, collected the wounded, and made their way back to Dinh Quan without further incident. Both King and Kirkbride were uninjured.

The following day Major Xuan, who had been away from the headquarters when the incident occurred, came to see me. I offered him a beer, and he sat down on the sofa next to me.

"You know, *Thieu-ta*, you did a bad thing yesterday." Without waiting for a response, he said, "You caused *Trung-uy* Dat to lose face. For a Vietnamese this is a very bad thing."

I waited for a moment, then said, "You are right. I lost my temper and exceeded my authority. For that I apologize. I am sorry that Lieutenant Dat has lost face, but his failure to act nearly cost lives, both Vietnamese and American. If my actions saved those lives, then I would do it again."

He nodded knowingly, then said, "Do not be too hard on Dat. He is young and has difficult responsibilities."

"I understand," I replied, "For me the incident is over."

"Yes," Xuan said, "But not for *Trung-uy* Dat."

Although the incident was never mentioned again, thereafter, and for the remainder of my tour, my relationship with Dat was changed. It is probably best described as proper yet strained. The open cordialness that we previously had enjoyed was gone.

PRIOR TO PERMITTING traffic on the roads each morning, it was the duty of the local RF and PF to make a physical sweep of the highway looking for mines, booby traps, sabotage, ambushes, or other signs of VC activity during the night. Small detachments would remain dispersed along the highway during the daylight hours. The casualness with which these sweeps were often conducted didn't provide me a lot of comfort, but by and large these daily activities were uneventful. Occasionally a mine or booby trap would be discovered, and even less frequently shots would be exchanged. However, periodically there would be evidence of large unit crossings of Highway 20 during the previous night. These crossings nearly always occurred near the location of the earlier major battle involving the 18th Division and the Airborne Division with the NVA 9th Division. Understandably, local RF units were reluctant to set up ambushes in this area for fear they would be overmatched. They explained that their mission was to protect the population centers, and they felt these crossings were not a direct threat to the local population.

In the evening the road security process would be reversed, the troops would return to the hamlets, and the highway was closed. In Dinh Quan, for example, the National Police would drag a barricade across the road. Occasionally a trucker would leave a populated area late in the afternoon and be unable to make the next area before the highway was closed. This invariably would invoke the wrath of the National Police, who would scrutinize the vehicle and cargo, as well as harangue and generally make life unpleasant for the culprit.

The final contribution to security that we were able to make was in the area of supplies and materials. Ammunition, sandbags, radio batteries, and medical supplies were always in short supply. While the red seal helped expedite requests, materials often were just not available in the Vietnamese supply chain. We were able to requisition some materials through the U.S. supply system, but more effectively, we were able to beg, borrow, trade, and steal from U.S. units—and of course, there was always the black market.

The essential security umbrella under which pacification efforts could go forward was in place in Dinh Quan District. The efforts of the 199th Brigade and 18th ARVN Division, augmented periodically with other U.S. and ARVN units, to keep main force units away from the population were, for the most part, successful. The Regional Force companies and Popular Force platoons operated against the local Viet Cong units, again, for the most part, successfully. Local VC units were being attrited and their effectiveness faded accordingly. Complementing these efforts were the successes of the Phoenix Program in identifying and eliminating the Viet Cong leadership infrastructure.

During my fourteen months there were breaches in the security umbrella. We experienced a limited number of assassinations and kidnappings, some mining and booby-trapping of roads, and some snipings and minor probes of village/hamlet security, but except for the attack on Artillery Hill there were no major attacks on the populated area. There was periodically some minor infiltration of hamlets, primarily for propaganda purposes or to collect taxes in the form of food, money, or other supplies. As a result of the improving security situation, ratings of the hamlets under the Hamlet Evaluation System Report steadily rose during this period.

Our major security problem came from our limited ability to protect the population working outside the secured areas, in the fields and paddies, and in the jungle. There they were exposed to the VC for tax collection, interrogation, propaganda, or forced recruitment. It was against these VC actions that we targeted our intelligence and military efforts. Success in this area was slow but steady.

It was in this environment of improving security that the pacification programs in Dinh Quan District were able to move forward successfully.

CHAPTER 30

Chopper Day

If it was Thursday, then it was chopper day in Dinh Quan District. Province headquarters would place a helicopter at our disposal for the entire day, operations and weather permitting. Sometimes it arrived late or had to leave early, but by and large we could count on having the helicopter available. Most often it was a standard UH-1, or Huey, from the air detachment at Xuan Loc, but sometimes it would be the smaller Light Observation Helicopter (LOH). On rare occasions, when operational demands had the province's choppers committed elsewhere, we might end up with an Air America helicopter. Air America was the worst-kept secret of the war—purportedly a private charter airline with a multitude of fixed-wing aircraft and helicopters, but well known to everyone as being owned and operated by the Central Intelligence Agency.

Chopper day was a special day for the team, always posing the question, "What shall we do this week?" What we did was an incredible variety of activities, running the gamut from reconnaissance to Christmas shopping. The weekly helicopter was a godsend, helping to satisfy both the professional needs of the district and the personal needs of the team members. The district chief was well aware of the availability of this wonderful asset and frequently offered suggestions for trips he would like to make. I naturally made every effort to accommodate him whenever possible.

Most frequently, we used the chopper to reconnoiter the district, particularly the more inaccessible parts, although we were careful not to stray too deep into War Zone D. It was easy from the vantage point of a thousand feet to identify new trails, spot new structures, and get a feel for what might be different. Suspicious areas were examined at even lower altitudes. This information helped us plan operations, select ambush sites, and identify target areas for our H&I fires. Whenever we flew these reconnaissance missions, we always had Vietnamese district officers aboard to permit them to observe for themselves. These weekly flights were also an excellent way to monitor the scope of the timber-harvesting efforts in the district.

From the chopper we could also clearly see the incredible damage wrought by Arc Light attacks. "Arc Light" was the code name for bomb strikes launched from U.S. Air Force B-52 Stratofortress bombers. Bombing from altitudes of 30,000 feet, the planes could neither be seen nor heard. Their lethal cargo of 500-pound bombs, 108 per aircraft, would cut a path of destruction hundreds of yards long, blowing down trees and creating huge craters. I recall receiving word one afternoon that there would be an Arc Light attack about ten kilometers south of Dinh Quan. A number of the team members and I drove to the top of Artillery Hill to observe. It was a bright, clear morning, and from that elevated vantage point we had an unobstructed view of the target area. It was an awesome and unforgettable event. Without warning, the earth erupted. We could see the shock wave from each explosion. Columns of smoke and debris exploded from the surface as the destruction marched laterally across our front. As best as we could determine, this particular attack consisted of bomb loads from only two B-52s, but it seemed to go on forever. The attack had the same effect on all of us who observed it. "My God," we thought, "how could anything survive that?"

I knew firsthand from my days as a company commander in the U.S. 1st Division the destruction these attacks wrought. On several occasions during that tour, my company had been inserted by chopper to sweep the area and mop up right after B-52 raids. It was a mission we hated. Movement through the area was extremely slow and difficult due to the tree blowdown, the huge craters, and the acres of loose soil. In addition, the tree blowdown removed the canopy that shaded us from the direct rays of that scorching Southeast Asian sun.

Many of these raids did little more than rip giant gashing scars in the countryside. Others, however, found real targets. When this occurred, the killing and destruction were nearly indescribable. We occasionally would find a VC or NVA soldier who had been nearby in a stupor, with blood pouring from his nose and ears from the concussion. Frequently, when VC or NVA gave themselves up as part of the *Chieu Hoi* Program, they cited the B-52 raids as one of the reasons. It was a real weapon of terror.

Our recon flights also provided us a firsthand view of the damage done through the spraying of the defoliant Agent Orange. Great swaths of the jungle were chemically peeled back, exposing the ground beneath. The theory behind the use of Agent Orange was that by killing the jungle cover, we could patrol the defoliated area by air, thus denying its use to the VC or NVA. It was also used to destroy crops in VC territories. I have no way of knowing if Agent Orange made any positive contribution to the war against the enemy, but I do know the devastating impact it had on crops when these sprays drifted into friendly areas. I also know of the intense emotion surrounding this issue and of the highly contentious allegations regarding its harmful impact on those soldiers, airmen, and civilians who were exposed to this chemical mix.

Most of our weekly reconnaissance flights were routine and uneventful; however, occasionally they resulted in memorable experiences. One legendary flight involved Captain Hughes, who took the new young lieutenant just assigned as commander of the MAT stationed at the bridge, on a reconnaissance flight along the western edge of the district. As the helicopter approached the bridge spanning the La Nga River, Hughes wondered aloud to the young warrant officer pilot if the helicopter could make it between the narrow support columns beneath the bridge. At that, the pilot dipped the chopper, and under they went at about 80 mph. The new lieutenant nearly wet his pants! We later measured the span and figured there was about six feet of clearance for the rotor blades as the chopper went under the span. That stunt was the subject of a lot of discussion, but no one tried it again. Although he never would admit it, I also believe that incident aged Hughes about ten years.

Chopper day also meant transportation for team members, either to or from Xuan Loc. All our support operations, from personnel actions to logistical support, were there, along with my boss and my counterpart's boss. In addition, most of the agencies with which we operated had field offices there—USAID, USIA, CIA, and others. Visits to Xuan Loc were frequent for all team members, and the helicopter was the principal means of transportation.

Liaison visits were another frequent mission. The district chief, Hughes, and I would visit adjacent district headquarters to meet with senior Vietnamese and American officers to exchange information, coordinate efforts, and catch up socially. We were also able to visit American units stationed or operating in the vicinity. Visits to U.S. units were always productive, as we were able to scrounge all sorts of goodies, from coffee to fresh meat to munitions to radio batteries. All the things that were in short supply for us were generally plentiful in the U.S. units. As trading materials, we would take along primitive crossbows made by our local Montagnards, small VC flags, and other captured weapons and materials.

Visits to U.S. units also generated a great deal of operational support for us. We might arrange for a medical team to visit and set up shop in one of our hamlets, or perhaps convince the U.S. unit to help us reconstruct a school or marketplace. In addition, through our visits we were able to coordinate operations and on rare occasions obtain some training for our local units.

Access to the helicopter also gave us access to some of the other goodies generally available to U.S. units but not to those of us in the boonies. The American Express bank in Long Binh was a frequent stop. Although most of the team members' pay went to their banks in the States for their families' use, a portion came to us directly each month to pay for food, laundry, haircuts, and so forth. Americans in Vietnam were issued not U.S. currency, but Military Payment Certificates (MPC). This currency, brightly colored and smaller in size than U.S. dollars, was dubbed "funny money" by U.S. troops. MPCs were introduced into Vietnam in 1965 in order to help curb inflation and to combat black market activities dealing in U.S. greenbacks. Periodically, and with little advance notice, the MPC was converted to a totally new series in order to sting those in the black market who were dealing in MPC. As my personal supply of MPC built up, I would periodically stop at the bank to have a cashier's check or money order made out so I could send it back to my family.

Probably the most enjoyable use of the chopper was our shopping sprees. Even the pilots enjoyed it when we launched one of these infrequent but memorable trips. We hit the PXs or commissaries at Saigon, Long Binh, Binh Hoa, and Vung Tau, as well as the major U.S. units' headquarters. In a two-pronged attack strategy, we frequently sent a couple of the NCOs ahead by jeep to scrounge and horse trade. When we arrived by chopper, the booty would be waiting for us at the helipad. This proved to be an effective technique for keeping the team supplied and for acquiring some of the items that were harder to come by. It also allowed us to get frozen food back to Dinh Quan and into our freezer before it thawed.

In order to ensure that our presents got home in time for Christmas, it was necessary for us to launch the Christmas shopping blitz in mid-November. During this frenzied search, no helipad was too small or too crowded for us to squeeze onto. No PX, however remote, was safe from our plunder. Not only were these Kamikaze shopping raids successful, they were fun as well. The pilots and crews who supported us on these missions loved them as much as we did. For a brief moment we all felt the exhilaration of being back home and rushing about getting our Christmas shopping done. I often wondered what the taxpayers would say, but I never wondered long—as the next PX helipad came into view, I would once again be caught up in the hunt!

CHAPTER 31

Phung Hoang:
The Phoenix Program

Except for the significance of Tet '68, the Phung Hoang (Phoenix Program) was the most misunderstood, misinterpreted, and misreported event or program of the Vietnam War.

Though the surprise Viet Cong offensive at Tet '68 was a psychological victory for the Communist forces, it was a devastating defeat for both the VC military forces and the VC infrastructure in the South. The Viet Cong forces, having come out of hiding and committed themselves, could not sustain their offensive and hold the objectives they had seized. They were overwhelmed by U.S. and ARVN forces and suffered tremendous casualties from which they never recovered. The Viet Cong infrastructure who surfaced during this offensive likewise suffered enormous losses, both from the fighting itself and from the fact that, now identified, they could be targeted and eliminated by the Phoenix Program. These losses and the successes of both the *Chieu Hoi* and pacification programs ultimately led the North Vietnamese government to abandon their guerrilla war strategy in favor of more conventional attacks.

The Phoenix Program certainly ranked high among the most controversial and notorious programs of the Vietnam War. Critics of Phoenix claimed it to be a barbarous program of assassination, abduction, and intimidation that resulted in the murder of thousands and the illegal incarceration and torture of thousands more (often innocent) civilians. Unfortunately, this was the view portrayed broadly by the U.S. media.

The program's proponents cited the necessity of attacking the Viet Cong infrastructure (VCI) as an essential component of a successful counterinsurgency strategy. North Vietnamese and Viet Cong documents, which have come to light in the years after the war, reflect deep concern on their part regarding the effectiveness of the Phoenix Program.

Phoenix was a creation of the U.S. Central Intelligence Agency. Implemented in 1967 as ICEX (Intelligence Collection and Exploitation), the program was intended to target the Viet Cong "shadow government," whose infrastructure existed from the very top of the government down through the village and hamlet level in every part of Vietnam. For example, in Dinh Quan District there was a VC district chief and staff, and similarly VC chiefs for every village and hamlet. There were VC tax collectors, propaganda and recruiting teams, and corresponding officials at all levels. These "officials" generally lived in the surrounding jungle areas, but frequently entered the occupied areas at night to tax, recruit, propagandize, or terrorize the population. In some cases members of the VCI were seemingly respectable loyal citizens by day, but clandestinely served as Viet Cong agents, supporters, or insurgents at night.

The Phoenix Program was an intensive intelligence operations program at the district and province levels that targeted these individuals. Each district had a District Intelligence Operations Coordination Center (DIOCC) at which information was collected, intelligence leads analyzed, and dossiers developed on suspected VCI. The DIOCC was an operational partnership between the police and military, with each party sharing information and jointly planning intelligence activities and operations. When sufficient evidence was amassed on an individual, he or she would be brought in for interrogation.

Special efforts were made to locate known members of the VCI who were targeted for arrest or elimination, and military operations were mounted to carry out their apprehension. Much of the public outcry against Phoenix was this latter aspect of targeting for elimination members of the "civilian" population. Critics never seemed to acknowledge that these "civilians" and the Viet Cong were one and the same. They somehow made a distinction between the Viet Cong operating in military units and living in base camps in the jungle, and the Viet Cong who posed as an innocent civilian by day and either picked up a weapon and served as a Viet Cong by night or provided clandestine leadership activities for the VC as a member of the shadow government. Both were the enemy of the Republic of

Vietnam and served in the revolutionary forces. My conscience never bothered me when one of the targeted VCI was killed as a result of a planned operation.

Each district advisory team had an intelligence officer whose main function was to advise and assist in the operation of the DIOCC. In Dinh Quan during my tenure that was initially Captain Backlin, and later Captain Hughes. The DIOCC coordinated activities of the district headquarters, the Special Police, the National Police Field Force (NPFF), and local military forces as necessary. In addition, Hughes coordinated his activities through the CIA officer assigned to the Province Intelligence Operations Coordination Center in Xuan Loc. Locally, Hughes relied on his counterpart, 1st Lt. Dong Van Thanh, the Vietnamese district intelligence officer (S-2), for coordination of intelligence activities. The district chief had delegated the day-to-day operation of the DIOCC to Lieutenant Thanh. Thanh was an older officer, not anxious to be too aggressive or to make waves. Working with him was pleasant but frustrating for Hughes because change was suspect and progress was slow. Captain Hughes's access to funds, however, provided him considerable influence in intelligence operations. In addition to paying the Provincial Reconnaissance Units and providing money to pay for agents and information, he had discretionary funds to use as he felt necessary. This issue was sensitive to the Vietnamese, so Hughes was careful to coordinate his activities with Lieutenant Thanh.

The action arm for the Phoenix Program was a volunteer force called the Provincial Reconnaissance Unit (PRU). These units, which ranged in size from company (100 men) to squad (10 men), were comprised of individuals with a variety of motivations: defectors from the Viet Cong or North Vietnamese Army, ardent anticommunists who sought revenge for some VC atrocity against their family members, draft dodgers, mercenaries, or criminals avoiding prison—an interesting bunch. In its own way, it reflected somewhat the mentality of the legendary French Foreign Legion. In some areas of Vietnam, U.S. Army Special Forces or Navy SEALS provided direct leadership for these groups—not so in Dinh Quan.

The PRUs had several distinct advantages in their efforts to recruit. First, since they were funded by the CIA, their pay was much higher than that of the Vietnamese soldiers. Second, since they operated only regionally, an individual could join and remain in his home area. And finally, the PRUs had somewhat of a mystique about them—they were tough by reputation, notably successful in their operations, and a valuable resource to the district. They made raids against the VC, captured VCI, conducted ambushes, and were a valuable source of intelligence through their reconnaissance, prisoners, and the documents they frequently recovered during their operations. The prisoners were interrogated and the documents were analyzed at the DIOCC before being forwarded through the intelligence chain to the province headquarters. They often provided critical leads on VC strength, equipment, morale, and operations. They also frequently identified other VC or VCI, often leading to their capture or elimination through subsequent operations.

In Dinh Quan, the PRUs consisted of a single squad-sized unit who worked directly for Captain Hughes in his role as intelligence officer. They were an interesting collection of individuals who had earned themselves a respected reputation within the district. Hughes oversaw the PRU operations through the DIOCC.

One particularly memorable event involving the PRU centered upon a bag of documents recovered during a PRU raid on a suspected VC cadre safe house in the jungle north of the predominately Chinese hamlet of Loi Tan. Among the sizable pile of documents was a scale drawing of the floor plan of our team house. Each room was accurately detailed and functionally described. Especially disturbing to me was the annotation on that portion of the sketch that represented my room at the right rear corner of the house: labeled neatly on the rectangular bed space was "*Thieu-ta* Becket." They not only knew who and where I was, they also knew exactly where I slept! Not a comforting thought. Of course, they had misspelled my name, so how good could their intelligence be?

Although other team members weren't identified by name, their bunk locations were accurately depicted. The discovery of this sketch made everyone, particularly me, a little uneasy for a time. How had the VC gotten this level of detail? Although we all trusted *Ba*, the two *Co*s, and our interpreters—those with total access to the team house—as we watched them go about their daily duties, we nonetheless secretly wondered if the information could have come from them. Jokingly we had often accused *Ba* of being a VC; this incident made us realize that in truth she, or any of the other Vietnamese, could be. In reality, a number of the Vietnamese officers, soldiers, and civilians were in our team house every single day, and during our movies—God alone knew who was there in the darkness. We never discovered the source, and the incident ultimately passed. The sketch was merely yet another uncomfortable reminder of our own vulnerability—a fact we tried not to dwell on, but knew all too well.

SHORTLY AFTER LIEUTENANT HUGHES's arrival, he decided to accompany the PRU on an ambush operation. It was to be his "cherry" mission. Through a number of intelligence sources, the DIOCC had gotten word that a VC political cadre and propaganda team was going to try to infiltrate one of the hamlets. An ambush was planned on the logical route leading into the hamlet. As Hughes reported later, all went well: they moved into the ambush sight just after dark, set up the Claymore mines, and deployed in a standard L-shaped ambush. Hughes and Houston positioned themselves at the bend in the ambush formation and settled in. Just before dawn, Hughes was sound asleep, as it was Houston's shift to be alert, when the dead stillness was shattered by the earth-shaking explosions of two Claymore mines detonating nearly simultaneously. At the same instant, the entire ambush formation erupted with automatic small-arms fire. Hughes, startled awake by the explosions, was groggy and totally disoriented. As he attempted to clear his head, the PRU members all around him were scrambling to their feet, screaming and charging across the opening to their front. Not knowing what the hell was going on, but determined not to be left behind out there in the jungle darkness, Hughes stumbled along behind them with heart pounding and adrenaline flowing. In the near light of the coming dawn, Hughes could make out the soldiers converging on a large dark mass on the edge of the clearing. By the time he arrived, they had knives and machetes out and were hacking away, each frantically working to get his share of the meat of the dead water buffalo that had wandered into the ambush. Hughes watched with amazement. There was no security, no unit discipline—this was meat for the table or for the market, and it was every man for himself.

The VC political cadre, whether tipped off about the ambush or not, had apparently changed their plans and had not come out that night. The PRU, however, did credit itself with one VC water buffalo. Hughes took gas from the team members for his "successful" ambush and from *Ba* for not bringing home any fresh meat!

THE NATIONAL POLICE Field Force located in Dinh Quan was another action arm of the Phoenix Program. They participated in intelligence collection and analysis, operated roadside checks, conducted searches and ID card checks during the frequent cordon and search operations, and were most frequently dispatched to arrest a suspect residing in one of the hamlets. The RF/PF also conducted operations in support of the Phoenix Program. In addition to their local security mission, they provided the cordon for cordon and search operations and conducted operations against larger suspected targets such as local VC units or armed VC tax collection teams.

The companion component of the Phoenix Program was the *Chieu Hoi* or Open Arms program. If Phoenix was the stick used against the Viet Cong, the *Chieu Hoi* Program was the carrot. This highly effective program offered rewards and incentives for individuals who defected from the VC or NVA to the Vietnamese government, including amnesty, security, resettlement, and cash. As the war wore on; as military pressure increased on the VC; as VC strength and morale were severely hurt by the Tet '68 outbreaks; as B-52 raids and artillery continued to rain down terror; as lack of supplies and medical aid worsened and living conditions deteriorated; as disenchantment grew within the VC ranks; and as the effectiveness of Phoenix increasingly identified and eliminated the VCI, the incentive to defect became greater and greater, and as such more and more ralliers (*hoi chanhs*) surrendered to the government.

The establishment of goals for the provinces and districts added increased pressures and assuredly contributed to false accusations and arrests as officials sought to meet those goals. I cannot speak to the alleged abuses by government officials—no doubt they existed and no doubt some number of innocent civilians were killed or imprisoned. I can only speak to Phoenix operations in Dinh Quan District. The Phoenix program there was a small-scale, reasonably effective program that successfully identified a number of the VCI cadre and resulted in their arrest or elimination. The net result was a weakening of the Viet Cong influence in the district. It also made recruitment by the VC more difficult and improved the credibility of the local government officials.

Captured Central Office for South Vietnam (COSVN), the North Vietnamese headquarters for Viet Cong forces in the South, documents and other documents subsequently released by the North Vietnamese after the war describe the deep concerns of the VC and NVA about the effectiveness of the Phoenix and *Chieu Hoi* Programs in decimating local VC units and limiting their ability to recruit and operate. It was this very effectiveness in eliminating the influence and strength of the Viet Cong that led the North Vietnamese ultimately to abandon their guerrilla war strategy and resort to a conventional war strategy—ironically, fighting and winning the very kind of war that the U.S. had unsuccessfully been trying to fight in all the years prior to our withdrawal.

IT DIDN'T TAKE me long to figure Dinh Quan's role in the VC scheme of things: Dinh Quan represented a lucrative tax base for the Viet Cong. I am convinced that it was precisely this role that kept VC attacks within the district to a minimum. There were three primary sources for these taxes: the farmers and villagers, the trucks moving on the highway, and the loggers.

The farmers would be "taxed" in the fields by armed VC tax collector teams and forced to pay piasters or, more often, a portion of their crops. To resist meant death. Occasionally a farmer would be abducted for service with the Viet Cong. The villagers would be subjected to taxes as they went into the jungle to hunt or gather firewood. Less frequently, the VC would enter the hamlets at night to collect taxes, recruit, and deliver propaganda messages. As security improved, these nighttime visits became more and more difficult for the VC.

Captain Backlin and I quite stupidly stumbled onto a VC tax cadre at work one morning. He and I were returning from an inspection of several tons of pierced steel planking that had been delivered at the airstrip when we noticed a number of people gathered at the edge of the woods about a hundred meters from the road. Curious as to what was going on, and without thinking, we pulled over, climbed out of the jeep, and proceeded toward the group of perhaps twenty people. We had only our .45-caliber pistols with us, and unsuspecting as we were, they were still snugly holstered. As we approached the group, they stopped talking and just stood there looking at us. At about thirty meters, after some apparent indecision on their part, the group split in half. About a dozen slipped back into the jungle, out of sight, and the remainder scurried back toward us. As they approached, they kept their eyes down and headed right past us toward the hamlet without a word. Just about then Backlin and I simultaneously uttered "Oh shit!" as the truth struck us like a bolt of lightning. We had walked right into an armed VC tax cadre collecting taxes from the villagers. Our suspicions were later confirmed through an intelligence report from an informant in the hamlet. They either thought we were the bravest dudes they had ever seen or the dumbest. More than likely the latter! In any event, after some indecision, they chose to slip away rather than take us on. Had they chosen to fire, I am convinced there was no way we could have survived. We were within thirty meters of them, in the open with no cover available, and armed only with pistols. Once again, fate had decided in my favor.

National Highway 20, which ran the width of the district and carried hundreds of cargo-laden trucks daily between Dalat and Saigon, was likewise a lucrative target for VC tax collection teams. They would spring from the cover of the jungle at some deserted stretch of highway, halt the vehicle, and demand a tax according to the cargo being carried. The driver would have no choice but to pay. The VC would then melt back into the jungle. The attitude of the drivers was that this was an irritating nuisance, but the price of doing business. If the driver bothered reporting the incident at the next checkpoint, by the time Vietnamese security forces reacted (if they did), the tax team would be long gone. The U.S. project to widen, straighten, and resurface Highway 20 later played a major role in reducing the vulnerability of these trucks and the effectiveness of the VC tax collection teams. The jungle was pushed back farther from the highway and the road was straightened, allowing security units greater visibility. These improvements allowed the trucks to move at greater speed and security units to react more quickly. In addition, there was an effort on the part of the district chief to improve highway security and more aggressively react to incidents on the highway. The net result was a marked decrease in the exploitation of truckers in Dinh Quan.

The greatest source of tax revenue for the Viet Cong, however, came not from the farmers or truckers, but from the loggers who worked the heavily forested areas north and south of Highway 20. As a group, the loggers represented the biggest target for the VC tax collection cadres in Dinh Quan. First, the loggers were the most vulnerable, as they worked deep in the surrounding jungle. Secondly, the teak, ebony, and other hardwoods they harvested were extremely valuable and brought premium prices in Saigon. The estimated wholesale value of the lumber harvested in the district exceeded 430 million piasters a year, roughly $3.7 million U.S. Approximately 25 percent of the population of Dinh Quan District was involved in the logging industry. It was not only the major economic engine of the district's economy, but also a significant source of tax revenue to the Vietnamese government. Loggers in Dinh Quan paid nearly 100 million piasters (more than $800,000) in taxes to the Vietnamese government each year.

In the spring of 1970, I did a study of the logging operations in Dinh Quan. Estimated taxes being collected by the VC averaged nearly 15 million piasters a month, or 180 million Ps per year. That was almost $1.5 million—nearly twice as much as what was being collected by the GVN. My study, which was forwarded to the province and subsequently up the chain of the CORDS organization, recommended several measures that I believed could severely cut back the taxes being collected by the VC.

The problem as I saw it was simple. The Vietnamese Ministry of Forestry, which controlled logging operations nationwide, had restricted logging operations in Dinh Quan to an area that ran 6 kilometers on both sides of Highway 20 across the width of the district. The belief was that security could be provided to loggers operating in this narrow band. Unfortunately, the designated 12-kilometer belt had long since been completely harvested of all significant hardwood trees. The loggers had to go deeper and deeper into the jungle in search of harvestable trees. The logging trucks were required to be brightly painted so they could be identified and monitored from the air. Unfortunately, when they left the authorized cutting areas and went into the restricted areas, they frequently became targets for U.S. and Vietnamese Air Force (VNAF) aircraft. There were repeated incidents of these aircraft engaging the lumber trucks without clearance from the district headquarters. Of course, the farther they went, the more vulnerable they were to the VC cadres. In addition to being

heavily taxed, their trucks often were commandeered to haul VC supplies and equipment. The profitability of the logging business, however, encouraged the locals to take the risks and to pay the heavy
taxes being exacted.

It seemed to me to be clearly in the best interest of the GVN to
promote and protect this profitable industry and deny this lucrative
source of taxes and in-kind services to the Viet Cong. The industry
could be promoted by extending the authorized logging areas farther than 6 kilometers from Highway 20. By such an extension of the
authorized area, the loggers could be protected from being fired
upon by patrolling aircraft. In order to deny access to the VC, I recommended that one battalion of the 43rd Regiment of the ARVN
18th Division, in whose tactical area of operation these loggers
worked, be assigned to heavily patrol these areas and provide necessary security to the loggers. The economic benefits to be gained were
obvious. I also assumed the tactical benefits were obvious. Because
the payoff was so high, I knew that the VC would take extraordinary
risks to collect taxes, thus increasing their own vulnerability in the
heavily patrolled area. This would result in some real tactical successes for the 43rd Regiment. I learned, however, that while everyone
seemed to agree my plan made a great deal of sense, like many other
great plans in Vietnam it was never implemented. Years later, in 1995,
I was pleasantly surprised to come across my handwritten study in a
dusty bin in the National Archives. It had been annotated favorably as
it had worked its way up the chain of command, but somewhere
along the line it had lost its way and was quietly buried in the bureaucratic morass of some higher headquarters.

CHAPTER 32

The Hamlet Evaluation System

In 1965, in response to a request from then Secretary of Defense Robert McNamara, the Central Intelligence Agency developed an evaluation system to measure the level of security being provided to the villages and hamlets of Vietnam. The system was intended to capture security trends in the countryside, and by so doing measure our success in this regard. Since, in a counterinsurgency environment, there are no front lines by which to assess the progress of the war, and most people felt body counts were a poor criteria, McNamara wanted a quantifiable measure of how well the government was doing in extending security into the countryside and protecting the people.

The instrument developed by the CIA was the Hamlet Evaluation System (HES), intended to measure security as well as the economic and political environment in each of the nation's villages and hamlets. The report required the American district advisor to answer a series of questions about each of the villages and hamlets within his district. The responses were in the form of check-off boxes on a large computer form. These responses were then scored, and a grade was assigned to each hamlet. There were six grades: A through E, and V. Hamlets with A ratings were considered totally secure and characterized by having a school, an effective local defense unit, an open marketplace, and demonstrated support for the government. At the other extreme, a rating of V meant the hamlet was under complete Viet Cong control. The intervening grades were merely intended to indicate the respective degree of security.

Because these reports were evaluated and reviewed at the highest levels of both the American and Vietnamese chains of command, there was great concern on the part of the district chief and the district senior advisor as to the progress of "their" hamlets. As and Bs were deemed okay, but Cs were worrisome, and anything less was unacceptable.

Each month, the computer worksheets would arrive, and I would sit down with the district chief to discuss with him my observations and ask him questions regarding progress in many of the evaluated areas. He would do his level best to explain away problems and to convince me that things in a particular hamlet were really better than they seemed on the surface. The final analysis was always mine, and though Major Xuan and I sometimes disagreed, he understood the basis for my evaluations, and being an intellectually honest man, he never protested too much.

The report's telling question, and the one providing the best indication regarding the security of the hamlet, was, "Does the hamlet chief sleep in the hamlet at night?" There were five categories of answers, ranging from "Always" to "Never." If the hamlet was not secure, hamlet chiefs frequently slept in military compounds or in nearby secure hamlets.

In order to effectively evaluate the hamlets, I had to visit them frequently, speak with the hamlet chiefs, and gather information regarding activities in the hamlet. Our own intelligence operations also provided information, as did commanders of local military units. In addition, district advisory team members as well as MAT teams were frequently in the hamlets working with both military and civilians in the course of their duties. Even though Dinh Quan's three villages and fourteen hamlets were widespread, we had a pretty good feel for what was going on.

I found that on ratings prior to my arrival, the district's hamlets were faring very well, with thirteen Bs and one C rating. Based on what little I had seen and the briefings I had received in Xuan Loc, my initial impression was that these appeared a little high, but I would have to wait and see. My first monthly ratings gave us seven Bs and seven Cs. The district chief nearly went into cardiac arrest! He was sure the report would result in his being fired or worse.

My report prompted a visit from my boss, Lieutenant Colonel Lake, and Lieutenant Colonel Long, the Vietnamese deputy province chief. The district chief and I explained that the previous ratings might have been slightly inflated and outlined the basis for these new ratings and our plan to address the shortcomings, most of which had to do with physical security. Both officers seemed to accept our appraisal and were satisfied with our plans for improvement. Over the next several months, we worked on security by providing additional training, used local Regional Force units to conduct ambushes, and provided local defense forces with additional weapons and munitions. In addition, I had team members periodically stay overnight with local militia units. After a number of months, we finally got the ratings up to a respectable twelve Bs and two Cs.

While I was not pressured by either Major Xuan or province headquarters regarding the HES report, I have talked to many former district senior advisors who were. The report had the potential of causing a great deal of ill will between the district senior advisor and his Vietnamese counterpart, and I know of cases where DSAs compromised their evaluations in order to preserve rapport with their Vietnamese district chiefs. I also know of cases where bad HES reports resulted in the removal of the district chief. In addition, some DSAs were pressured by their own bosses (the province senior advisor) to inflate the reports, either because the PSA felt a lower score would reflect on his own performance or because the province advisor was being pressured by the province chief. That was not the case in Long Khanh Province. To the best of my knowledge, both Lieutenant Colonel Lake and Lieutenant Colonel Scott, who succeeded him, supported their DSAs and stood by their evaluations; although Captain Hughes, who prepared the Dinh Quan District HES report after my departure, told me that on a subsequent visit to Saigon he had an opportunity to see his HES reports, and to his surprise and dismay, they had been altered and much improved. By whom, he had no way of knowing.

Additional pressure also came to bear on DSAs from commanders of U.S. units who had operational responsibility for the area. As support of pacification became an essential part of their mission, some U.S. commanders pressured advisory elements to reflect higher HES ratings. These higher ratings would demonstrate the effectiveness of the U.S. unit's pacification efforts. Again, in Dinh Quan this did not happen. The 199th Brigade was concerned and supportive, but did not attempt to influence the ratings, at least at my level.

One of the troubling aspects regarding all the reports we submitted was that we seldom got any feedback. We were never sure to what use, if any, all this information was being put. I did learn, however, that the HES report was a major determinant in deciding which hamlets would participate in the national elections of 1969. Although the information was not made available to us at the time, I have subsequently read that in 1969 approximately 90 percent of the hamlets nationwide were rated as C or higher, with only 50 percent being B or higher. Although we didn't know it, by the spring of 1970, compared nationally Dinh Quan was doing well. We had 100 percent of our hamlets at C or higher and 86 percent at B or higher.

The HES report was only one of several monthly reports that we were required to submit. In addition, there was the District Senior Advisor's report on various activities in the district, the Territorial Forces Evaluation System report, and a monthly "counterpart letter" that DSAs were required to write to their district chief, critiquing him and offering suggestions for improvement. There were also required reports on the Phoenix Program, a variety of intelligence reports, reports on our expenditures of various discretionary funds, and reports on the progress of various projects for USAID, USIA, or other American agencies. Generally, these reports all came due at the first of each month. To the extent that I was permitted, I shared these reports with Major Xuan. My diary entries reveal that nearly two days each month were consumed in completing required reports. My search of team records at the National Archives turned up a 1969 Disposition Form issued by Dick Hretz, the deputy province senior advisor, entitled "Reporting Requirements," and citing sixty-one separate reports due each month. Fortunately, all these reports did not originate in the districts, although we had more than our fair share. Even in a combat zone you can't escape bureaucratic reporting.

PART SIX

Memorable Events

CHAPTER 33

The Great Ambush

The Vietnamese soldier came sprinting across the compound, yelling excitedly. After his hurried conversation with Sergeant Cuong, our interpreter, Cuong ran into the team house shouting that SFC King and SP4 Houston had been ambushed on Highway 20 about ten miles north of Dinh Quan. They had been visiting Phu Lam hamlet in the northern part of the district and were on their way back when their vehicle was and overturned. A nearby PF platoon was now on the scene and had radioed the district headquarters, but details were sketchy and confused. There was no word regarding King's and Houston's fate, nor that of the interpreter and the two Vietnamese soldiers accompanying them.

We grabbed our weapons and radio, piled into the two remaining jeeps, and roared out of the compound. A ¾-ton truck carrying a squad of RF soldiers from the 621st Company in the neighboring compound joined us as we raced up the highway toward the ambush site.

My greatest concern was for King, Houston, and the others in the jeep, but I was likewise concerned with what we may be racing into. I realized that our reaction, speeding up the highway to our comrades' aid, was very predictable and that this could well have been a setup. We might be racing headlong into phase two of a well-laid ambush. There was only one road leading to the ambush site, and the sun was going down. There just wasn't enough time to wait on a helicopter from province, so on we sped.

I was encouraged by the presence of soldiers along the road; apparently the district headquarters had them turn out to provide some measure of security. I wasn't sure of the exact location of the ambush, but I knew the general area and while en route plotted the coordinates for potential artillery support. I passed these back to Lieutenant Wingo at the team house to relay to the Vietnamese artillery section that provided support to the northern portion of the district.

As we approached the ambush site, I could see the overturned jeep in a swale on the left side of the highway, with an indistinguishable group of figures surrounding it. As we got closer, I was relieved to make out both King and Houston standing at the rear of the jeep. I made a quick check of the local security and noted that the accompanying RF soldiers were moving into positions around the ambush site. I dismounted and approached SFC King to see if everyone was all right. After being assured that except for bumps and bruises resulting from being thrown from the overturned jeep, everyone (Vietnamese and American) was uninjured, I started questioning King about what had happened. Meanwhile SFC Kraft was inspecting the jeep to see if we could tow it back to the compound. He determined that we couldn't tow it and would have to ask the engineers to retrieve it for us the following day.

King said they had completed their visit with hamlet officials and the PF platoon at Phu Lam and that they were hurrying back down the highway to Dinh Quan because it was getting late. The engineer road project had not yet reached this far north. This section of Highway 20 was narrow, marred by a broken surface, and full of potholes, so any speed above 25 mph was hazardous. King by his own admission was driving about 45 mph when automatic weapons opened fire on them from the wood line about a hundred feet away. When the fire erupted, King swerved, and when its wheels ran onto the shoulder of the road, the careening jeep flipped over. Fortunately, they were all thrown clear, and even more fortunately, their ambushers did not come out of the woods to finish them off.

Soldiers from a nearby PF platoon had arrived on the scene shortly thereafter. I found it strange that neither Houston, the interpreter, nor the Vietnamese soldiers had anything to add to King's story. Because darkness was rapidly approaching, we gathered up everyone and their equipment, left the damaged jeep for the night, and headed back down the highway to Dinh Quan, arriving there just at dark. District headquarters detailed the PF platoon on the scene to secure the jeep overnight.

Once back at the team house, *Bac-si* tended to the minor cuts and scratches, while I made a radio report of the incident to Lieutenant Colonel Scott. After dinner I questioned all of them again and got exactly the same story. I noted that King's eyes were bloodshot, but that wasn't unusual for him, and since he had been ambushed and thrown out of a tumbling jeep, I gave him the benefit of the doubt. I also noted that King did all the talking, that there was a surprising lack of detail about the incident, and that worried glances were being exchanged among King, Houston, and the interpreter. When I asked the others for confirmation, they nodded or grunted their agreement with King's account. I was beginning to smell a rat. Sergeant King's drinking had gotten him into trouble with me twice before, once for driving while drunk, and once for getting drunk and failing to return from a visit to Xuan Loc.

The next morning, once the highway was cleared for travel, I took all of them back to the ambush site. A close inspection revealed no bullet holes in the jeep, and a thorough sweep of the area from which the fire had allegedly come produced no spent cartridges or any other evidence to corroborate King's story. My suspicions, which I could not confirm, were that there was no ambush, but that King and party, as guests of the Phu Lam hamlet chief, had inhaled one too many Bière Larues and that while speeding back they were either clowning around or simply lost control and flipped the jeep. Lacking further evidence to the contrary, the incident was officially listed as "vehicle damaged as a result of automatic weapons fire." The engineers towed the jeep in the next morning. It was ultimately retrieved by province headquarters, and about a week later a replacement arrived.

There was very little discussion among team members, at least in my presence, about the incident. SFC King's tour was up about three weeks later, but in the interim I quietly limited his unsupervised travel. He offered no objection.

About two weeks after King's departure, the truth came to light. As I had suspected, there were no shots. King not only had too much to drink, but also had a "roadie" in his possession when he lost control while speeding and horsing around. They had cleaned up the crash site before we arrived, and King had sworn everyone to secrecy. They all agreed not to talk because, since he had only a few weeks to go, no one wanted to see him get into serious trouble. When I informed

Major Xuan as to what had really happened, he smiled sheepishly and said, "I know." It turned out he also had known the truth all along.

THE POTENTIAL FOR ambush was real for anyone serving in Vietnam, but it was especially real for those serving as advisors. In such an environment, luck and fate played a major role in deciding who survived and who did not. You were an easy target: highly visible, lightly armed, usually traveling alone or in small groups of two or three, frequently in an isolated location, traveling a limited road network, and often following a very predictable pattern. For those of us in Dinh Quan, if you traveled anywhere outside the village there was only one road—Highway 20—that we could travel, both going out and coming back. Conventional wisdom was that if the VC decided to get you, they could. There certainly were a great many opportunities. Although we tried our best to be alert and not do anything stupid, the nature of our job and the environment in which we operated placed us constantly at risk. Every advisor has his own story to tell. In addition to my own experiences, my other West Point roommate, Capt. James Blesse, similarly benefited from a fateful intervention.

Jim was a Special Forces officer in 1966, serving as an A Detachment commander in Chau Doc Province in the IV CTZ. While traveling by jeep to meet with the commander of a Khmer Kampuchea Krom (ethnic Cambodian) battalion that had recently rallied to the Vietnamese government, he unknowingly drove through a VC ambush site. As was later learned, the ambush was in position alongside the road waiting for him when a runner arrived and told them not to execute the ambush. There was no time for them to pull out prior to the arrival of Blesse's jeep, so the VC stayed in position and watched as he drove by. It turns out the local VC who had established the ambush were part of a VC platoon that was quietly negotiating with the Vietnamese for their entire platoon to rally to the Vietnamese government. The VC platoon leader at the last moment had decided that he didn't want to do anything that might risk the success of those negotiations, so the ambush was called off literally seconds before it was to be triggered. This was all confirmed the following month when the VC platoon consisting of seventeen men and twenty-seven weapons surrendered without incident under the *Chieu Hoi* Program.

CHAPTER 34

The Crash

Staff Sergeant Michels watched the plane make lazy circles overhead as the pilot sized up our landing strip. Landing anything other than a helicopter in Dinh Quan was quite a challenge.

There was an unmanned district landing strip about a mile northeast of the team house. The airfield had been constructed years earlier and consisted of a built-up laterite strip, which as I recall was roughly six hundred to seven hundred feet long and thirty-five feet wide. The surface of the runway was four to six feet above the surrounding area. Trees had been cut down at both ends of the runway, but their trunks lay where they had fallen and the large stumps, which had not been removed, protruded upward several feet above the ground. Because of the runway's inadequate length, the strip was seldom used. In addition, the availability of helicopters from the mid-1960s onward greatly reduced the use of fixed-wing aircraft for logistical support or passenger travel. The air force had closed the Dinh Quan strip to its traffic, but the army with its lighter "short field" aircraft still listed it as open.

The area surrounding the airstrip was a lowland that during the several months of the monsoon season filled with water. The airstrip sitting in the middle of the flooded area resembled an aircraft carrier without its superstructure. The airfield was unmanned; there was no tower, no parking area, and no buildings or support facilities. Only a tattered windsock stood vigil. It was the responsibility of the Vietnamese road security force to check the runway each morning to look for any evidence that it may have been mined or booby-trapped.

The normal procedure for any aircraft wanting to land was simply to contact us on the province radio net. If the pilot didn't know the proper frequency, he was to make a low pass over our team house, alerting us to put one of our radios on the established aircraft frequency. Upon establishing radio contact, we would advise the pilot of any security concerns around the airfield, caution him about the short length of the runway, and dispatch a vehicle to the landing strip to pick up passengers or cargo.

On this occasion, the plane did neither—no radio contact and no low overhead pass. It was an army U20 Beaver with a pilot and four passengers aboard. The passengers were senior officers of the U.S. 18th Engineer Brigade on their way to inspect the Highway 20 construction project and visit the local engineer company doing the work.

Michels happened to be outside working on one of the vehicles when he noticed the plane circling as if preparing to land. On the final pass, it circled low, well out beyond the village, and disappeared behind the bunkhouse, which was blocking Michels's line of sight. A few minutes later a motorbike sped up to the fence opposite where Michels was working. The driver was shouting excitedly and pointing frantically back up the highway in the direction of the landing strip. "Airplane! Airplane!" he shouted.

Michels ran into the team house, grabbed his medical bag, and yelled for me to join him. "I think a plane just crashed at the airstrip!" he shouted. I had been working on the monthly reports at the dining room table. In an instant I was out the door and into the jeep, and we were speeding away from the team house. As we cleared the compound, we could see an ugly black column of smoke climbing into the sky above the airstrip. The man on the motorbike raced ahead of us, waving us on.

Arriving at the airfield, we could see the plane, about a hundred feet off the western end of the airstrip, laying astride a huge tree trunk. One wing was broken off, the bottom of the plane had been ripped open by a jagged tree stump, the fuel cells had been ruptured, and the plane was burning furiously. The crash had broken the fuselage apart, and two of the passengers were lying on the ground beside the wreckage. Numerous explosions filled the air as the intense heat from the flames set off munitions aboard the plane. The pilot had managed to free himself, and although badly burned, crawled out of the wreckage and slumped to the ground just as we arrived. Two other passengers were still in the plane. With the flames and the explosions intensifying, there wasn't a minute to spare. Without thinking, Michels and I crawled into the plane and pulled the two officers out and onto the ground, dragging them and then the others a safe distance from the burning aircraft.

It was only then that we could begin attending to their injuries. All exposed flesh was severely burned. The epidermis from their faces had literally melted away and was hanging down below their chins like a grotesque translucent necklace. While Michels treated them as best he could, I got on the radio and called for help. Fortunately, there was a helicopter operating about twenty miles to our southeast; it responded to my "Mayday" call and was on the scene in about fifteen minutes.

As we helped these badly injured men into the helicopter, I was struck by the calm they displayed. I don't know if it was shock or incredible composure, but they weren't showing any signs of the terrible pain that I was sure was to come, and as we got the last one aboard, the senior officer of the group thanked us for our help. I never knew their names, or what ultimately happened to them, although the local engineer company commander said he heard they had been evacuated to a burn treatment facility in Japan. *Bac-si* and I were very fortunate. Except for some minor burns, we escaped uninjured, though the loss of hair from our faces and arms and the bright-red sunburn-like glow did leave us looking strange for a while.

The Vietnamese established security around the area to keep people away from the burning aircraft. With no firefighting capability within the district, the plane's fire was simply permitted to burn itself out. Having spent a previous Vietnam tour in an aviation unit, I knew that an accident investigator would soon be on the scene, so I asked that security be maintained at the site and that no one be allowed near the aircraft or to remove anything from the area. I walked the landing strip itself, noting the tire prints and marking the beginning and ending of the tracks. Even to me it was obvious what had happened: the pilot had used up nearly half of the strip before his wheels touched down, and when he realized that he couldn't stop the plane before he ran off the edge, he applied full power in an effort to get airborne once again. The plane lifted off the runway momentarily, but because of insufficient airspeed was unable to climb and crashed onto the stumps off the end of the runway.

The investigator would subsequently rule it "pilot error"; how-ever, both the airfield and the aircraft itself may have been major con-tributors to this accident. The short landing strip with tall trees at both ends forced a fixed-wing pilot to "fly into the runway." Other-wise, as apparently happened in this case, the plane would be well down the runway before touching down. Further, the Beaver, an army aircraft built by de Havilland, was famous (or infamous) for its glide capability. Pilots have told me that you could be just above the runway and chop power and the aircraft would continue to glide; it just wouldn't settle in. I suspect that is what happened in this case.

Staff Sergeant Michels was awarded the Soldier's Medal, the army's highest award for valor not involving combat, for his actions during this incident.

The army subsequently closed the Dinh Quan airstrip to fixed-wing aircraft.

CHAPTER 35

R&R

As she entered the room, a low murmur arose. Conscious that all eyes were on her, she walked gracefully to the deserted far end of the bar and took her place on a stool where she could observe the entire room and likewise be observed. She was arguably the most beautiful woman I had ever seen—long black hair, delicate Eurasian features, beautiful eyes, and a gorgeous body. She was stunning!

I sat at the bar with my two comrades, an American lieutenant also in Hong Kong on R&R and Edward, a New Zealander living in Hong Kong who was a regular at this particular bar, quietly admiring this lovely creature. After a long moment the lieutenant broke the silence by summoning the bartender to tell him he wanted to buy the lady a drink.

The bartender grinned slyly, exchanged knowing glances with the New Zealander, and said, "Sure." He ambled down the length of the bar and said something to the lady. She responded by raising her head, nodding, and giving the lieutenant a warm smile.

At that, the lieutenant grinned at us and said, "That's my cue! Don't wait up!"

As he was sliding off the bar stool, our Kiwi companion casually said, "I wouldn't do that if I were you."

The lieutenant stopped. "Why not?" he asked. "She's gorgeous!"

"What you see is not always what you get," Edward replied.

Looking slightly confused, the lieutenant said, "What the hell are you talking about?"

At that, a broad grin lit up Edward's face. "She's not a she," he said.

"What are you talking about?" the lieutenant demanded.

"It's simple—she's a he!"

"Cut the crap," our lieutenant friend responded. "You're trying to tell me that beautiful creature is a man?"

"That's exactly what I'm telling you." By this time the bartender had joined us. "Tell him, mate," Edward said, gesturing toward the bartender.

"It's true," responded the bartender. He reached under the bar and pulled out a newspaper. He rummaged through it for a few seconds and slapped it on the bar. "Here, see for yourself."

It was a large ad by a Hong Kong night club announcing their world famous nightclub production featuring the world's most beautiful female impersonators. In the left corner of the ad was a picture of "the lady" at the bar. She was the feature attraction! There was a moment of disbelief, then the lieutenant let out an "Oh my God!" and climbed back onto his bar stool.

The "lady" had observed all this and understood immediately what had happened. She grinned at us and raised her glass in salute. With great solemnity we returned her toast. We watched her carefully for the rest of the evening as Edward, who prided himself on knowing Hong Kong, gave us endless advice on where to go, what to see, where to get the best bargains, best food, and best prostitutes. You name it, Edward knew where to get it!

Several times during the evening, our lady friend danced with the unsuspecting; she was as graceful as a cat. Around 9:00 P.M., a U.S. Navy captain, looking dashing in his white uniform, entered the bar, surveyed the scene, and moved without hesitation onto the vacant bar stool next to her. As the evening wore on, they danced, they drank, they whispered, they kissed, and they laughed—it was a sight to behold. I had promised myself I was going to turn in early that evening, but there was no way I was going to miss this.

Around midnight, the captain, beaming like the proverbial cat that ate the canary, strutted out of the bar with our lady friend securely attached to his arm. As soon as they cleared the door, a roar went up in the bar—apparently, we weren't the only ones in in the know. I've often thought back to that incident, wondering just how it all played out and trying to picture the captain's reaction at the inevitable moment of truth.

Experiences like this became legend and contributed to making R&R the most popular activity available to those serving in Vietnam.

The program was intended to give servicemen in Vietnam a brief respite from the combat zone. There was an in-country program that allowed soldiers a week at R&R centers in Vung Tau or China Beach, basking in the sun and enjoying the beaches, movies, live entertainment, and good chow. However, the most popular R&R destinations were those out-of-country. Trips were available to Hawaii, Bangkok, Singapore, Australia, Hong Kong, Manila, Tokyo, Taipei, and Kuala Lumpur.

At these sites, the troops could completely escape the war. They were flown in and given five to seven days on their own. For many, it was a non-stop orgy of wine, women, and song. For others, it was an opportunity to get away from the war, to relax and regroup, and to do a little sightseeing and shopping. Some flew to Hawaii to meet their wives or girlfriends for a week of reunion and renewal.

Among the GIs, Bangkok was perhaps the most popular. It was the city for fun and sex. The practice of "buying" a bar girl for the entire week of the R&R was common and, of course, the thing of which legends are made!

For the serious shopper, however, Hong Kong was the destination of choice. Invariably those destined for Hong Kong were laden with everyone's shopping lists. Hong Kong was a shopper's paradise—a place where you could find everything from tailor-made clothing to Rolex watches to photographic equipment to the latest in electronics, and it was all available at duty-free bargain basement prices. It was a city that thrived on trade and services, and almost anything you wanted could be had. During my three tours to Vietnam I made three trips to Hong Kong, each time armed with multiple shopping lists and several thousand dollars.

Among the greatest pleasures of R&R was the opportunity to stay in a first-class hotel and to experience clean sheets, air conditioning, a delicious quietness, and the feeling of complete security. And, of course, the *coup de grâce* was the opportunity to gorge yourself in top-notch restaurants.

Sightseeing in Hong Kong was easy. The competition among tailors was so intense that they solicited the troops at the R&R in-processing center and in the hotel lobbies. They all offered free escorted tours of the city to include the Tiger Balm Gardens, the harbor, Victoria Point, Kowloon, and the out country. They offered advice on the best girls and the best deals. What they hoped for in return was your business. Tailor-made clothing was a bargain. A suit could be produced in three or four days with only a couple of fittings. The tailors also profited from kickbacks as they referred their customers to the "very best place in Hong Kong" to buy whatever it was that the GI wanted to buy, so haggling in these referral shops was the norm. To make things a little easier for U.S. servicemen, the U.S. Navy operated a "ship's store" in Kowloon where all sorts of goods could be purchased. They would pack and crate all purchases for shipping. If a copy of your orders was included, your crate of treasures could be shipped to the United States and not be taxed by U.S. customs. Sometimes, after arduous bargaining with local merchants, you could beat the ship's store prices, but in most cases it was either a draw or the ship's store did better. At least with the ship's store you were assured of the quality of the product you were purchasing. More than one GI purchased a bargain-priced Rolex from an unscrupulous vendor, only to learn later that it was a cheap knockoff.

I was able to get my wife a Canadian EMBA mink stole at duty-free prices, even though the stole was made in Canada and shipped directly from there without ever being in Hong Kong. Simply placing the order in Hong Kong somehow saved me several hundred dollars. I didn't understand it, but I took full advantage of it. Mikimoto pearls from Japan, precious stones from Thailand, wool from England, and Japanese cameras and audio equipment were among the many treasures I acquired during my three trips.

Probably my favorite personal purchase was a pair of handmade shoes. The process started with me standing barefoot on a blank piece of poster board while the outline of my feet was carefully traced. I returned the next day for an intermediate fitting of the shell of the shoe. The shoes were completed on the fourth day. The final product was terrific—the perfect fit. Those were the most comfortable shoes I ever owned. I wore them for years, replacing the heels and soles seven or eight times. Finally, the uppers became so disreputable that my family refused to appear in public with me wearing them. It was a sad day when the trash man hauled them away.

Hong Kong was an amazing place. It was the hotbed of free trade and capitalism, but located in the very heart of all this imperialist decadence was the Chinese Communist store. This communist venture into capitalism was very successful. They offered a plethora of Chinese-made goods at extremely good prices. The store was an interesting place to visit. Heroic paintings of Schwarzenegger-physiqued communist workers adorned the walls, and Party slogans were everywhere. While songs extolling the virtues of the communist workers blared in the background, the cash registers rang out in true capitalist fashion. I never gave more than a passing thought to the irony inherent in the fact that two days before I had been engaged in a struggle to kill communist insurgents armed and equipped by the same Chinese government that commissioned this store from which I was so freely purchasing goods!

I recall they had beautiful lace and magnificent furs. Having already purchased my wife's Canadian mink, I was admiring the many fur hats available in the store. These were incredibly beautiful, and I was just about to purchase one when an Australian gentleman walked over to me, cleared his throat, and said, "You really don't want to buy that!"

"Why not?" I inquired. "These furs are gorgeous!"

"Indeed they are, but the Chinese cure the skins with the uric acid from human urine, and when the furs get wet they smell like a dirty restroom urinal—quite ghastly!" he advised.

I thank him, and armed with this good advice, I passed.

Major Xuan had saved up for nearly a year for a Panasonic stereo system: tuner/amplifier, turntable, and speakers. The night before I went to Hong Kong, he came over, thrust into my hand a wad of money—a combination of greenbacks and MPCs—and gave me his order. Fortunately, I was able to find everything he wanted and somehow managed to get it all back in one piece. For him it was just like Christmas. He invited everyone in to see his new stereo system, and from then on, each evening, music from his quarters could be heard drifting across the compound.

During my final visit to Hong Kong, I inadvertently experienced an incredibly moving moment—one I have never forgotten. I was eating a late dinner one evening in the hotel dining room, one of those penthouse restaurants that afforded a spectacular view of the Hong Kong harbor. It had been a long day, so I was enjoying a leisurely meal, taking in the view, and enjoying the music provided by strolling violinists. Because it was late, most of the tables were now empty, but two tables away sat an elderly couple who appeared to be equally enjoying the evening. As the violinists approached their table, they began to play "Edelweiss." I recognized the song and was aware of its significance as the unofficial national song of Austria, because in Dinh Quan just a few days prior, we had watched *The Sound of Music*, and that song was prominent in the film. As the violins played, the elderly woman began to sob uncontrollably. Confused, the violinists halted the song. The elderly gentleman apologized and asked them to continue. The man and woman sat there and cried through the entire song. The maître d' came over to inquire about the problem and offer his assistance. With a heavy accent, the man explained that he and his wife were Austrian Jews who had fled their homeland in 1940 to escape the Nazis. They had left everything behind and had never returned. They were now on a trip to return to Austria for the first time after nearly thirty years. "Edelweiss" had triggered an outpouring of emotion that had been bottled up for three decades. They asked the violinists to play it once more, and as they did everyone in the restaurant cried. In the nearly thirty years since that experience, whenever I hear the haunting strains of that beautiful song I am carried back to that memorable and moving moment in Hong Kong in 1970.

The week of R&R was always up too soon, and the flight back was far more somber than the flight out. Watching the plane unload in Saigon reminded me of watching the unloading of those tour buses that take women's clubs on trips to outlets—the pile of boxes and crates unloaded appeared to be bigger than the plane itself!

Team members returning from R&R always offered sage advice to the others on where to go, what to buy, and the pitfalls to avoid. But most importantly, they entertained the rest of the team for several days with tales of their respective adventures, providing vicarious pleasures for those who had stayed behind. As with everything else, the tales got a little better with each recounting.

CHAPTER 36

The Thai Traveling Show

O f all the strange events that took place during my tour as district senior advisor in Dinh Quan, surely the most bizarre was the arrival of a troupe of Thai dancers. They had been booked in Dinh Quan by the USO entertainment office to provide entertainment for the troops of the 4th Battalion, 12th Infantry, of the U.S. 199th Brigade, which was occupying Firebase Nancy about a quarter mile northeast of Dinh Quan.

In planning the troupe's itinerary, the powers that be had failed to make any arrangements for them to stay overnight. So on a Saturday afternoon they rolled into Dinh Quan looking for a hotel. Dinh Quan had many things to offer visitors, but a hotel was not among them. The troupe consisted of a manager, a sound man, a singer and five dancers. The girls were young and pretty and spoke only a little pidgin English.

Nightfall was rapidly approaching, and it suddenly occurred to the manager that he was deep in "Indian Country," as we used to say, and with no place to stay. He first tried the U.S. firebase. The battalion commander wouldn't let them to stay on the firebase because of security concerns and the fact that there was no place there to accommodate females. Quite nervous and upset, the troupe manager came to see me late in the afternoon, pleading for a place to stay. I reluctantly agreed to take them in for the night.

In front of our team house we had a small bunkhouse, which the engineers had constructed for us to house a small team who operated a rock crusher just on the outskirts of Dinh Quan. By living with us, the rock crusher detachment didn't have to make the 6-mile trip between the quarry and the engineer compound in early morning

and late afternoon. Fortunately for the Thai troupe, the crusher operation had shut down several months before, so the bunkhouse, which
could sleep eight people, was available. Despite the availability of bunk
space, team members, in a moving gesture of compassion, had all volunteered to share their bunks with the girls! Not only did I nix that,
but in anticipation of hormones run amok, I made it clear that the
bunkhouse and the girls were off limits—another popular decision.

In return for the overnight accommodations, I insisted that the
troupe give a free performance that evening for the people of the village. Major Xuan thought this was a wonderful idea and hurried to
get the word out to the local villagers and nearby military units. By
performance time, several hundred Vietnamese men, women, and
children were present.

The performance was to be conducted on a raised platform in
front of district headquarters. The platform, generally used as a
reviewing stand for VIPs during military ceremonies, also served as
the focal point for punishments administered under the authority of
the district chief. It was not unusual to find a Vietnamese soldier
kneeling bareheaded on that concrete platform for hours through
the heat of the day as punishment for some minor infraction.

In preparation for the performance, Major Xuan had a number
of chairs moved into the yard for me, himself, his senior staff, and the
local village and hamlet chiefs. Small tables were brought out and put
in place for the cognac and beer that would be available for his special guests during the show. Lights were rigged and electricity provided to the Thai sound man so he could operate his tape player,
amplifier, and giant speakers. As the Vietnamese soldiers and villagers arrived, they crowded close behind the VIP row and hunkered
down in typical Vietnamese style. There was eager anticipation, a
near carnival atmosphere, among the growing crowd. Children were
running around excitedly. Dinh Quan didn't often have professional
entertainment, and this show was provided by the *Co Van My* (American advisor), so it was surely going to be something special! They
were not to be disappointed—special hardly describes it.

Following a brief speech by Major Xuan praising me and thank-
ing me for providing this entertainment, there was wild applause
from the crowd. Then, with a musical fanfare blaring from the
troupe's oversized speakers, the show began. The show was billed as

ninety minutes of quality entertainment, featuring some of Thailand's most promising young singers and dancers. As it turned out, what followed proved to be the longest forty minutes of my life.

As the singer wailed out a Thai version of "Proud Mary," a popular American rock tune at that time, the dancers began to gyrate around the stage. As they did, my discomfort level rose exponentially. Soon they were pulling off pieces of their clothing, until clad only in the skimpiest of halter tops and G-strings, they began bumping and grinding grotesquely. My immediate reaction was, "Oh my God!" I didn't know whether to crawl under my chair or call a halt to the show. By this time, the Vietnamese were howling with delight. I leaned over and embarrassedly explained my concern to the district chief, but he just grinned and said let it continue.

So on it went, and the longer it went, the worse it got! With dozens of giggling Vietnamese children crowded around the platform, the dancers began to writhe around the floor and to "dry hump" the microphone stand, the corner of the stage, the speakers, and anything else that was standing still. I looked over at the Thai manager who was standing beside the stage; he was grinning proudly, his gold front tooth gleaming in the stage lights. The crowd was roaring, but I didn't know if it was in approval or in protest. All I knew was that I was dying a slow, painful death.

Those who know me will vouch for the fact that I am anything but a prude, but the show was getting raunchier by the minute, and I dreaded to think where it was heading. The dancers seemed totally unfazed by the presence of women and children. As the show continued, two of the dancers began to rub their genitals against each other, while moaning and clutching their breasts. Frantically I signaled one of the team NCOs who was standing near the stage and discreetly gave him the slash across the throat sign. He grabbed the troupe manager, and at the end of the song, the plug was pulled. I immediately leaped to my feet and began shaking hands with the assembled dignitaries, giving a clear sign to all present that the show was over. It had lasted only forty minutes, but to me it seemed like forty days! While the Vietnamese, who thought it was wonderful, hooted and applauded, I quietly slunk away.

After that show, I was tempted to put an armed guard at the door of the bunkhouse, both to keep members of the troupe inside and to keep my team members and the Vietnamese soldiers out. To the best of my knowledge, the night passed uneventfully.

The next morning I was anxious to see the troupe on its way. They were to give two performances at the U.S. firebase before returning to Saigon that afternoon. I had a previously scheduled visit with the battalion commander at the firebase that day to coordinate an upcoming operation in which some of the district Regional Force companies would join with U.S. forces. When I arrived at the firebase in late morning, the second and final show was well underway.

The troops were sitting on sandbags arrayed along the hillside above and surrounding on three sides, a makeshift stage at the bottom. The stage was backed right up to the perimeter wire and minefields surrounding the firebase. From what I could observe, my fears the previous evening about where the show was heading were justified. The dancers had shed their tops and were slithering around clad only in G-strings. The scene was general pandemonium. The several hundred assembled GIs were "in heat"—screaming and groaning. Those gathered about the foot of the stage were lunging at the girls every time they came near. The girls deftly avoided the clumsy lunges and didn't miss a beat. As expected, soon the G-strings came off and were tossed into the crowd, causing a near riot as the troops scrambled to recover these treasures. I started to worry about how they were going to get those naked girls out of there—the only routes out were through the concertina wire and minefield to their rear or through the crowd of now sex-crazed soldiers!

At the absolute height of the frenzy, the show suddenly stopped for a brief intermission. Almost magically, the girls, troupe manager, and sound man immediately produced cartons of 12-inch by 18-inch framed pictures, which the girls proceeded to sell as they moved among the troops. Although the girls—draped now only in short, filmy robes that concealed nothing and that they made no effort to close—were being groped and pawed as they moved through the crowd, they were undeterred, appearing not to even notice. They were too busy taking the money from the GIs. Soldiers were crowding, pushing, shoving, and literally throwing money at them in an effort to buy the pictures.

As the girls worked their way up the hill toward my vantage point, I was finally able to get a good look at the pictures they were peddling.

Proving the old adage that "Truth is stranger than fiction," these nude girls were selling cheaply framed gold and silver metallic paintings of Jesus! Worse yet, the eyes of Jesus appeared to follow you wherever you went. After selling more than a hundred at some outlandish price, intermission ended, and the rest of the show went on. Time didn't permit me to stay for the second half, but throughout my meeting with the battalion commander I could hear the roar from the GIs. I tried not to think about what might be going on!

I am sure that today in households across America there are still scores of those pictures adorning walls or tucked away in attics. I have often wondered what the mothers and girlfriends to whom these pictures were lovingly shipped would do if they had the slightest inkling of their colorful origins.

My three tours in Vietnam included a number of absurdities, but the visit of the Thai troupe has to rank at the very top.

CHAPTER 37

My Lai

About the mid-point of my tour, details of the My Lai massacre began to surface little by little. Although the incident had occurred more than twenty-one months previously, it was not until Ron Ridenhour, a former GI who had heard accounts of the incident from participants, made it public that the army launched its investigation.

It was difficult to get a great deal of information in Vietnam because the army was trying to keep a lid on the incident, and the two official information sources in Vietnam, the *Stars and Stripes* newspaper and the Armed Forces Radio and Television Network, were controlled by the Department of Defense. Additionally, the incident didn't receive much play in the Vietnamese media because the Vietnamese government didn't want to embarrass the U.S. and took the public position that it was simply a regrettable consequence of the war.

What we did manage to learn, however, was that elements of the 1st Battalion, 20th Infantry (most specifically Company C), of the Americal Division had taken part in a cold-blooded mass murder of nearly 500 unarmed Vietnamese civilians, mostly old men, women, and children. Methodically rounding up the terrified noncombatant residents of the hamlet of My Lai in Quang Ngai Province, American soldiers had brutally subjected many to rape, torture, and sodomy before herding them into ditches where they were summarily executed.

Among members of our advisory team there was genuine shock and remorse. We talked about this incident a great deal, trying to understand how it could have happened. I had commanded an infantry company in Vietnam and was aware of the frustrations experienced as casualties are inflicted by an elusive and often unseen enemy. Additionally, I knew the general attitudes in those units toward the Vietnamese.

But there was no excuse, no explanation, no rationalization that could justify the soldiers' conduct at My Lai—it was murder, pure and simple.

Some have argued that the soldiers who participated were simply following orders, that they had no choice. That defense didn't work in Nuremberg at the end of World War II, and it was equally hollow in justifying the actions at My Lai. The order to kill civilians was an unlawful order, the soldiers knew it, and many in that unit rightfully refused to obey it.

The conclusions (if you can call them that) we in Dinh Quan reached placed the blame on poor leadership and what appeared to us to be the continuing disintegration of U.S. units in Vietnam. The army's personnel policies, the one-year tour, and the exodus of potential talent through liberal deferments and draft evasion had by the late 1960s resulted in a diminution of quality in the newly commissioned officers, thus allowing into the officer ranks many who by normal standards would have been rejected. Likewise, the noncommissioned officer corps was weakened by such expedient measures as the "shake and bake" sergeants (individuals right out of training promoted to fill needs) and massive field promotions that accelerated advancement to higher grades, all of which produced an inexperienced, often immature, and frequently inept leadership from sergeant up through the junior officer level. Added to these issues were the officer turnover rate generated by six-month commands, the pressure to produce results during these abbreviated command tours, and the "body count" mentality that equated enemy bodies with success.

Further, the absence of unit training played a role; individual replacements had only Basic Combat Training and Advanced Individual Training to prepare them. Missing was the unit training that produced teamwork, sharpened skills, ingrained values, instilled discipline, and thereby polished the young soldier.

The disintegration of the U.S. units in Vietnam was shockingly clear to those of us who had served tours with U.S. units early in the war. I dealt frequently with the U.S. 199th Infantry Brigade and had contact with other U.S. units when they operated in our area of operations. In addition, I recall that Maj. Bob Boyd, the province G-3 advisor, and I visited the U.S. 1st Infantry Division in Dian. Bob and I had served together as infantry company commanders in the 18th Infantry Regiment in the 1st Division in 1965–66. After our visit we commented on the sharp contrast between 1965 and 1969. We had deployed to Vietnam with the 1st Division from its base at Fort Riley, Kansas. At the time of deployment we were a cohesive unit complete with professional and experienced officers and noncommissioned officers. We were a well-trained and disciplined organization. We believed in our unit and our mission.

The turnover, individual replacements, lack of adequate training, unpopularity of the war, and decreasing quality of leadership often resulted in ragtag units where soldiers often looked like guerrillas, discipline was lax, drugs abounded, and cohesiveness was nearly non-existent. The blatant drug use and the growing incidences of "fragging"—tossing live grenades into the quarters of unpopular officers or NCOs—attest to this disintegration. Thus, My Lai—probably the most shameful American event of the entire war.

Amazingly, the Vietnamese in Dinh Quan remained clear of the My Lai incident. There was some passing reference that acknowledged the affair, but the outrage I expected never visibly materialized. Perhaps the Vietnamese concern with not wanting to embarrass their "guests" came into play. Major Xuan and I did discuss it one evening, and while he also couldn't understand it, he was willing to dismiss it as an unfortunate event—one of many that could be expected in such a brutal war.

My Lai bothered me then, and it continues to bother me now from the distance of nearly three decades. I am most troubled by the Army's unwillingness to aggressively pursue it and by the subsequent whitewash attempts associated with the whole affair. I am likewise disappointed in the American political leadership that alibied for Lt. William Calley's actions and attempted to turn him into a national hero.

Not surprisingly, the incident was seized by the political left as more evidence of the war's insanity and the corruption of U.S. policy in Vietnam. The resulting public outcry further pressured the Nixon administration to accelerate U.S. disengagement under the guise of Vietnamization.

Not only did the My Lai incident and its subsequent handling irrevocably stain the proud history of the U.S. Army, it also severely damaged the integrity of the officer corps and cast an undeserved pall over all those honorable men who served their country during the Vietnam War.

PART SEVEN

Closing Scenes

CHAPTER 38

Vietnamization: The Beginning of the End

My arrival in Vietnam in the spring of 1969 coincided with the high-water mark of U.S. military presence in Vietnam. More than 550,000 Americans were on the ground, and the U.S. advisory effort was at its peak, with more than 14,000 advisors in the field. Unfortunately, U.S. casualties had also reached record highs for the war.

In the United States, the escalating casualties, resistance to the draft, and lack of discernable progress in the war were fueling the fires of discontent, prompting demonstrations and protests that likewise had risen to new levels. The Chicago 8 were on trial and the "Age of Aquarius" was upon us. President Nixon had just taken office after being elected on a promise to bring U.S. forces home from Vietnam.

Amid increasing pressure to act, President Nixon met with Vietnamese President Thieu on the island of Midway on June 8, 1969. The communiqué reporting the meeting announced that the United States would withdraw 25,000 U.S. soldiers from Vietnam before the end of that August. Both Thieu and Nixon emphasized that the U.S. forces would be replaced in the field by Vietnamese units. Thus began the transition. The war effort was being handed over to the Vietnamese. Vietnamization, as it came to be known, had begun.

The Vietnamization program was consistent with the Nixon Doctrine, which President Nixon had espoused as the new American foreign policy shortly after he took office in January 1969. In short, the Nixon Doctrine said that while the United States would provide arms and logistical support to its allies who were engaged in internal counterinsurgency operations, we would no longer provide U.S. combat troops.

For Vietnam, the writing was on the wall. The United States was withdrawing, and the burden of fighting the war was being handed to them—ready or not. Despite promises that the rate of U.S. military withdrawal would be determined by General Abrams's assessment (Abrams had replaced Westmoreland as COMUSMACV) of the readiness of the Vietnamese military to assume the combat role, American withdrawals, driven by domestic political considerations rather than military ones, came rapidly. On September 16, 1969, came the second troop withdrawal announcement. This time a 35,000-troop drawdown was announced, and yet another announcement for an additional 50,000 troops came on December 15. The United States had reduced its combat presence by more than 20 percent in less than six months.

In the United States, the spring of 1970 brought protest and campus unrest to new heights, culminating in the tragic shootings at Kent State. Succumbing to increasing pressures and criticisms, the administration chose to ignore assessments of Vietnamese capabilities and continued the withdrawals at an accelerated pace.

For the advisory effort, the Vietnamization announcement meant redoubled efforts to train and prepare the more than 900,000 Vietnamese serving in ARVN, Regional Force, and Popular Force Units. In the months to come, the Vietnamese forces would grow to over one million men in the field. Considerable effort was to be focused on the already improving Regional and Popular Forces so that they could relieve the regular ARVN forces from security duty, freeing them for a more mobile combat mission. In addition, the CORDS' focus was to strengthen efforts at pacification and nation-building, and through the Phoenix Program, to press the attack against the local Viet Cong infrastructure.

For us at Dinh Quan, the announcement of the Vietnamization program had a sobering effect. Among the advisory team, our assessment was unanimous—we felt it was too soon and all happening too quickly. Locally, we determined to do what we could to prepare Dinh Quan District for what lay ahead. Between our team efforts and the four MAT teams now assigned to our district, we assisted the RF and PF forces as best we could. We worked with them on local operations, were able to arrange several joint operations with the U.S. 199th Brigade, and continued efforts to obtain M16 rifles for all local forces.

We constructed a rifle range to assist in the familiarization with and training on the new weapons. Additionally, we scrounged every piece of equipment and supplies we could get our hands on from U.S. units—sandbags, grenades, Claymore mines, weapons, and munitions of all sorts—if it wasn't nailed down we went for it. Although I felt good about the progress our local units were making, I knew from my previous tour with the U.S. 1st Infantry Division that they were far from being ready for prime time, and the clock was running.

Concurrently, Captain Hughes stepped up efforts of the Phoenix Program to identify and eliminate the leadership of the local Viet Cong cadres. On the nation-building side, efforts continued to move forward with the many projects underway: roads, schools, sanitation, hospitals, and economic development were all making slow but visible progress.

The announcement of the Vietnamization program had a devastating effect on the Vietnamese officers and officials of the district. I recall one evening shortly after the announcement, Major Xuan and I were sitting alone in the team house enjoying a drink and quietly discussing district business and the events of the day. After a few drinks, he slumped forward, turned slowly to face me and said, "You know, *Thieu-ta,* I am a dead man." I will never forget the sadness in his voice or the pain in his expression. Surprised at this sudden turn, I asked him what he meant. He responded by saying it was all over for Vietnam. He was certain that when the Americans withdrew, the Vietnamese army would be unable to withstand the simultaneous internal attack from the Viet Cong and the external offensive of the North Vietnamese Army. I tried my best to assure him that the Vietnamese Army had made great progress and that America was not just going to abandon Vietnam after all we had been through, but I must not have been very convincing. He went on to say, "You know well that I am not a corrupt man. I have not stolen from the people of Dinh Quan or from the government. I am therefore not a wealthy man. I will not be able to buy my way out when the end comes, and I am not high enough in the Vietnamese hierarchy to be evacuated by your government. In the course of my duties, I have prosecuted and persecuted the Viet Cong in Dinh Quan. I am a marked man with a price on my head. When the end comes, I and my family will all be killed." The depth of his despair was overwhelming.

We sat there in the heavy silence, each deep in our own thoughts. Suddenly the impact of his words hit me. "My God," I thought, "it's true. We are going to abandon these people. We encouraged and supported them, and they committed. Now we are going to just walk away—leaving them at the mercy of the communists." I couldn't even respond. I wanted to reassure him, to tell him it would be all right, but I couldn't. I just sat there with him. After some time he got up, and without saying a word walked slowly back across the compound to his quarters. We never spoke of it again.

As events were ultimately to unfold, Major Xuan's assessment and prognostication that August evening were remarkably accurate. The end came just as he had foreseen it—the army did collapse, and the wealthy and influential Vietnamese did escape.

After the war, I was unable to learn what happened to Major Xuan and his family. I didn't know if he was able to get out of Vietnam or not. It was only after completing this book that I finally learned Major Xuan died from starvation after five brutal years in a communist "re-education camp." I will never forget his words or that moment when he shared his despair. As an advisor living among the Vietnamese and working with them daily for fourteen months, I had come to know them well. I knew them personally and professionally. I knew their families, I knew their strengths, and I understood their weaknesses. They trusted me and accepted me. They were my colleagues and my friends. Twenty-nine years later, I still carry my private share of our country's guilt for the shameful abandonment of our friends and allies. It is a guilt I will carry with me to the grave.

CHAPTER 39

The Painting

The jeep bounced across the tarmac at a high speed, coming directly toward the helicopter. It screeched to a halt just beyond the arc of the rotor blades, and out jumped Lieutenant Colonel Diem, the province chief. He had come personally to see me off and to present me with a special gift. It was a touching and awkward moment.

The events leading to this gesture went back to the beginning of my fourteen months in Long Khanh Province. Early in my tour I was summoned to province headquarters in Xuan Loc to attend a meeting of senior advisors. The morning portion of the meeting was a joint session with our Vietnamese counterparts, and when we broke for lunch, Lieutenant Colonel Diem invited Xuan (still a captain at that time) and me over to his home for dinner that evening. Naturally, we accepted. Captain Xuan advised me that this was a great honor, since Diem rarely invited people to his home.

We arrived on time, and I was surprised to find that his home was a western-style villa (previously French-owned) tastefully appointed in a mixture of western and Vietnamese furniture and decorations. The dining room was decorated in a formal European style.

After the usual rounds of cognac and appropriate toasts, a Vietnamese-style dinner was served by the females of the house. In accordance with Vietnamese custom, the females did not join us at the table but remained in the kitchen throughout the evening, making appearances only to serve food or remove dishes from the table. I was introduced to Mrs. Diem, but she stayed only briefly before retreating back to her post in the kitchen. After an excellent meal, we sat around the table sipping cognac and puffing on Cuban cigars that Diem had somehow acquired.

At one point in the conversation, Diem pointed to a large painting on the wall of the dining room and asked me if I recognized the subject. I recognized it immediately as a painting of the unique rock formations in the center of Dinh Quan. It was an unusual and beautiful painting in various shades of blues and grays, depicting the Dinh Quan area as it may have looked a hundred years before. As I examined the painting closely, I noted that it was painted on some unusual material. My wife was an artist, and I knew immediately that this painting was not done on traditional artist's canvas. I asked the province chief if he knew what the material was. He laughed and explained that art canvas was impossible to find in Vietnam; this particular picture was painted on an old pulldown-type window shade, the kind that comes rolled around a spring-loaded rod. The canvas-like material had been removed from the rod and fashioned onto a frame for painting.

Lieutenant Colonel Diem searched through a drawer in a serving stand and produced a small pamphlet describing the artist and a short history of his painting career. Surprisingly, it was in English. The painting was done by Lam Huynh Long, a draftee serving as a private in one of the Regional Force companies in Long Khanh Province. Painting under the pseudonym Nguyen Lam, Private Long had enjoyed a distinguished artistic career prior to his military service, earning numerous Vietnamese and international awards. In addition, his works had shown in art exhibitions in Paris, New York, Kuala Lumpur, Sao Paulo, and New Delhi. Diem was using him as the artist-in-residence for the province. His paintings adorned a number of senior homes and official offices in the province capital of Xuan Loc.

After a while, the conversation at the table turned to other topics and the camaraderie continued for another hour or so. When the party broke up, Captain Xuan and I expressed our gratitude for a most enjoyable evening and made our way back to the headquarters compound where we would spend the night before returning to Dinh Quan on the resupply chopper the following morning.

Except for a comment by Lieutenant Colonel Diem several months later, nothing more was ever said about the painting. On that single occasion, Diem and Lt. Col. Joseph J. Scott, the new province senior advisor, were visiting us in Dinh Quan. We happened to be standing in front of the district headquarters when Diem turned to me, pointed toward the rock formation, and asked if I recalled the oil painting of those rocks. I told him I had not forgotten and commented that the artist's perspective of the rocks was from approximately the front of my team house. I told him that I had taken several photographs from that spot in an attempt to replicate the scene depicted in the painting.

The remaining months of my tour passed, and in early June 1970 it was time for me to return home. I had orders to report to the Pennsylvania Military College in Chester, Pennsylvania, where I was to teach international relations and U.S. foreign policy as part of an experimental program designed to save the army ROTC program. The Option C Program, as it was called, substituted fully credited courses in International Relations, U.S. Foreign Policy, and Military History for the more traditional ROTC courses such as leadership, map reading, tactics, and weapons. The notion was to make the program more attractive to students, thus enhancing enrollments and retention in the program. The leisurely pace of campus life would permit me to get reacquainted with my family and spend with them some of what has come to be known as quality time. I was ready.

My replacement had already arrived and was living with us and learning the ropes in anticipation of my departure. There had been several dinners in my honor, and a number of Vietnamese gifts and military awards had been bestowed on me. These had been included in my personal possessions, which were all packed, crated, and shipped to my family, residing at that time in Fayetteville, North Carolina, just outside of Fort Bragg.

Finally the day came. I bid farewell to the team, Major Xuan, and as many of the Vietnamese officials and residents as I could find, and climbed aboard the helicopter for the trip to Xuan Loc. I was to out-process there and spend the night before proceeding to Saigon for the flight home. The province team in Xuan Loc likewise honored me with a dinner and drinks and presented me with a few parting mementos. I slept like a dead man.

I was up early the next morning, wolfed down breakfast, and sat, leaning forward, waiting for the scheduled 10:00 A.M. flight to Saigon. After what seemed like an eternity, I said my farewells, was driven to the airfield, and climbed aboard the chopper, which was already cranked up ready for takeoff. I sat back in my canvas seat and buckled my seat belt. The chopper, however, did not take off. It continued to sit on the tarmac with its rotor blades whirling. After nearly fifteen minutes, I asked the pilot, a young American warrant officer with whom I had flown on numerous occasions, what the holdup was. He responded that the tower had told him to hold; apparently we were to have another passenger. After another five minutes or so I spotted a jeep racing across the airfield.

Clutching his cap to his head to prevent it from being blown away by the rotor wash, Lieutenant Colonel Diem sprang from the jeep and ran up to the helicopter. He took my hand, shook it, and still holding it, said he was sorry to see me go, that I had been a good advisor, a good soldier, and a friend, and that I had made many contributions to Dinh Quan and its people. He wished me luck and said he would like to personally thank me. At that, the Vietnamese soldier accompanying him stepped forward and handed me the large oil painting. It was not wrapped and had apparently just been taken from the dining room wall of Diem's house. I was moved by the gesture and awkwardly tried to express my gratitude. He nodded in understanding, stepped back, and saluted as the helicopter lifted off. As we climbed higher en route to Saigon, I watched Xuan Loc and Long Khanh Province disappear behind us. The Vietnamization program had already started, and U.S. troops were systematically being withdrawn. Like many of my advisor friends, I knew what the outcome was certain to be, so as I watched the province disappear, I knew deep inside that I would never see this place or these people again. It was a tough parting.

I was jolted out of my melancholy by the sudden realization that my personal goods had long since been shipped and that I was now in possession of an oversized painting that I had no idea how to get home. My flight was scheduled for early the following morning.

When the helicopter landed in Saigon, I hit the ground running. By late afternoon, I had found a place to have a crate constructed. I stuffed a set of my orders inside with the painting, stenciled my name and stateside address all over it, and turned it over to the appropriate military detachment who promised me faithfully that it would be shipped back for me. With that accomplished, I headed into Saigon, where I spent the evening with George Laudato and friends at their villa. Sometime that evening I crashed into a vacant bed and slept fitfully, waiting for morning to come.

I don't recall much of the flight home, but I do remember experiencing a feeling of finality. This was my third such trip, and I knew it was my final one, that I would not be coming back. My thoughts gradually shifted to what lay ahead. My wife and six-year-old daughter, Natasha, were waiting for me in North Carolina. I had been away for fourteen months. It was going to be a great homecoming!

Much to my surprise, all my personal items, as well as the painting, arrived safe and sound within a few weeks. In the intervening years my family and I have lived in eight different homes. At each location there was always a debate over where this painting should hang. The picture did not hold the same significance for my wife as it did for me, and the painting's style and colors did not fit well with the decor of the house.

I subsequently have remarried, and in my current home in Grasonville on Maryland's eastern shore, I have secured a place of honor in the study for the painting. As I sit and gaze at it from time to time, I feel the rush of those many months and many experiences in Dinh Quan flowing over me. My time there was both personally and professionally rewarding and represents one of the most memorable times of my life. And while more than twenty-nine years have passed, I cannot shake the inevitable guilt I feel for our nation's abandonment of those many good and decent people who trusted us and made the ultimate commitment.

CHAPTER 40

Final Thoughts

E ven though more than a quarter of a century has elapsed since my final departure from Vietnam in 1970, I still find it difficult to draw conclusions, reconcile feelings, and "put it all away." I suspect that perhaps I never will.

If anything, writing this book over the past several years has awakened forgotten emotions and heightened my anger and sense of frustration. I said in the preface that I thought the current trend toward honest and open discussion about Vietnam was both healthy and historically appropriate. I truly believe that, and I believe our society, and particularly those who served in Vietnam, will be the better for it. I, nonetheless, remain troubled by the experience.

It is pointless to argue whether or not the United States ever should have committed its sons and daughters, resources, honor, and reputation to the defense of the South Vietnamese government. The fact is it did. More than 58,000 names on the wall, thousands more with shattered bodies and minds, and the expenditure of billions of U.S. dollars attest to the depth of our commitment.

As a professional soldier, it was my duty to go when called. I answered that call three times—in 1963, 1965, and 1969. I have no regrets. I am proud to have served. I served with good men—professionals, volunteers, and draftees—most of whom did not want to be there but nonetheless did their duty.

Still, after all this time, I am angry. Angry at the draft and its inherent unfairness, at its economic bias in favor of those who had money and influence and were able to obtain educational and other deferments. Angry at a system that exempted 16 million of the approximately 27 million draft-age men of that era. Angry at a government that initiated Project 100,000 and other measures that protected college deferments at the expense of the poor and disadvantaged. Roughly one-third of those serving in Vietnam were conscripted; thus the predictable consequence of this bias was a class division that resulted in the "have-not" draftees fighting the war in the place of the "haves."

I am angrier still with those who fled the country, falsified records, feigned homosexuality, or used influence to unfairly avoid the draft. Their actions were reprehensible. As American citizens enjoying the bounty of this country, they had every right to oppose the war, but they had a legal and moral obligation to serve if called. By shirking their responsibility, they sent others—less affluent, less influential, but arguably more honorable—in their places. Many of those who went in their places did not return; others returned physically or emotionally damaged. My personal belief in the concepts of "Duty, Honor, Country," taught to me at West Point so many years ago makes it impossible for me to understand how those who have so dishonored themselves have been able to reconcile the consequences of their behavior. Worse yet, they have further dishonored themselves by claiming vindication as a result of Secretary McNamara's later disgraceful confessions.

Likewise, I am angry about the treatment accorded to Vietnam veterans. For too many years, the American people have not been able to distinguish between an unpopular war and the soldiers who were called upon to fight it. The country did not welcome us home, acknowledge our sacrifices, or honor us in any way. Because the war was hateful and divisive at home, there was an effort to pretend it didn't happen and to somehow distance our nation from it. By ignoring those who served, it was apparently hoped that they and memories of the war would quietly fade away. Vietnam veterans have been discriminated against in the workplace, and the treatment of them by the Veterans Administration has at times been disgraceful, as have Congressional cuts in programs to assist Vietnam veterans.

In the years following the war, Hollywood and the media have exacerbated the problem by portraying Vietnam veterans as drug-ridden psychopaths and misfits unable to assume their places in American society. This irresponsible stereotyping, though not supported by any legitimate research, and despite credible evidence to the contrary, has been embedded in the minds of the American public. Unfortunately, a number of veterans and Vietnam imposters, whom I have labeled the "professional mourners," have contributed to the image problem by their own conduct and shoddy personal appearance. Hardly a Vietnam-related event takes place that these individuals don't appear and capture media attention. The public loses sight of the fact that these are not the typical Vietnam veteran. I am angrier still at the Vietnam Veterans of America (VVA) for their role in perpetuating this loser image for Vietnam vets. If the VVA wants to truly represent the 2.5 million Vietnam veterans in this country, they should be in the forefront telling the factual story: the vast majority of Vietnam veterans returned home without serious emotional problems and quietly resumed productive lives.

I am angry with our country's handling of the MIA issue. While I personally do not believe any of the nearly 2,200 servicemen officially listed as missing in action are still alive, I am just as certain that the U.S. government failed to do all it could in applying leverage to get information from the North Vietnamese regarding the fate of those individuals. It appears only in recent years has there been genuine progress in this regard. Just as inexcusable has been the unwillingness of the government to deal candidly and honestly with the MIA families, allowing the myth to perpetuate in spite of significant evidence to the contrary.

Most troubling to me, however, was our government's ultimate abandonment of Vietnam and especially those Vietnamese who, with our encouragement and support, made a commitment—a commitment they could not walk away from when the end came. Once the Vietnamization program was in place and American withdrawals had begun, our government yielded to political pressure and took the expedient, easier course over the right, but more difficult course. Our rush to exit ignored the very guidelines that had been established to determine the rate of withdrawal. We simply pulled the plug. Predictably, the Vietnamese Army collapsed, and those who were left behind paid the price. This is our national shame and my own personal guilt. I believe that those of us who lived and worked closely with the Vietnamese people feel it most deeply. For me, it has not abated over these twenty-eight years, and I doubt I will ever overcome it.

The good news is that slowly there is a growing genuine public recognition of the sacrifices and contributions these men and women made for their country and of the injustices they have endured. I am convinced that the tremendous outpouring of emotion, patriotism, and support for the Gulf War and those who served in it was in large part fueled by the latent sense of guilt that many in this country have carried for years over their attitudes and treatment of those who served in Vietnam. I believe this same recognition accounts for the continued attraction the Vietnam Memorial holds for visitors to our nation's capital.

I would like to return to Vietnam—to Dinh Quan—for one final visit. I have been back many times over these past twenty-nine years in my mind, and the painting in my study is a constant reminder. My hopes for those we left behind are for the peace and happiness they deserve. If anyone there should still have memories of us during our time there, I hope they are fond memories of men who cared and tried to help.

POSTSCRIPT

Worst Practices

Current management theory touts a technique known as "best practices," where organizations examine the successes—best practices—of similar organizations to learn what others are doing well and how they are doing it. I have labeled this final chapter "Worst Practices," for I catalog not the successes, but the failures in the army's selection, training, support, and assignment of advisors for the Vietnam War.

I have not attempted, in the course of writing this book, to analyze the strategy of the war, discuss the role of the media, or engage in any debate over the correctness of the policy of containment or the domino theory. Others more qualified than I have written in those arenas. But in keeping with the focus of this book, I do wish to share some thoughts and observations regarding the advisory side of the war. Most of these observations have already been touched upon in various parts of the book.

An advisor's perspective of the Vietnam War was far different than that of those whose Vietnam experience was limited to service in U.S. units. Many of my friends who served only in American units never understood the people, the country, the culture, or, in fact too often, the war itself. I believe this lack of understanding, more than anything else, has contributed to the collective confusion and guilt felt by many Vietnam veterans. It was unfortunate that all who served in Vietnam—officers, NCOs, grunts, and support types—did not have the opportunity to serve in an advisory position prior to being assigned to an American unit. It would have markedly changed their view of the Vietnamese people, and I believe it would have provided some sense of what the war was all about. I know it would have had a profound effect on the conduct of the war.

In a larger sense, it was this same lack of knowledge of Vietnam—the people, culture, history, and politics—that enabled American policymakers to blindly take our country down the path that led to our ultimate bewilderment and failure. We ultimately fought a war in a country we knew nothing about, in support of a government we neither knew nor respected, to assist a people we didn't understand and whose culture we could not appreciate, against an enemy we completely underestimated and misinterpreted.

In earlier chapters I highlighted a number of frustrations resulting from what I believe were flawed policies regarding selection, training, support, and assignment of advisors. There are no new discoveries among these observations; I only echo the thoughts of others before me. However, as the Vietnam experience fades over time and new generations assume the leadership and policy development roles in our military and in our government, it is good that we remind ourselves once more of these mistakes.

Length of Tour. The decision for a twelve-month tour was disastrous in U.S. units, and doubly so in the advisory effort. Although defended in terms of preventing "burn out," all it really did was cycle officers through command and other key combat assignments to punch their tickets and enhance their careers. About the time that an officer was starting to learn his job, he was moved to another position or his tour was over. We were constantly being led by the inexperienced, and the men serving under these officers paid the price. This practice led John Paul Vann to observe, "We didn't fight a ten-year war, we fought a one-year war ten times."

For a district- or province-level advisor to be most effective, at minimum a two-year tour would have been necessary to absorb all the knowledge that was essential, to establish rapport, and to build trust and confidence. Eighteen months should have been the minimum for those assigned as advisors to tactical units. The standard twelve-month tour was simply an insufficient length of time.

Compounding this problem was the army's decision, in the face of mounting criticism over repeated tours, to fill many advisory positions with officers below the required grade: lieutenants in captain positions, captains in major positions, and majors in lieutenant colonel positions. The net result was inexperienced junior officers frequently being assigned to advise experienced officers senior to them. The implicit message was that a young, inexperienced American officer was somehow more capable than an older, experienced, and more senior Vietnamese officer, and could therefore effectively advise him—hardly the basis for the trust, respect, and rapport required. The enhancements in advisor training and the extension of the advisory tour to eighteen months in the latter part of the war were recognitions of this fact. While these were important improvements, they were too little, too late.

Selection of Personnel for Advisory Duty. The army failed to recognize that not everyone is cut out to be an advisor; a unique combination of skills and personality traits is required. The assumption that any U.S. officer or NCO—regardless of background, training, interpersonal skills, or combat experience—could just step in, be immediately accepted, and be an effective advisor was a delusion born of American arrogance. The lack of screening had predictable results in many cases. The post–Vietnam establishment of the Foreign Area Officer career specialty is a step in the right direction, but could not produce the quantity of advisors needed in a large-scale advisory effort. The army needs to develop some method of identifying those personnel who possess the necessary traits and skills to serve effectively as military advisors.

Recognition for Advisory Duty. The army not only failed to assign its best to the advisory effort, but also through its personnel practices discouraged those who might have wanted to serve as advisors from seeking such assignments. Worse yet, it penalized those who did serve as advisors by refusing to recognize and credit advisory duty as equivalent to duty in U.S. units. This discrimination, evidenced through promotions, assignments, and selection for command and senior service schools, was well recognized in the officer corps with predictable consequences. Advisory duty was to be avoided at all costs.

Language Training. Failure to properly train advisory personnel in the language was, in my judgment, perhaps the major deficiency. Many advisors, myself included, received only a cursory introduction to the language as part of the MATA course at Fort Bragg. A few who were more fortunate received extended language training at Monterey, Fort Bliss, or at the State Department in Washington. Some received none. The rapid turnover, resulting from the one-year tour policy, didn't allow sufficient time for adequate training. The results were predictably disastrous. The inability to speak the language isolated the advisor socially, culturally, professionally, and in all the unofficial subtleties. The reliance on often inferior interpreters gave rise to misinterpretation, delays, and frequent lack of candor as the interpreter softened or modified the translation so as not to offend. It also interjected a layer between counterparts that made rapport and trust much more difficult to build and sustain. It's a no-brainer—language training for advisors is a must.

Cultural Training. Perhaps the most difficult adjustment of all was that necessary to live and work in another culture. This book is replete with examples of American failures to understand and appreciate the Vietnamese culture, which led directly to failures of U.S. programs. Nowhere was serious attention given to this critical shortcoming.

Preparation for Advisory Duty. Since selection for specific advisor assignments often occurred after arrival in Vietnam, in most cases officers and NCOs did not know what their jobs would be; they knew only that they were being assigned to MACV. Without prior identification, critical preparation for specific jobs was impossible. The training that would have been most helpful for district and province advisory teams was far different from the training that would have been best for advisors going to combat unit advisory teams. The MATA course at Fort Bragg was the army's catch-all course; it was inadequate on all counts. Once arriving in Vietnam, some going to advisory assignments received short in-country orientations prior to joining their units. Most did not.

Support for Advisory Teams. As this book illustrates, a great deal of the advisory teams' time and effort was devoted not to advising or assisting the Vietnamese, but to the fundamental tasks of supply, repair, and support of the team itself. The advisory organization from the MATs through the district and province to the corps had no logistical support elements. Food had to be scrounged from U.S. units or purchased either locally or at the commissaries, if they were accessible. The same for repair materials for the team house. Except for weapons, radios, TA-50, and vehicles, it was all self-help. Even those items frequently required supplementing through scrounging. There is a clear need for a support element to be included in any future advisory organization to ensure adequate support and to relieve advisors of this time-consuming distraction.

Commitment to Training the VN Armed Forces. Finally, although not directly falling into the categories of selection, training, support, or assignment of advisors, the lack of commitment of U.S. forces to the mission of supporting advisory efforts through the training of the Vietnamese armed forces represents another key shortcoming that must be overcome in future advisory efforts. To a great extent, the lack of cultural understanding contributed to the failure of U.S. units to properly train and support the Vietnamese units in their sectors of operation. There was a reluctance to conduct joint operations, Vietnamese officers were often not trusted and thus not included in the planning, and Vietnamese units were given trivial roles in operations. American officers in U.S. units were critical of the ARVN, but regrettably did little to prepare the Vietnamese Army to assume responsibility for the ultimate conduct of the war. The Americanization of the combat role had, in fact, an opposite effect. It contributed to the unwillingness and the unpreparedness of the Vietnamese Army to pursue the war, and the trivialization of the Vietnamese role in planning and operations not only failed to prepare them, but also widened the cultural chasm and added to the resentment.

THE FAILURES NOTED above were as obvious then as they are today. There has been no sudden clarity of hindsight. A true lack of understanding on the part of policymakers, arrogance, self-interest, and an expediency born of political pressure all contributed to the evolvement of policies disastrous not only to the advisory effort, but also to the conduct of the war and to the U.S. Army itself. My hope is that from this failure we learned lessons that will not be repeated at the expense of future generations.

Despite these shortcomings, CORDS and the advisory effort were successful. Pacification worked, the Phoenix Program worked, the Viet Cong were being defeated and rooted out, and the war in the villages and hamlets was being won. The change in strategy of the North to more direct conventional warfare attests to those successes. Given time and meaningful commitment, I believe Vietnamization could have worked.

Glossary

ABBREVIATIONS AND ACRONYMS

AFVN	Armed Forces Vietnam Network
AFRTS	Armed Forces Radio and Television Service
AG	adjutant general
AK-47	Kalashnikov assault rifle
AO	area of operation
Arc Light	code name for B-52 strike
ARVN	Army of the Republic of Vietnam
AWOL	absent without leave
boonies	the jungle
B-52	U.S. Air Force Stratofortress Bomber
CIDG	Civilian Irregular Defense Group
CORDS	Civil Operations and Revolutionary Development Support
COSVN	Central Office for South Vietnam (Control HQs for the VC)
CTZ	Corps Tactical Zone
DA	Department of the Army
DEPCORDS	Deputy for CORDS
DIOCC	District Intelligence Operations Coordinating Center
DoD	Department of Defense
DSA	district senior advisor
dust-off	medical evacuation helicopter
FNG	fucking new guy
grunts	infantry soldiers or marines
GVN	Government of Vietnam
H&I fire	harassment and interdiction fire
HES	Hamlet Evaluation System
HQ	headquarters
IN	Infantry
J-3, G-3, or S-3	staff officer for Plans, Operations, and Training
J-4, G-4, or S-4	staff officer for Supply and Logistics
M14	7.62mm rifle (replaced the M1)
M16	5.56mm automatic rifle (replaced the M14)
MACV	Military Assistance Command Vietnam

MAT	mobile advisory team
MATA	Military Assistance Training Advisors Course
NCO	noncommissioned officer
NLF	National Liberation Front
NPFF	National Police Field Force
NVA	North Vietnamese Army
P	piaster (Vietnamese currency)
PRC-25	portable radio
PRU	Provincial Reconnaissance Unit
PF	Popular Forces
PSA	province senior advisor
PSDF	People's Self-Defense Force
PX	post exchange
R&R	rest and recuperation leave
REMF	rear echelon motherfuckers
RF	Regional Forces
RPG	rocket-propelled grenade
RTO	radio telephone operator
RVN	Republic of Vietnam
SFC	sergeant first class
SP4	specialist fourth class
TA-50	standard-issue individual field gear
UH-1	Bell helicopter (Huey)
U-20	fixed-wing aircraft (Beaver)
USAID	United States Agency for International Development
USIA	United States Information Agency
VC	Viet Cong
VCI	Viet Cong Infrastructure
VN	Vietnam
War Zone D	free-fire zone northeast of Saigon

VIETNAMESE WORDS AND PHRASES

(Spelling is without diacritical marks.)

Ao Dai	Traditional Vietnamese woman's dress
Ba	married woman, Madame
Bac-si	medic, doctor
Chao	greeting
Co	unmarried woman, miss
Co Van My	American advisor
Nuoc mam	fermented fish sauce
Ong	mister or sir
Phung Hoang	Phoenix
QL	national highway
Tet	Lunar New Year
Thieu-ta	major
Trung-uy	first lieutenant

Bibliography

Andrade, Dale. *Ashes to Ashes: The Phoenix Program and the Vietnam War.* Lexington, MA: Lexington Books, D. C. Heath and Co., 1994.

Baritz, Loren. *Backfire: A History of How American Culture Led Us into Vietnam and Made Us Fight the Way We Did.* New York: William Morrow and Co., 1985.

Bergerud, Eric M. *The Dynamics of Defeat: The Vietnam War in Hau Nghia Province.* San Francisco: Westview Press, 1991.

Bonds, Ray, ed. *The Vietnam War: The Illustrated History of the Conflict in Southeast Asia.* New York: Crown Publishers, 1979.

Boston Publishing Co. *The Vietnam Experience: War in the Shadows.* Boston: Boston Publishing Co., 1988.

Bowman, John S., ed. *The Vietnam War: An Almanac.* New York: World Almanac Publications, 1985.

Campbell, Tom. *The Old Man's Trail: A Novel about the Vietcong.* Annapolis: Naval Institute Press, 1995.

Caputo, Philip. *A Rumor of War.* New York: Ballantine Books, 1978.

Clarke, Jeffrey J. *United States Army in Vietnam, Advice and Support: The Final Years 1965–1973.* Washington, DC: Center for Military History, US Army, 1988.

Cohen, Barbara. *Vietnam Guidebook, 3rd Edition.* Boston: Houghton Mifflin Co., 1994.

Colby, William. *Lost Victory: A Firsthand Account of America's Sixteen-Year Involvement in Vietnam.* Chicago: Contemporary Books, 1989.

Cook, LTC John L. *The Advisor: The Phoenix Program in Vietnam.* Toronto: Bantam Books, 1987.

Donovan, David. *Once A Warrior King: Memories of an Officer in Vietnam.* New York: Ballantine Books, 1985.

Dougan, Clark, David Fulgham, et al. *The Vietnam Experience: The Fall of the South.* Boston: Boston Publishing Co., 1985.

Doyle, Edward, Samuel Lipsman, et al. *The Vietnam Experience: A Collision of Cultures.* Boston: Boston Publishing Co., 1984.

————. *The Vietnam Experience: Setting the Stage.* Boston: Boston Publishing Co., 1981.

Duncanson, Dennis, Richard A. Yudkin, and Barry Zorthian. *Lessons of Vietnam: Three Interpretive Essays.* New York: American-Asian Educational Exchange, 1971.

Gallucci, Robert L. *Neither Peace Nor Honor: The Politics of American Military Policy in Viet-Nam.* Baltimore: Johns Hopkins University Press, 1975.

Guidebook for PF Platoon Leaders, translated from Vietnamese. APO San Francisco: United States Military Assistance Command Vietnam, 1968.

Halberstam, David. *One Very Hot Day.* Boston: Houghton Mifflin Co., 1967.

Hardy, Gordon, et al. *The Vietnam Experience: Words of War.* Boston: Boston Publishing Co., 1988.

Hargrove, Thomas R. *A Dragon Lives Forever: War and Rice in Vietnam's Mekong Delta 1969–1991, and Beyond.* New York: Ivy Books, 1994.

Hemingway, Al. *Our War Was Different: Marine Combined Action Platoons in Vietnam.* Annapolis: Naval Institute Press, 1995.

Hoa, Nguyen Dinh. *Vietnamese–English Dictionary.* Rutland, VT: Charles E. Tuttle, 1968.

Hunt, Richard A. *Pacification: The American Struggle for Vietnam's Hearts and Minds.* San Francisco: Westview Press, 1995.

Just, Ward. *Military Men.* New York: Alfred A. Knopf, 1970.

Katakis, Michael. *The Vietnam Veterans Memorial.* New York: Crown Publishers, 1988.

Kinnard, Douglas. *The War Managers.* Wayne, NJ: Avery Publishing Group, 1985.

Know Your Enemy: The Viet Cong. Department of the Army Pamphlet 360-518. Washington, DC, 1966.

Krepinevich, Andrew F. Jr. *The Army and Vietnam.* Baltimore: Johns Hopkins University Press, 1986.

"Long Khanh Province, Civil Operations and Revolutionary Development Support." Information brief, III CTZ, Vietnam, 1969.

Long, Robert Emmet. *Vietnam Ten Years After.* New York: H. W. Wilson Co., 1986.

Luce, Don, and John Sommer. *Viet Nam—The Unheard Voices.* Ithaca, NY: Cornell University Press, 1969.

Maitland, Terrence, Peter McInerney, et al. *The Vietnam Experience: A Contagion of War.* Boston: Boston Publishing Co., 1983.

Maurer, Harry. *Strange Ground: Americans in Vietnam 1945–1975, An Oral History.* New York: Henry Holt and Co., 1989.

McMahon, Robert J. *Major Problems in the History of the Vietnam War.* Lexington, MA: D.C. Heath and Co., 1990.

Moskos, Charles C. Jr. *The American Enlisted Man.* New York: Russell Sage Foundation, 1970.

Newman, Bernard. *Let's Visit Vietnam.* Toronto: Burke Publishing, 1983.

"Organization of the Government of Vietnam, Civil Operations and Revolutionary Development Support." III CTZ, Vietnam, February 1970.

Pratt, John Clark. *Vietnam Voices: Perspectives on the War Years, 1941–1982.* New York: Penguin Books, 1984.

Reinberg, Linda. *In the Field: The Language of the Vietnam War.* New York: Facts on File Publications, 1991.

Revolutionary Development: A Plan for a New Vietnam. Command Information Pamphlet 4-67. APO San Francisco: MACV Information Office, 1967.

RF/PF Handbook for Advisors. APO San Francisco: Headquarters, United States Military Assistance Command Vietnam, 1969.

Sheehan, Neil. *A Bright Shining Lie: John Paul Vann and America in Vietnam.* New York: Random House, 1988.

Smith, Eric. *Not By the Book: A Combat Intelligence Officer in Vietnam.* New York: Ivy Books, 1993.

Summers, Col. Harry G. *On Strategy: The Vietnam War in Context.* Carlisle Barracks, PA: Strategic Studies Institute, US Army War College, 1981.

———. *Vietnam War Almanac.* New York: Facts on File Publications, 1985.

Tour 365. APO San Francisco: United States Army, Vietnam, 1969.

Vietnam Information Booklet. Fort Benning, GA: US Army Infantry School, 1967.

Willenson, Kim. *The Bad War: An Oral History of the Vietnam War.* New York: New American Library, 1987.

Wolff, Tobias. *In Pharaoh's Army: Memories of the Lost War.* New York: Vintage Books, 1994.

Wood, Specialist 4C Steve. "Dinh Quan's Ice Age Legacy: Geological and Legendary Mystery." *The Hurricane.* Publication of II Field Force, Vietnam (August 1969).

World Almanac and Book of Facts, 1995. Mahwah, NJ: Funk and Wagnalls, 1994.

Wright, David K. *Vietnam.* Chicago: Children's Press, 1989.

Acknowledgments

This book was many years in the making, and I am indebted to many people for the help and encouragement they provided along the way. Of particular note: the staff at the National Archives for their research assistance; Jim Blesse, Theresa Cadell, Paul DeVries, Wade Elrod, Ken Lawson, and Martha "Bunny" Hood for their comments and helpful suggestions; Nan Beckett, my former spouse, for urging me to begin this endeavor; my daughters, Natasha and Natanya, for their patience and support throughout; Steve Grey and Jennifer Houck for their assistance with the photos; and Bob Hughes and Chuck Backlin, both featured in this book, for their invaluable recall, suggestions, photos, and material assistance.

I am especially indebted to my wife, Jane Walker Beckett, for her encouragement, support, research assistance, editorial comments, thoughtful suggestions, love, and understanding, and for her diligence as proofreader of this book.

Finally, I am indebted to my many friends over the years, who upon hearing these stories, made me believe they were worth recording.

Thank you all.

Stackpole Military History Series

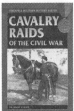

CAVALRY RAIDS OF THE CIVIL WAR

IN THE LION'S MOUTH
Hood's Tragic Retreat from Nashville, 1864

WITNESS TO GETTYSBURG
Inside the Battle That Changed the Course of the Civil War

DOUGHBOY WAR
The American Expeditionary Force in WWI

AFTER D-DAY
Operation Cobra and the Normandy Breakout

AIRBORNE COMBAT
The Glider War / Fighting Gliders of WWII

ARMOR BATTLES OF THE WAFFEN SS 1943-45

ARMOURED GUARDSMEN
A War Diary from Normandy to the Rhine

ARNHEM 1944
The Airborne Battle

B-24 IN CHINA
General Chennault's Secret Weapon in WWII

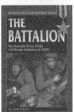

THE BATTALION
The Dramatic Story of the 2nd Ranger Battalion in WWII

THE BATTLE OF FRANCE
Six Weeks That Changed the World

THE BATTLE OF SICILY
How the Allies Lost Their Chance for Total Victory

BATTLE OF THE BULGE
Volume One: The Losheim Gap / Holding the Line

BATTLE OF THE BULGE
Volume Two: Hell at Bütgenbach / Seize the Bridges

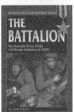

BATTLE OF THE BULGE
Volume Three: The 3rd Fallschirmjäger Division in Action, December 1944–January 1945

BEYOND THE BEACHHEAD
The 29th Infantry Division in Normandy

BEYOND STALINGRAD
Manstein and the Operations of Army Group Don

BLACK BULL
From Normandy to the Baltic with the 11th Armoured Division

BLITZKRIEG UNLEASHED
The German Invasion of Poland, 1939

BLOSSOMING SILK AGAINST THE RISING SUN
U.S. and Japanese Paratroopers at War in the Pacific in WWII

BODENPLATTE
The Luftwaffe's Last Hope

BREAKING POINT
Sedan, and the Fall of France, 1940

THE BRIGADE
The Fifth Canadian Infantry Brigade in WWII

THE CANADIAN ARMY AND THE NORMANDY CAMPAIGN

CLAY PIGEONS OF ST. LÔ

CRITICAL CONVOY BATTLES OF WWII
Crisis in the North Atlantic, March 1943

DANGEROUS ASSIGNMENT
An Artillery Forward Observer in WWII

D-DAY BOMBERS
The Stories of Allied Heavy Bombers during the Invasion of Normandy

D-DAY DECEPTION
Operation Fortitude and the Normandy Invasion

Real battles. Real soldiers. Real stories.

D-DAY TO BERLIN
The Northwest Europe Campaign, 1944–45

DECISION IN THE UKRAINE
German Panzer Operations on the Eastern Front, Summer 1943

THE DEFENSE OF MOSCOW 1941
The Northern Flank

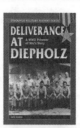
DELIVERANCE AT DIEPHOLZ
A WWII Prisoner of War's Story

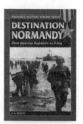
DESTINATION NORMANDY
Three American Regiments on D-Day

DIVE BOMBER!
Aircraft, Technology, and Tactics in WWII

EAGER EAGLES
The U.S. Eighth Air Force in Europe, 1941–43

EAGLES OF THE THIRD REICH
Men of the Luftwaffe in WWII

THE EARLY BATTLES OF EIGHTH ARMY
Crusader to the Alamein Line, 1941–42

EASTERN FRONT COMBAT
The German Soldier in Battle from Stalingrad to Berlin

EUROPE IN FLAMES
Understanding WWII

EXIT ROMMEL
The Tunisian Campaign, 1942–43

THE FACE OF COURAGE
The 98 Men Who Received the Knight's Cross and the Close-Combat Clasp in Gold

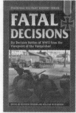
FATAL DECISIONS
Six Decisive Battles of WWII from the Viewpoint of the Vanquished

FIST FROM THE SKY
Japan's Dive-Bomber Ace of WWII

FLAME ON
U.S. Incendiary Weapons, 1918–1945

FLYING AMERICAN COMBAT AIRCRAFT OF WWII
1939–45

FOR EUROPE
The French Volunteers of the Waffen-SS

FORGING THE THUNDERBOLT
History of the US Army's Armored Forces, 1917–45

FOR THE HOMELAND
The 31st Waffen-SS Volunteer Grenadier Division in WWII

FORTRESS FRANCE
The Maginot Line and French Defenses in WWII

THE GERMAN DEFEAT IN THE EAST
1944–45

GERMAN ORDER OF BATTLE
Volume One: 1st–290th Infantry Divisions in WWII

GERMAN ORDER OF BATTLE
Volume Two: 291st–999th Infantry Divisions, Named Infantry Divisions, and Special Divisions in WWII

GERMAN ORDER OF BATTLE
Volume Three: Panzer, Panzer Grenadier, and Waffen SS Divisions in WWII

THE GERMANS IN NORMANDY

GERMANY'S PANZER ARM IN WWII

GI INGENUITY
Improvisation, Technology, and Winning WWII

GOODBYE, TRANSYLVANIA
A Romanian Waffen-SS Soldier in WWII

THE GREAT SHIPS
British Battleships in WWII

Stackpole Military History Series

GRENADIERS
The Story of Waffen SS General Kurt "Panzer" Meyer

GUNS AGAINST THE REICH
Memoirs of a Soviet Artillery Officer on the Eastern Front

HITLER'S FINAL FORTRESS
Breslau 1945

HITLER'S NEMESIS
The Red Army 1930-45

HITLER'S SPANISH LEGION
The Blue Division in Russia in WWII

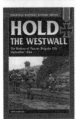
HOLD THE WESTWALL
The History of Panzer Brigade 105, September 1944

INFANTRY ACES
The German Soldier in Combat in WWII

IN THE FIRE OF THE EASTERN FRONT
The Experiences of a Dutch Waffen-SS Volunteer, 1941-45

IRON ARM
The Mechanization of Mussolini's Army, 1920-40

IRON KNIGHTS
The U.S. 66th Armored Regiment in WWII

JAPANESE ARMY FIGHTER ACES 1931-45

JAPANESE NAVAL FIGHTER ACES 1932-45

JG 26 LUFTWAFFE FIGHTER WING WAR DIARY
Volume One: 1939-42

JG 26 LUFTWAFFE FIGHTER WING WAR DIARY
Volume Two: 1943-45

KAMPFGRUPPE PEIPER AT THE BATTLE OF THE BULGE

THE KEY TO THE BULGE
The Battle for Losheimergraben

KURSK
Hitler's Gamble, 1943

LUFTWAFFE ACES
German Combat Pilots of WWII

LUFTWAFFE FIGHTER ACE
From the Eastern Front to the Defense of the Homeland

LUFTWAFFE FIGHTER-BOMBERS OVER BRITAIN
The Tip and Run Campaign, 1942-43

LUFTWAFFE FIGHTERS & BOMBERS
The Battle of Britain

LUFTWAFFE KG 200
The German Air Force's Most Secret Unit of World War II

MARSHAL OF VICTORY
Volume One: The WWII Memoirs of Soviet General Georgy Zhukov through 1941

MARSHAL OF VICTORY
Volume Two: The WWII Memoirs of Soviet General Georgy Zhukov, 1941-45

MASSACRE AT TOBRUK
The British Assault on Rommel, 1942

MECHANIZED JUGGERNAUT OR MILITARY ANACHRONISM?
Horses and the German Army of WWII

MESSERSCHMITTS OVER SICILY
Diary of a Luftwaffe Fighter Commander

MICHAEL WITTMANN
and the Waffen SS Tiger Commanders of the Leibstandarte in WWII
VOLUME ONE

MICHAEL WITTMANN
and the Waffen SS Tiger Commanders of the Leibstandarte in WWII
VOLUME TWO

MISSION 85
The U.S. Eighth Air Force's Battle over Holland, August 19, 1943

Real battles. Real soldiers. Real stories.

MISSION 376
Battle over the Reich, May 28, 1944

THE NAZI ROCKETEERS
Dreams of Space and Crimes of War

NIGHT FLYER/ MOSQUITO PATHFINDER
Night Operations in WWII

NO HOLDING BACK
Operation Totalize, Normandy, August 1944

OPERATION MERCURY
The Battle for Crete, 1941

PANZER ACES
German Tank Commanders of WWII

PANZER ACES II
Battle Stories of German Tank Commanders of WWII

PANZER COMMANDERS OF THE WESTERN FRONT
German Tank Generals in WWII

PANZER-GRENADIER ACES
German Mechanized Infantrymen in WWII

PANZER GUNNER
A Canadian in the German 7th Panzer Division, 1944–45

THE PANZER LEGIONS
A Guide to the German Army Tank Divisions of WWII and Their Commanders

PANZER WEDGE
Volume One: The German 3rd Panzer Division and the Summer of Victory in the East

PANZER WEDGE
Volume Two: The German 3rd Panzer Division and Barbarossa's Failure at the Gates of Moscow

PANZERS IN WINTER
Hitler's Army and the Battle of the Bulge

THE PATH TO BLITZKRIEG
Doctrine and Training in the German Army, 1920–39

PENALTY STRIKE
The Memoirs of a Red Army Penal Company Commander, 1943–45

POLAND BETRAYED
The Nazi-Soviet Invasions of 1939

RED ROAD FROM STALINGRAD
Recollections of a Soviet Infantryman

RED STAR UNDER THE BALTIC
A Soviet Submariner in WWII

RETREAT TO THE REICH
The German Defeat in France, 1944

ROMMEL RECONSIDERED

ROMMEL'S DESERT COMMANDERS
The Men Who Served the Desert Fox, North Africa, 1941–42

ROMMEL'S DESERT WAR
The Life and Death of the Afrika Korps

ROMMEL'S LIEUTENANTS
The Men Who Served the Desert Fox, France, 1940

THE SAVAGE SKY
Life and Death on a Bomber over Germany in 1944

THE SEEDS OF DISASTER
The Development of French Army Doctrine, 1919–39

SHIP-BUSTERS
British Torpedo-Bombers in WWII

THE SIEGE OF BREST 1941
The Red Army's Stand against the Germans during Operation Barbarossa

THE SIEGE OF KÜSTRIN
Gateway to Berlin, 1945

THE SIEGFRIED LINE
The German Defense of the West Wall, September–December 1944

Stackpole Military History Series

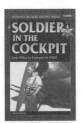

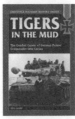

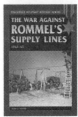

Real battles. Real soldiers. Real stories.

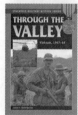
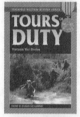

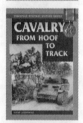

Stackpole Military History Series

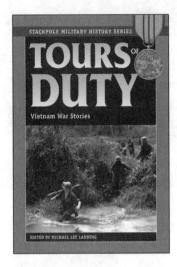

TOURS OF DUTY
VIETNAM WAR STORIES
Edited by Michael Lee Lanning

These are the stories Vietnam vets tell over beers at Legion halls and VFW posts—stories of young men tangled up in the chaos of landing zones and nameless jungle hills, in the boredom of base camps, in the confusion of a controversial war. Raw, often gut-wrenching, sometimes funny, these war stories describe slices of individual tours of duty, from the firefights to the friendships, and combine to capture the kaleidoscope of the American experience in Vietnam. As one vet put it, "There is only one story about the Vietnam War—we all just tell it differently."

Paperback • 6 x 9 • 288 pages • 1 map

WWW.STACKPOLEBOOKS.COM
1-800-732-3669

Stackpole Military History Series

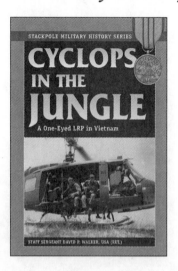

CYCLOPS IN THE JUNGLE
A ONE-EYED LRP IN VIETNAM
Staff Sergeant David P. Walker, USA (Ret.)

Dave Walker enlisted in the U.S. Army at seventeen, full
of patriotism and eager to play his part in Vietnam.
Trained for long-range patrol (LRP) operations, he
received a debilitating shrapnel wound to his eye barely
a month after arriving in Vietnam. Medically discharged
and sent home to a country he decreasingly recognized,
Walker—now missing an eye—maneuvered his way back
to the jungles of Vietnam, where he survived another
eighteen months conducting patrols and special
operations with an elite Ranger unit.

Paperback • 6 x 9 • 240 pages • 30 b/w photos

WWW.STACKPOLEBOOKS.COM
1-800-732-3669

Stackpole Military History Series

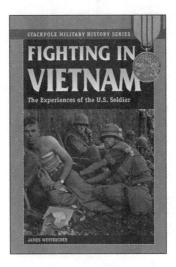

FIGHTING IN VIETNAM
THE EXPERIENCES OF THE U.S. SOLDIER
James Westheider

The Vietnam War differed from previous American wars of
the twentieth century. It was an undeclared and limited war
that divided the country and was fought disproportionately
by minorities and working-class whites, many of whom did
not want to serve. This is the story of the men and women
who participated in this generation-defining conflict overseas
and stateside—a war of search-and-destroy missions and
combat with an ill-defined enemy, but also a war of drug use,
fragging, and antiwar protests. With sweeping scope and
careful detail, James Westheider captures the many
dimensions of what it was like to fight in the Vietnam War.

Paperback • 6 x 9 • 256 pages • 32 b/w photos, 1 map

WWW.STACKPOLEBOOKS.COM
1-800-732-3669

Stackpole Military History Series

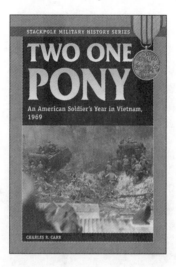

TWO ONE PONY
AN AMERICAN SOLDIER'S YEAR IN VIETNAM, 1969
Charles R. Carr

At the height of the Vietnam War, Charles Carr left graduate school to serve in the army in Southeast Asia, knowing that if he didn't, another man would go—and possibly die—in his place. He was assigned to the 2nd Battalion of the 47th Infantry (Mechanized) in the northern Mekong Delta for a tour of forcing himself through rice paddies and jungles all day and then setting ambushes at night. He concluded his tour with a stint at battalion headquarters. More than just a war memoir, this is the story of one soldier trying to find his way in uncertain times—and to survive his year in Vietnam.

Paperback • 6 x 9 • 208 pages • 16-page color insert with 25 photos

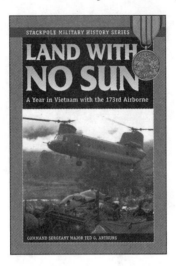